Brazilian Hip Hoppers
Speak from the Margins

Brazilian Hip Hoppers Speak from the Margins

We's on Tape

Derek Pardue

BRAZILIAN HIP HOPPERS SPEAK FROM THE MARGINS
Copyright © Derek Pardue, 2008, 20011.
All rights reserved.

First published in hardcover in 2008 as ideologies of marginality in brazilian hip hop by PALGRAVE MACMILLAN® in the United States - a division of St. Martin's Press LLC, 175 Fifth Avenue, New York, NY 10010.

Where this book is distributed in the UK, Europe and the rest of the world, this is by Palgrave Macmillan, a division of Macmillan Publishers Limited, registered in England, company number 785998, of Houndmills, Basingstoke, Hampshire RG21 6XS.

Palgrave Macmillan is the global academic imprint of the above companies and has companies and representatives throughout the world.

Palgrave® and Macmillan® are registered trademarks in the United States, the United Kingdom, Europe and other countries.

ISBN: 978-0-230-12071-6

Pardue, Derek, 1969–
  Ideologies of marginality in Brazilian hip hop / Derek Pardue.
    p. cm.
  Includes bibliographical references and index.
  ISBN 0-230-60465-X
  1. Ethnology—Brazil—São Paulo. 2. Hip-hop—Brazil—São Paulo. 3. Hip-hop dance—Brazil—São Paulo. 4. Social classes—Brazil—São Paulo. 5. Ethnicity—Brazil—São Paulo. 6. Sex role—Brazil—São Paulo. 7. Marginality, Social—Brazil—São Paulo. 8. Dance—Social aspects—Brazil—São Paulo. 9. São Paulo (Brazil)—Social life and customs. I. Title.

GN564.B6P37 2008
306.4'846098161—dc22   2007051215

A catalogue record for this book is available from the British Library.

Design by Scribe Inc.

First PALGRAVE MACMILLAN paperback edition: October 2011

10 9 8 7 6 5 4 3 2 1

Transferred to Digital Printing in 2011

This book is dedicated to all the young men and women of São Paulo coming of age in the *periferia*. I hope you can find in hip hop what I have discovered—*axé*, a force of life.

Contents

List of Illustrations	ix
Preface	xi
Acknowledgments	xv
1 Introduction and Frame	1
2 Assembling Brazilian Hip Hop Histories	33
3 Making Territorial Claims: São Paulo Hip Hop and the Socio-geographical Dynamics of *Periferia*	59
4 Putting *Mano* to Music: Testing Hip Hop *Negritude*	91
5 *Mano/Mana*: The Engendering of the *Periferia*	121
6 *Fechou?* (I'm Out/The End?): Concluding Remarks about a Crisis and an Opportunity	159
Epilogue	167
Notes	175
References	195
Index	215

Illustrations

Figure 1.1	"Nóis na fita." Derek Pardue, 2002	10
Figure 1.2	Rap em Festa. Derek Pardue, 2005	12
Figure 1.3	Graffiti at Rap em Festa. Derek Pardue, 2005	13
Figure 1.4	Rapper at Rap em Festa. Derek Pardue, 2005	13
Figure 1.5	Map of São Paulo. Dipro/Sempla, 2007	18
Figure 2.1	Galeria 24 de Maio. Derek Pardue, 1999	53
Figure 3.1	Consultant's domestic courtyard. Derek Pardue, 1999	63
Figure 3.2	A favela around the Billings Reservoir on the south side	64
Figure 3.3	Hip hopper leaning against the Cidade Tiradentes Library wall. Derek Pardue, 2001	73
Figure 4.1	*Senzala* (Slave quarters). Derek Pardue, 2002	96
Figure 4.2	Poster of André Rebouças	103
Figure 4.3	Afrika Bambaataa with King Nino Brown at Zulu Nation Brasil Headquarters. Diego Pereira, 2007	107
Figure 5.1	*Posse Hausa* scrapbook 1. Derek Pardue, 1999, drawing by Zulu King Nino Brown, 1999	139
Figure 5.2	*Posse Hausa* scrapbook 2. Derek Pardue, 1999, drawing by Zulu King Nino Brown, 1999	140
Figure 5.3	Former member of rap group Alvos da Lei. Derek Pardue, 1999	145

Preface

For more than twenty years, scholars have engaged in the formal study of hip hop culture. These efforts resulted in the formation of Hip-Hop Studies, an interdisciplinary field that has created intellectual and institutional space within the Western academy for the study of rap music, turntablism, tagging, b-boying, fashion, language, and a range of other expressive cultural practices broadly subsumed under the rubric of hip hop.

In its first ten years, Hip-Hop Studies scholarship held a very narrow intellectual and methodological focus. Because of the relative youth of hip hop, many scholars and journalists devoted their attention to writing brief histories of the culture, situating it firmly within the context of post-Fordist New York City. Many hip hop scholars operated from a more defensive posture, defending hip hop against the moral panics of the day. This resulted in the birth of humanistic scholarship that spotlighted the literary merit of rap music in relation to Western canonical texts. Many scholars responded to the moral panics of the day, which focused on the socially degenerative effects of gangster rap, through intense cultural criticism (and a few empirical studies) that challenged the notion that hip hop culture was the cause of violence, hypersexuality, or anti-intellectualism.

More recently, Hip-Hop Studies has grown both in scope and rigor. A new generation of "native" hip hop scholars—those who grew up consuming hip hop culture and entered graduate programs with the intention of studying hip hop culture—entered the academy and stretched the field into new directions. Scholars like Imani Perry, Mark Anthony Neal, William Jelani Cobb, Gwendolyn Pough, Ian Condry, Samy Alim, and others forced the field to confront new questions, locate new units of analysis, adopt new methodological approaches, and link to broader intellectual trends in a range of areas and disciplines. Derek Pardue's book, *Ideologies of Marginality in Brazilian Hip Hop*, is a bold and important piece of Hip-Hop Studies scholarship that serves as a clear index of the field's intellectual maturity as well a map for future routes of intellectual inquiry.

This book joins a small but growing body of ethnographic studies on hip hop culture. Pardue helps to usher the field beyond its traditionally humanities-centered approach, which has resulted in the rigid textual analyses that have predominated the academic and popular study of hip hop. Instead of succumbing to dogmatic textualism, Pardue privileges localized, emic understandings of various sites of hip hop cultural production. This is not to suggest, however, that Pardue avoids the necessary work of analyzing the various rhetorical and aesthetic texts that are produced and consumed by the participants in his study. Rather, he articulates his analysis of texts to the broader social, political, and economic contexts in which they are constituted. Through this methodological and conceptual shift, he allows us to discover a complex and unexpected array of meanings, purposes, and functions for hip hop within the lives of youth in Sao Paulo's *periferia*.

For the youth in this book, hip hop culture is more than a site of play, pleasure, escape, or even resistive expression. Rather, it functions as a critical and often contradictory social, political, and pedagogical project that allows practitioners to negotiate race and class-based forms of social marginality; articulate various forms of social misery; and fashion new individual, community, and (trans)national identities. By framing hip hop culture in this way, Pardue encourages hip hop scholars to forsake their parochial commitments to "close readings" of rap music lyrics and to interrogate the broader contexts, subjects, and systems in which hip hop cultural production occurs.

Ideologies of Marginality in Brazilian Hip Hop also pushes the field of Hip-Hop Studies beyond a narrow and romantic focus on cultural politics. Following the cue of cultural studies, many Hip-Hop Studies scholars have located sites of "resistance" and "opposition" through everyday cultural practices. While such work is both legitimate and necessary, it has often come at the expense of more grounded and material analyses of the relationship between cultural practices and the contexts in which they are situated. In this book, Pardue resists to make such a move.

Although this book highlights the ways in which an engagement with hip hop cultural practices serves as a site of resistance, Pardue refuses to paint hip hop as a purely salvific or even romantic politico-cultural project. Instead he exposes the deep contradictions embedded within spaces of hip hop production, consumption, and even distribution. For example, Pardue shows how *periferia* ideologies around race and social marginality have created fecund space for critical social critique and the production of more stable and healthy subjectivities. At the same time, however, Pardue demonstrates how these approaches can reproduce the very conditions that are ostensibly being challenged through the social critiques of Brazilian hip hoppers.

Ideologies of Marginality in Brazilian Hip Hop also makes a sorely needed contribution to the growing body of international research on hip hop culture. As Pardue himself argues, much of the scholarship on global hip hop fails to advance theory in substantive fashion and, many times, merely uses hip hop as a metaphor for other phenomena. Pardue, on the other hand, manages to link hip hop culture to broader discourses within Latin American Studies, anthropology, and musicology, as well as pressing social issues within Brazilian Studies, without compromising its critical attention to hip hop culture.

This book also avoids the common tendency to frame non-American hip hop culture as purely derivative or mimetic. Instead, it demonstrates how local actors appropriate Western forms of hip hop and baptize them within their own cultural, social, and political traditions. At the same time, Pardue shows how the cultural logics and epistemological frameworks of hip hop culture remain (somewhat) stable as they flow across the global landscape.

Ideologies of Marginality in Brazilian Hip Hop is one of the most important books ever written in the field of Hip-Hop Studies. Its value rests in the fact that Derek Pardue doesn't merely tell us *what* hip hop means, he also tells us *how* hip hop means. In doing so, he adds multiple layers of complexity, nuance, and rigor to the study of Brazil and to the study of hip hop culture. If the field of Hip-Hop Studies is to thrive and grow, texts like this must lead the way.

Marc Lamont Hill
May 2011

Acknowledgments

Acknowledgment and recognition are some of the greatest struggles in social life. Hip hoppers know this all very well, and, in fact, they insist on recognition as an essential part of respect and community building. In this spirit, I give my utmost respect as I recognize all the rappers, DJs, hip-hop producers, B-boys and B-girls, graffiti artists, Non-Governmental Organization (NGO) representatives, community activists, state employees, event promoters, local hip hop scholars, and local *periferia* youth. In particular, I want to thank the contributions of Zulu King Nino Brown, Marcelinho Backspin, Drica, and everyone at the Casa de Cultura Hip Hop for all their time and patience with me over the past years. I want to give a special thanks to DJ Erry-G, who always had time to not only chat about hip hop but to really debate key issues. I thank André, Gil, and Fábio of Bocada for giving me a column and space on their hip hop Web site.

I want to recognize my mother and father, without whose support and understanding I would have never had the chance to develop a spirit of inquiry and criticism. I give thanks to my wife and best friend Selma. Always both critical and loving, Selma has always been there for me. To little André, my son, I acknowledge the future—may it be bright. Family and field come first.

This project would not have been possible without the support of SSRC (Social Science Research Council) and Wenner-Gren Foundation for Anthropological Research, which funded fieldwork research in 2001–2. In addition, I thank the Department of Anthropology at the University of Illinois, Urbana-Champaign for providing me with summer funding in 1999 to return to São Paulo and conduct preliminary research. I give thanks to Greg Diethrich, Fernando Rios, Tony Perman, Bjorn Westgard, and Jack Forbes for our conversations in and out of graduate school. I give special thanks to Claudio Moreira, my friend as well as avid *Corintiano* and activist-scholar for the Brazilian working classes. Claudio has stood up for me and given me respect for what I try to do both in and out of the academy. I very much value his opinion. I want to give another special acknowledgement to Will

Leggett, who became a true friend and colleague and whose insights into anthropology and popular culture are natural, not contrived.

At Union College, I would like to thank Sharon and George Gmelch for their advice on publishing and general professionalism. I want to thank Tom Turino, Bill Kelleher, Andy Orta, Alex Dent, and John Burdick for providing critical comments on earlier versions of portions of this text. And finally, I want to acknowledge Joanna Mericle at Palgrave Macmillan for her editorial work.

Chapter 1

Introduction and Frame

> *Sabe quem eu sou?, então me diga quem você é. (Do you know who I am?, then tell me who you are.)*
>
> —Thaíde e DJ Hum, "Afro-Brasileiro"

With more than two decades of academic research, hip hop scholarship has reached a point of reflection. Likewise, in the commercial scene itself, rap performers over the past few years have become increasingly nostalgic and yearn to revisit the old days of raw performance and neighborhood battles. Such reflection is evident in the lyrics quoted above. Thaíde, one of the most widely recognized rappers and pioneers of hip hop in Brazil, created a catchy refrain for the 1996 hit song "Afro-Brasileiro" (Afro-Brazilian). "Who am I?" is one of the apparently simpler questions of conversation, yet it is one that preoccupies all of us periodically throughout life. For hip hoppers around the world, the question of identity is a beginning for demonstrating "reality" knowledge and aesthetic skills.

In Brazil, hip hop is a form of identity expressed through the politics and pleasure of marginalized youth. In São Paulo, Brazil's largest metropolitan area of over twenty million inhabitants (IBGE 2005), tens of thousands of adolescents and young adults look to hip hop as a hopeful opportunity to encounter someone who actually cares who they are.

I am not aware of any organized poll or study of the hip hop population in terms of demographics or other statistics, although Kall of the posse Conceitos de Rua (Street Concepts) once referred to a study suggesting that there are five thousand hip hop performance groups in São Paulo. I estimate that there are two hundred thousand hip hoppers currently in the São Paulo area. I arrived at this calculation based on observations from public concerts, record sales, and the number of regular weekend events throughout the metropolitan area. During any token weekend, for example, there are approximately forty public events sponsored by community or governmental organizations. Such activity does not take into account shows of entertainment, which occur at night in clubs and include a ticket price.

It is important to qualify the above estimate of hip hoppers in São Paulo. Hip hoppers are a heterogeneous social group and members' involvement is extremely varied. For the purposes of this project, I follow the local, unwritten but implicit definition of a hip hopper, which is a person who not only consumes hip hop (e.g., CD purchase and MTV viewing) but also practices in some active manner one or more "elements" of hip hop. These include rap, DJ (disc jockey), graffiti, and street dance.

Hip hop thrives in São Paulo, especially in the periphery neighborhoods (*periferia*), because youth see hip hop as an alternative to being Joe Shmo, so-and-so, or "little thing" (*zé ninguém, fulano,* or *coisinha* respectively). As South African hip hoppers Shaheen Ariefdien and Nazli Abrahams stated in their "Cape Flats Alchemy" text, "hip hop is about seeing the *something* in what we are often told is nothing" (Ariefdeen and Abrahams 2006, 262). Similarly, insignificance and marginality is what *periferia* dwellers represent to the Brazilian middle class, traditional historiography, and all too frequently to each other. Marginality is what hip hoppers seek to change in their belief in and performance of hip hop.

I wrote this book for two reasons. First, I want to contribute to the literature on hip hop by provoking discussion on both general theories about popular culture, especially within the disciplines of anthropology, ethnomusicology, and Latin American studies, and adding to the growing knowledge about hip hoppers around the world. Second, I wrote this book as an "alternative" view of contemporary Brazilian society, especially in an urban context. I follow what I take to be the strengths of ethnographies such as *Travesti* (Kulick 1998) and *At Home in the Street* (Hecht 1998). Both of these texts are successful at integrating general theories of gender and childhood into ethnographic local knowledge of the Brazilian cities of Salvador and Recife, respectively. For the literature on Brazil, they are important, critical accounts of social agency from two marginalized populations—transvestites and street kids.

This book is an ethnography of Brazilian hip hoppers[1] as they have attempted to institute an alternative system of ideology. As they constitute and develop their identity as "hip hoppers," Brazilian youth try to take control and refashion burdensome cultural categories such as Brazilian (*brasileiro*) and Brazilian-ness (*brasilidade*), often defined vis-à-vis *gringo*, ideas and people from the United States, Europe, and to a lesser extent anywhere outside of Brazil. Furthermore, Brazilian hip hoppers attempt to redesign social categories of race, class, and gender as well as sociogeographical categories such as *periferia* and marginality (*marginalidade*). They do this explicitly through a range of material (image and sound) and ideology (discourses, narratives, networking practices). I have organized this book according to three pertinent categories: space, race, and gender. In the case of Brazilian hip hop, history and class systematically contextualize the meaning of these categories; therefore, I systematically underscore my analysis as historically grounded and class inflected.

I certainly appreciate that meaning is context-driven; however, I also believe that meaning is highly dependent on intention. Hip hoppers make this fact acutely apparent. While I found most hip hoppers to be humble (an important class marker to be discussed later) and relatively easy going on a personal level, hip hoppers represent the world as "reality" and "truth" in extremely dogmatic ways. They foreground intention as the force of change. To create and maintain a high level of intentional force, one has to believe in the design. Hip hoppers are *crentes*, a term that literally translates as "believers" but more specifically refers to "evangelical" or non-Catholic Christian devotees in Brazil. The ideological and institutional connections between "evangelicalism" and Brazilian hip hop will be discussed later, but for right now, I want to convey the feeling and power of belief as essential to hip hop.

As I state later, hip hop is a process of becoming, full of moments of recognition. It is a process of developing, often for the first time, an empowered sense of self. Disenfranchised Brazilian youth see hip hop as a sociocultural system with which they can take control and potentially redesign their lives and conditions. Before I outline the chapters of the book and introduce in greater detail the pertinent debates and fieldwork methodologies, I want to demonstrate through a short vignette the logic of hip hop as a "salvation."

On June 12, 1999, I attended an organizational meeting sponsored by CEDECA (Center for the Defense of Children and Adolescents) in Jardim Sapopemba on the east side of São Paulo. CEDECA was legally established in 1991 as an NGO supported in part by

United Nations International Children's Emergency Fund (UNICEF) and the São Paulo Archdiocese. In practice, the organization began in 1986 as a community initiative to protect teenage prostitutes and offer shelter to adolescents suffering daily acts of violence in the Sapopemba district. In 1995 CEDECA expanded its program to include hip hop as a vehicle to engage local adolescents in issues of health, politics, vocation, and history. I had been to several similar meetings of CEDECA, in which participants debated and negotiated the preparation of *Rap em Festa*. This annual "rap party" draws hip hop performance groups from the states of São Paulo, Minas Gerais, Rio de Janeiro, and Paraná. The event takes place during a weekend, usually in August. CEDECA coordinators, Fábio and Neuza, as well as lawyer and long-time community activist, Wanda, use the event to recruit potential volunteers for the NGO in not only hip hop but also its other sectors of community activity.

DJ Gog was a volunteer and an occasionally paid workshop instructor for CEDECA's DJ classes. He told me about the get together. It had been three years since I had last visited CEDECA. Somewhat lost, I asked a passing clergyman if he knew the whereabouts of CEDECA. He explained that he indeed worked with one of CEDECA's original founders, Padre Salvério Paulillo (Padre Xavier), and showed me the way. As per usual, the meeting started with a round of introductions. People stated their names, their places of residence, the names of hip hop groups, how long they had been in the "movement," and what attracted them to come to CEDECA this particular day. I noticed quite obviously that most participants thanked God for being able to make it to the meeting. Yet, it was Razor's introduction that was remarkable to me. "Razor" was his nickname and stage name. He was from Mogi das Cruzes, a periphery suburb east of São Paulo municipality. Razor introduced himself not unlike someone in Alcoholics Anonymous (AA) or Narcotics Anonymous (NA) or a *crente* from church:

> Greetings. Satisfaction to you all (*satisfação*). It's [my story] like this. I used to be part of the movement during the early '90s, but in 1995 I began to steal cars, use drugs, steal from family members and abandon my children. Three "dark" years passed my friends. It was a time of feeling lost with no direction. I was on the bad side of things (*eu era de mal*). I was that guy on the corner, who you used to look away from, who you used to discount as nothing (*não vale nada*). I didn't believe in anything. Nothing was real; nothing was true. I don't remember

even time passing by. But, recently, I was "saved" and am on my way out of dependency. I am on a new path (*caminho*). Hip hop is that path. I'm glad to be here at CEDECA today and am glad to have the opportunity to sit here and exchange information with all of you. I am here representing myself and all the lost souls out there in Mogi [short for Mogi das Cruzes city], who turned the tables and now embrace with a full heart and mind the power of hip hop. This is what is real. Hip hop is all about reality and truth.

Razor's confessional introduction of self and his sense of membership in the hip hop community are similar to conventional Pentecostal narratives in that the discourses articulate "real-life accounts" to "direct evocation of God" (Novaes 1999, 88). Although Razor's account was slightly more dramatic than most, it was certainly not unique.

Brazilian hip hoppers periodically refer to hip hop as a "salvation" (*salvação*), a force and set of beliefs that helped reorient their lives. For rapper Necaf, hip hop "saves" one from "falling into samba" (*cair no samba*)—an expression, in this case, symbolizing a step backward into mainstream notions of black, periphery males, namely *malandros* or hustlers with little to offer to society other than a little ditty. "*Cair no samba*" is a popular saying referring to standard lyrics of 1930s *sambistas*, samba composers and musician, such as Noel Rosa and Ary Barroso. Hip hoppers are, in effect, deconstructing this phrase and recasting it with contemporary criticisms of what they hold to be national ideologies of race, class, and citizenship. For many, hip hop "saved" (*salvou*) them from wrong and the despair of quotidian life in the urban peripheries. In short, hip hoppers use the material and discourse of marginality to save themselves from further negativity and by extension transform the periphery into a place and concept more akin to empowerment than marginality.

Salvation comes in the process of becoming a hip hopper. Moments of, not only performing on stage or on the street as a rapper, DJ, B-boy or B-girl, or graffiti artist, but also of watching videos, joining hip hop *posses* or organizations, or discussing music and style are transformative. They are moments of enlightenment, and Brazilian youth feel a sense of confirmation that they are hip hoppers and are evolving (*evoluindo*). Hip hoppers understand this as both an individual and collective process. The idiom of spirituality is thus logical as burgeoning and established hip hoppers mark their identities. For example, early pioneers of what is currently termed "positive hip hop" (*hip hop positivo*), such as *Filosofia de Rua* (Street Philosophy) and

Alpiste, sought to establish the Gospel as a trope for hip hop community building. According to Ugli, former member of *Filosofia de Rua*, the Gospel refers to the "spiritual state [of mind or existence] in which we all meet" (pers. comm.).

Research and Ethnographic Objectives

In their personal introductions, local hip hoppers directly connect "salvation" to "reality." Hip hop becomes a cultural matrix with which practitioners attempt to represent and thus change the current state of things. In local terms, hip hop involves the "concept" (*conceito*) of imagining and acting on real changes. In this book, I draw from the energy and spirit of the majority of São Paulo hip hoppers and argue that in the process of transforming *periferia* reality, hip hoppers create and codify an alternative ideology.[2] Hip hop as a design for "reality" includes formal aesthetics and ideological ethics for the structuring of daily life. As they organize and coordinate a range of images, sounds, and narratives around the key themes of marginality and violence, hip hoppers comment on and contribute to a contemporary understanding of race and gender in Brazil. Therefore, Brazilian hip hop is about a dynamic material "design" and "making of" society (Pardue 2005).

Virtually all Brazilian hip hoppers are invested in retelling periphery "reality" through narratives of marginality, with the aim of both legitimating the *periferia* as a potentially empowering space of identity, and revealing problems of mainstream Brazilian views of social difference mostly around the markers of class and race (to a much lesser extent, gender and sexuality). According to hip hoppers, rather than a daily life filled with meaningless violence and insurmountable corruption, ubiquity should be about respect, honesty, and neighborhood pride or general "attitude."

With that said, there exists a basic difference in approach, one that has led to two general types of hip hop in Brazil: the "marginal" and "positive." For "marginal" hip hoppers, the operative ideology consists of spreading the "truths" of reality through acute and transparent detail. "Transformation" comes naturally; or as local "marginal" hip hoppers often claim, change comes as a follow up (*na seqüência*). There are very few concrete "solutions" (another keyword in hip hop discourse) offered, because the primary concern is simply to make sure people understand what reality is. This translates into lengthy reports or indictments (*denúncias*) of police violence, precarious living conditions, racial discrimination, homicide related to drug trafficking, and police and general state corruption.

During the late 1990s, many hip hoppers argued that this approach was not enough. Through rap recordings, fanzine interviews, meeting discussions, and so on, "positive" hip hoppers claimed that they were, in fact, prepared to provide "solutions" to the periphery reality. Some of these included a rejuvenated and activist sense of spirituality through various "evangelical" denominations rooted in the hundreds of local churches throughout the periphery. Hip hop positivism also includes orientations toward information and sound technology as a way to escape the limited resources of the periphery. Veteran hip hoppers such as Thaíde and Nino Brown see technology as a powerful force to create transnational and translocal "unity" among hip hoppers through organizations such as Zulu Nation. Others, such as Web site pioneers André and Fábio, concern themselves more with the techniques of technology as a force that can potentially enable hip hoppers to become more "informed" (another keyword discussed at length in Chapter 2) and thus more conversant with hip hoppers outside of Brazil. In both cases, "positivism" implicitly involves new processes of identification in which hip hoppers imagine their particular issues of locality (detailed so well in "marginal" hip hop), as similar to other peripheral or marginalized communities in other places and other times. In short, "positivists" see hip hop as more diasporic and historical in scope. Such a perspective is important, because it means that the ideas and material for local change can come from afar.

My representation is both general and specific in purview. I address issues of performance and production, which refer to hip hop transnationally. Furthermore, I demonstrate specific procedural and conceptual aspects of hip hop and hip hoppers in São Paulo that are particularly "Brazilian." I posit that both the manner in which I have framed my analysis and the topics of inquiry that I have identified make significant interventions into more general anthropological and musicological discussions in urban anthropology and the relations of performance and power. With the guiding principle of hip hop as ideology and practice, I hope to combine what hip hop scholars have referred to as the two sides of the current literature, that is, the historical and sociological with the aesthetic, artistic, and ideological aspects (Perry 2005, 3).

The flows of hip hop material and ideas, based on a notion of "reality," "truth," and "respect," offer a layout of circuits of expressive culture and markets of identification. Therefore, the "global issue" within hip hop and, more generally speaking, popular culture studies necessarily structure this book. How does Brazilian hip hop compare and contrast to hip hop in the United States? How can one describe that "mothership connection" (to borrow from the oft trite but, in this case, still apt phrase of George Clinton and the funk band Parliament), linking the dominant U.S. hip hop sphere to her satellites of influence around the world? Is the globalization of hip hop a form of homogenization, or is it more akin to what some hip hop scholars have argued, a "reterritorialization" or "glocalization"[3] of powerful and empowering symbols? If it is the latter, what are the most effective strategies to describe and explain the parameters and concerns of, for example, "Brazilian" hip hop?

These are rhetorical questions in the sense that they force the analyst or interpreter to choose a theory or set of theories and try to persuade the reader that his or her story is plausible not as the absolute "right" answer but as a contribution to the cumulative scholarship on hip hop. For the most part, scholarly texts on global hip hop are confined to the occasional journal article or edited volume. Either authors spend a great deal of time clearing space by describing the context and history of hip hop in a particular location that one feels cut short of any theoretical impact (Durand 2005; Mitchell 2001; Chang 2006), or scholars extrapolate hip hop as a metaphor or as a lens for some larger issue, such as "indigeneity" in Bolivia (Goodale 2006), so that one might question the empirical legitimacy of any contribution to hip hop scholarship per se.

One might notice that most global hip hop texts in book form are edited volumes. In fact, with regard to U.S. hip hop, the format of the edited volume is a marketing and discursive favorite. Implicitly, this signals that hip hop is a relatively challenging subject matter for detailed empirical and theoretical treatment. Few authors work to provide analytical cohesion. There are missed opportunities. For example, in Jeff Chang's recent collection of essays, *Total chaos*, there is a potentially provocative transcript of a roundtable discussion, "Native Tongues: Hip-Hop's Global Indigenous Movement" (Chang 2006, 278–90). At one point, Grant Saunders, a B-boy and MC from New South Wales described the "whitening" of hip hop in Australia since the rise of Eminem and the resulting strategic shifts of Aboriginal peoples (Saunders 2006, 289). Saunders's statements provide an opportunity for either Chang as editor or Cristina Verán, the journalist, Rock Steady Crew and Zulu Nation member, and mediator of the roundtable discussion, to flesh out issues of racialization and difference as a dynamic process among hip hoppers, particularly in the "in-between" category of indigenous hip hoppers.

This is not to say that all of global hip hop has been relegated to a "covering-the-bases" approach to representation. The global is not epiphenomenal, and its flows are not unidirectional. The edited volume *The vinyl ain't final* departs from the premise that all locales of hip hop production are themselves results of complex global flows in terms of actors, economies, politics, ideologies, and so on. In this manner, "globalization" or "glocalization" become epistemological rather than topical in nature, and that is significant. Furthermore, scholars, such as anthropologist Ian Condry (2006) and sociologist Sujatha Fernandes (2006), have written compelling ethnographies of Japanese and Cuban expressive art and hip hop, respectively, that provide descriptive detail of local actors and theoretical rigor in the interrogation of shared issues of race, class, gender, the role of the state, media circuits, and popular consumption practices. Whether through the "Elvis effect" (Condry 2006) or the *Orishas* rap group (Fernandes 2003, 2006), hip hop scholars cannot simply ignore the global dimensions of hip hop as a system of knowledge and cultural practices. I reiterate that the "global issue" is a *necessary* one; it is not one that I embraced from the beginning.

I left the United States for Brazil in 1995 looking for a different way of thinking about the world. I remember having conversations with graduate students, librarians, and faculty members at PUC (Pontific Catholic University) and USP (University of São Paulo). I wanted them to point me in the right direction so that I could become acquainted with Brazilian paradigms of social theory. While, of course, the content of the research projects discussed was Brazilian, new paradigms were not forthcoming. In fact, the more I studied and participated in seminars, I realized that Brazilian scholarship in the social sciences (especially anthropology) was and continues to be, for the most part, dependent on trends in British history, French sociology, and American cultural anthropology. I remained frustrated until I discovered that dependence does not require imitation. Dependence and adaptation are not, of course, mutually exclusive. Many early Brazilian scholars (Freyre 1933, 1936; Buarque de Holanda 1936; Cunha 1903) distinguished themselves by reworking European and U.S. theories of "culture," which themselves were based on observations or imaginations about "other" places such as Brazil. In fact, relations of dependence, whether in intellectual theories or in popular culture, reflect much more about relative positions in transnational markets

Figure 1.1 Bumper sticker photo taken on street on the south side of São Paulo, March 2002.

of material and ideological production than about issues of cultural meaning or use.

I dwell on this point because I believe that many hip hop fans and scholars approach hip hop outside of the United States as essentially derivative and thus ultimately trivial. In the fall of 2005, I attended a hip hop conference at City University of New York (CUNY) Lehman located in the northern section of the Bronx. While there were many fascinating presentations and debates about contemporary artists, trends, and styles covering several centers of hip hop production around the world, I was struck by the pervasive logic throughout the conversations that the dominant position that the United States holds in global hip hop production corresponds to a position of ideological control over non-U.S. hip hop practices. Presenters were quick to discuss the particular issues and concerns of Japanese, Jamaican, and South African hip hop performers, yet they continued to refer to such local recordings or other activities as stemming from a U.S. "template" of how to create local or national distinction. As Livio Sansone has argued with regard to race and identity work, it is the perceived status of "super blacks" (Sansone 2003, 98), ascribed to U.S. "blacks" by black and marginalized people outside of the United States, that is then mobilized for locals to mark distinction. There is no template or model but rather a cross-culturally shared idea of "skills/z," "respect," "reality," and performative authority with multiple origins and uses. For example, it is not any sort of U.S. hip hop model of "nationalism" (political, cultural, aesthetic, or otherwise) per se, but rather a translocal sense of "blackness" and "attitude" moving among metropolitan areas of New York, London, Rio, Salvador, São Paulo, Capetown, Kingston, Miami, and Paris that is important.

It is from this contentious position that I address the theme of hip hop and globalization. Instead of bracketing my discussion of the relation of Brazilian hip hop to American hip hop as a separate chapter or subheading, I will provide comparative information and interpretation along the narrative, ethnographic path. The chapters of this text are organized in terms of ideological categories. Within such components of history, race, class, place, and gender, various "marginal" and "positivist" hip hoppers in São Paulo borrow and recast hip hop signs they associate with the United States via actual performers (e.g., Tupac, Common, Crazy Legs, DJ Premiere) or generalized imaginations (e.g., "Wild Style" graffiti, DJ cuttin', "Black Power"). These components are contextual and thus are treated as significant factors in Brazilian hip hop. In other words, I intend to foreground Brazilian hip hoppers, who are obviously influenced by their counterparts in the United States. However, this condition remains a significant background context. Brazilians are the figure, and the United States (along with France, the UK, Japan, and Nigeria) is the ground. (See Figure 1.1.)

The title of this book refers to a ubiquitous phrase invented by Brazilian hip hoppers. The phrase *nóis na fita*, we's on tape, is purposefully incorrect Portuguese, but the message is clear: "we represent ourselves on this recording." The bumper sticker in the above photograph is a ubiquitous sight, especially in the *periferia* of São Paulo. Perhaps more significant than hip hoppers' creative differentiation[4] with regard to standard Portuguese grammar is their expansion of the idea of cassette tape (*fita*) into a general narrative category. "*A fita á o seguinte, mano* [It goes like this, brother]." The cassette tape is a metaphor for the situation, the business plan, and the project. The *fita* is the product of the committee or "crew" (*banca*). It is the catch-all term for hip hop representation regardless of which "element" (rap, DJ, graffiti, B-boy) is actually in question.

Hip Hop Culture in Brazil

In Brazil, hip hop functions as a general concept of culture, a dynamic and generative set of practices through which practitioners formulate a system of identity concepts, beliefs, ethics, aesthetics, and politics. In general, I understand hip hop in Brazil to be an ideology of representation and personhood positioned in relation to a cluster of primarily national hegemonic discourses and practices represented in such terms as cordial,[5] racial democracy,[6] tropicalism,[7] and tradition. Hip hoppers refer to this national hegemonic formation as the system (*o sistema*),[8] and they understand this "system" as part of Brazil's problematic socialization process.

Hip hop is an "alternative system" (*sistema alternativo*) of cultural production and identity formation grounded in what practitioners call the four "elements." Street dance includes break dancing, lockin', and poppin'. Although there is some debate over these terms, most aficionados agree that what distinguishes breakin' from poppin' and lockin' is the performative emphasis on spins (head, back, and other body parts) rather than footwork. In addition, breakin' originated on the East Coast, while poppin' and lockin' came from California. Local

Figure 1.2 "Four elements" banner, which greeted visitors to the Rap em Festa, July 2005.

Figure 1.3 Local "east side" teenagers do spray art related to the theme of "Violence."

Figure 1.4 Rapper from Voz Feminina on stage at Rap em Festa.

hip hoppers usually refer to all of this as B-boy or B-girl activities ("B" refers to "break," as break became the umbrella term to refer to all forms of street dance).[9]

In Brazil, hip hoppers are particularly aware of these four elements and stress their integration during performance and conversation. For example, in an interview, the organizers of the annual event *Rap em Festa* (Rap Celebration) from the nongovernmental organization CEDECA (Center of Defense for the Rights of Children and Adolescents) insisted during the 2005 event that "integration of the four elements" was "one of the major goals" of *Rap em Festa* (pers. comm.). Figures 1.1–1.4 were taken in a span of minutes as I walked and scanned the premises of a local public high school on the extreme east side of São Paulo. From the initial banner at the entrance of the school gymnasium to the improvisational street dance (too blurry for my camera's still shots) to the parallel graffiti workshops, one is struck by the coterminous nature of the four elements during the hip hop event. According to the organizers and some attendees, "it is important to have all four elements going on at the same time, because we create more unity (*união*) that way. Nowadays, this is fundamental, because there is pressure on hip hoppers to concentrate on just one of the elements and forget about the others. This alienates us from each other (*a gente fica alienado*)."

The keywords of "unity" and "alienation" are part of most Brazilian hip hoppers' vocabulary, and they employ them in a wide array of contexts. In general, younger hip hoppers lack the historical knowledge (sometimes glossed as "consciousness" or *consciência*) to offer any meaningful explanation of these words; they simply use them because they know they carry authority. Older hip hoppers, roughly participants over the age of twenty, often feel an obligation to explain such terms, because they see these concepts as central to the notion and practice of hip hop as a "culture" and not simply a form of entertainment or what is locally referred to as art (*arte*). Of course this is a generalization, and there are numerous exceptions at the individual level; however, I think age classification is significant. The operative ideologies and attitudes of Brazilian hip hop (just as anywhere else) are formations; they require performative articulations. In my experience, "older" hip hoppers tend to invest more time—as a matter of course, not necessarily propaganda—in explaining hip hop as they take up roles of pedagogues, community leaders, NGO workers, and fanzine publishers.

It is from these terms of "knowledge, "consciousness," and "unity/alienation" that Brazilian hip hoppers articulate systems of value, aesthetics, and ethics. While there are certainly many rappers, DJs, *grafiteiros*, B-boys, B-girls, and fans who honestly do not really care about "unity" or see hip hop as another way to be a criminal, all hip hoppers are in some significant way positioned by the ideological structure embedded in the integration of the four elements. For example, very few rappers can survive if they rhyme about marijuana, excessive consumerism ("bling"), or just partying. Individuals feel at least rhetorically oblige, to (re)present themselves as part of and conversant with hip hop's central concepts of unity, consciousness versus alienation, reality, truth, the system, social change (*transformação*), and homage to other "elements" (in the instance that B-boys or graffiti artists are not visibly present at the event). Whether it is lip service or genuine consciousness, rap discourse reveals the ideological power of unity. In this sense, Brazilian hip hop is relatively orthodox to other hip hop communities around the globe. In my opinion, one of the reasons that hip hop has been so successful around the world is precisely the inclusive structure of the ideas and activities involved in the "four elements." The activities require years of dedication and are varied to the extent that there is a somewhat natural tendency for hip hop in general to be inclusive. Furthermore, the keywords of "unity" and so on, similar to all ideological concepts, are inherently both vague and powerful. They "hail" youth from around the world to participate actively in life and show off expressive skills.

Hip hop is also a style. In more popular terms, hip hop is (an) attitude. Local hip hop organizer Oliveira explains, "It's not enough to just sing; you gotta do something. This is what it is to have attitude, to be coherent with the kind of life we preach in the songs" (Oliveira 1996, 4). Hip hoppers exercise their "attitudes" to articulate material production (e.g., compact disc recordings, clothes and fashion, flyers and posters) and ideological practice (e.g., a set of mantras, common historicities, narrative genres) to a recognized set of tastes. In popular parlance, performers and fans refer to such formations as "grooves," "beats," "looks," or "walks."

The production and interpretation of hip hop demonstrates that there are correlations between aesthetics, ethics, and politics. Hip hoppers make choices and strive for, at least rhetorically and performatively, what Oliveira refers to above as "coherence" by creating and arranging graphic typographies, composition schemes, and sound engineering techniques in accordance with key phrases and stories of community including perspectives regarding the *periferia*, Brazilian state agencies, and U.S. (*gringo*) influence. For example, within the local category of *marginal* hip hop, sometimes referred to as *gangsta* or *perifa*, performers and proponents have established a set of typefaces, colors, timbres, and rhythmic pulse adjustments that consumers recognize. Marginal fans expect certain kinds of stories about periphery daily life that oppose the state and sometimes, controversially, the United States as monolithic and pernicious "systems" of exploitation and control (Pardue 2005).

METHODOLOGY

The fieldwork for this ethnography started in June of 1995. I spent three years living and working São Paulo from 1995 to 1998, another year of dissertation research in 2001–2, and several two-month stays (1999, 2003, 2004, 2005, 2006, 2007). During this time I spoke with forty-eight rappers. All of these individuals except for five were or are members of a rap group as opposed to being solo artists. Another three rappers transitioned into solo careers during our acquaintance. I conversed with thirty-one DJs at various stages of proficiency and experience, who ranged from students in hip hop workshops to national DJ champions to acclaimed DJs. Most of those from the final category have since transitioned into the role of studio producer. I talked to seventeen graffiti artists, all of whom were or are part of a "crew." They worked in groups, and while they all had "tag" names (individual identities), they all strongly asserted their role as a group member. I chatted with twenty-six B-boys and B-girls. Street dance is most present in São Paulo in the forum of workshops and classes, whose participants graduate and perform on stage (for example, in the CEDECA-sponsored event). The issue of age was most pronounced in this group. There were "young" students and "old" teachers. The great majority of hip hop street dancers are young, relative to practitioners of the other "elements." However, due to the fact that street dance was the first hip hop element to be developed in Brazil (as is the story elsewhere around the globe), many of the street dance instructors are "old," again relative to the other elements. Many of the professors I met began dancing pop, lock, boogaloo, and break dance style starting in the early 1980s.

Other significant factors that shape hip hop in São Paulo and that have structured my experience, data collection, and ultimately my analysis include hip hop hierarchy and geographical location. Similar to any other cultural system, hip hop is hierarchical with respect to "emic" or "insider" categories such as knowledge, respect, and skills, as well as in relation to "etic" or more general categories such as market forces within the Brazilian and international music industries and nationalist conceptions of art, folk, and Afro-Brazilian and pop culture. Of course, this division of emic/etic is an abstraction, since, in practice, there is a great deal of influence and overlap between insider and outsider classifications. For example, current notions of "blackness" at a national level of discourse significantly affect hip hoppers as they position themselves as racialized subjects in their performance. Such affects are reflected in hierarchical judgments directed at visible hip hoppers such as Bispo, Naldinho, DJ Tano, Thaíde, Marcelo D2, Rappin' Hood, or Mano Brown and lesser known or anonymous hip hoppers. Members of the hip hop community express judgment often in terms of being more or less "conscious," having or not having a *consciência*. In short, hip hop hierarchy is multifaceted and dynamic given various macro-level contextual factors. Part of the analytical challenge I address in the following chapters is to attempt to track hip hop hierarchy from the perspective of ideology and position.

With that said, I can provide some useful quantifiable data with respect to the group of hip hop consultants pertinent to this text. Especially with regard to the elements of rap and DJ, one's position in the hip hop economic market is an important influence on representation, access to social networks, and ideological investment.

This ethnography is not, for the most part, a study of rap celebrities and other hip hop icons, of which there are a small but growing number in Brazil. Although I have been able to have conversations with Thaíde, King Nino Brown, Marcelinho Back Spin, Banks, Os Gêmeos, DJ Hum, Mano Brown, Pregador Luo, Xis, and other well-known hip hoppers or former hip hoppers (case of the Os Gêmeos), most of my data and analysis is based on interactions with relatively anonymous hip hoppers. There are a couple of reasons for this approach. One is that I believe that hip hop, in general, is about the performance of everyday life and that a hip hop ethnography should involve the reader in the primary tools and experience of performance. Second, I believe that popular culture accounts should provide space for common practitioners to speak. In the case of Brazilian hip hop, this is a case of subaltern studies and representation.[10] Of the forty-eight rappers I spoke with directly, forty were "independent" (i.e., they have no contract with any professional recording label and thus had limited access to professional studio equipment). Of these forty, fifteen had never produced a demo tape or CD. Since approximately the year 2000, more and more Brazilian youth have gained access to increasingly cheaper music production software so that they can produce at least a demo CD. The other twenty-five rappers in this group of forty

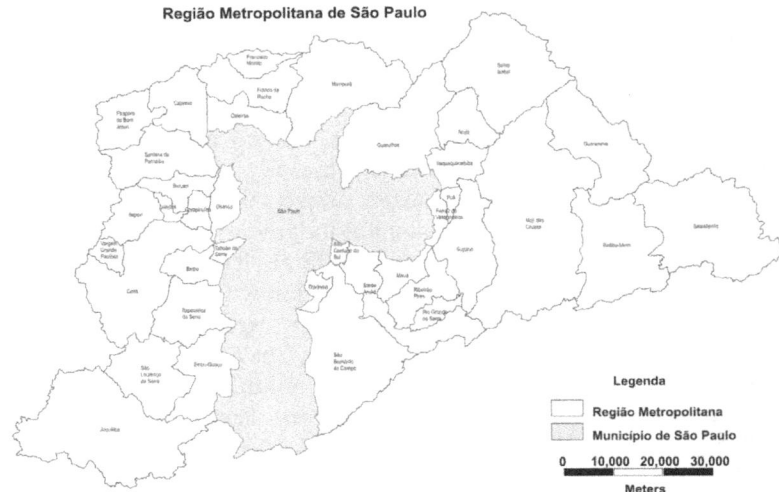

Figure 1.5 Map of São Paulo (Source: City of São Paulo governmental Web site)

invested more time, material, and attitude and created their own label, such as Guerreiros Productions. From a purely economic perspective, a step above the demo but still a cut below the recognition of being recorded at Trama, Sony, or El Dorado.

I have focused my research on the everyday life of youth and how they use hip hop to try to comment on or correct not only their individual lives but also Brazilian urban society as a whole. Beyond the conversations with performers, I conducted over one hundred interviews with hip hop consumers and fans, producers, show promoters, Web site managers, and others involved in hip hop commerce. I attended 117 events and recorded thirty-five hip hop performances in image and sound.

As will become apparent in Chapter 3, the notion and practice of space constitutes an important part of hip hop ideologies. It is also a significant contextual aspect outlining my ethnographic methodology. For reasons of networking tendencies, I spent most of my time within the municipality in various neighborhoods in the east and south "zones" of São Paulo. The map in Figure 1.5 represents the São Paulo metropolitan area with the municipality of São Paulo highlighted. As is apparent in the map, the east and south zones are the largest geographic areas of the municipality. Within the larger São Paulo metropolitan area, I became quite familiar with the central and periphery districts of Santo André, São Bernardo do Campo, and

Diadema, located southeast of the São Paulo municipality. My network of consultants for this project was restricted to these areas. Certainly there were times when I accompanied a group from, for example, São Bernardo in the southeast section of the metro area, to Perús, a district of Sào Paulo in the extreme north zone, for a hip hop event, or to Jandira, a municipality on the extreme western end of the metro area, for a series of hip hop workshops. However, I never made strong connections with those areas.

Arrival and Positioning

The following passage is intended to give the reader a sense of arrival. Anthropologists, as well as journalists, make a point of describing entry points into the field, as they reveal, often in hindsight, significant aspects of society. In this case, my "arrival" in 2001 was a "return" to the field for my official dissertation fieldwork.

> Cumbica Airport, 9:15 AM, August 16, 2001
> One signal of tourist attraction is the appearance of modern technology. This was the case this morning as I watched a computer-simulated video of how to fill out my immigration and customs forms. Having gone through these checkpoints several times before, I surprisingly paid attention and indeed was impressed by the image graphics. The Cumbica (Guarulhos) airport, which handles most international flights in southeastern Brazil, took on a newer sheen as we went through baggage claim, met Selma's parents, and exited to the car. *Mano a mano* and *mulher com mulher* (man-to-man and woman-with-woman), we made our way out of the parking lot and on toward Zona Leste (east side São Paulo). Senhor Antônio, Selma's father, started his usual set of questions about the duration of the flight, the cost of cars, and minimum wage in the United States. Normally, I try to use these questions to query his perspective on contemporary Brazilian socioeconomic conditions. However, I was distracted by the series of billboards on the exit avenue of Cumbica. Like the customs video, these advertisements for airlines, cellular phones, Internet providers, and other markers of cosmopolitan life had been updated. Well-crafted. I imagined a clean continuity for the international traveler moving from Chicago to São Paulo—a relatively uninterrupted sense of place and position. I remembered the "Let's get down to business" article in the on-board reading material about a Uruguayan-born Asian market representative of United Airlines. I stalled Senhor Antônio for a moment as we passed the billboard clusters. Leaving airports reminds me of the virtual trip one takes at corporate cinemas with the perspective of a space traveler navigating through rows of advertisements of consumption and promotions.

Splash!! A bucket of popcorn appears as the driver daydreams of spending his/her frequent flyer miles on a trip to the Cayman Islands. *Come to the island and enjoy the snorkeling adventures and waving palm trees. Close your palm pilot and use it as a lid cover for your Cuba libre, your Hawaiian breeze cooler.* While the corporate cinema promises an excursion into the Hollywood imagination, our exit this morning promised at least a trace of change as a result of Cumbica's makeover.

During my arrival, it was apparent all too quickly that the fresh veneer of globalized São Paulo represented in the produced films of United/Varig Airlines and the avenue billboards had not spread to the vast areas of "periphery" we traveled through on the way home. The trip was immediately familiar as the poor roads, the begging unemployed, the overcrowded buses, and the same architecture hailed me to recognize that *contradiction* is one of Brazil's most plentiful resources. Even the most elite residents of the São Paulo metro area (*Paulistanos*) use "contradiction" as a primary keyword in describing the sense of place in São Paulo. It is the result of haphazard urbanization. It is the result of administration organized around economic stimulation rather than human management. Contradiction is the slippage between modernization and modernity. It is the *favela* neighborhood surrounding the gated and patrolled towers of Ericsson, Tupperware, and Avon regional corporate headquarters. It is the intimate relationships (cordial and spatial) of impoverished service workers with cosmopolitan citizens and the growing distance between socioeconomic classes and life purviews.

The contradictions of Brazil, not unlike relations in India or Mexico, remain the catalyst for production, which has catapulted these countries periodically to high rankings regarding world economies (based on simplistic indicators such as GDP). In Brazil, São Paulo is the strongest example of the contradiction embedded in the national flag's slogan of "order and progress." These terms contradict each other, because due to the manner in which they have been defined, there has not been any measurable or felt "progress" without significant disorder or what Paulistanos generally refer to as São Paulo's constant state of chaos (*caos*). The nervousness of disorder or the rush-rush (*correria*) of São Paulo daily life is not just a feeling and a discourse; it is made material in the "autoconstruction" of the *periferia* and the decaying institutions of the state.

The materiality of *caos* is perhaps most visible in the project *Fura-Fila* (literally "cut in line"), one of the cornerstones of the administration of Mayor Celso Pitta (1996–2000). *Fura-Fila* was an attempt to alleviate the madness of São Paulo metro traffic by constructing an extended highway elevated above the already existing Avenida do Estado. Unfortunately, within a year of construction, there were suddenly no more funds, and the project was abandoned. Literally, the ruins of *Fura-Fila* remain. The project heralded as a step toward "modernization," and "progress" resulted in a scene reminiscent of postwar Dresden, Germany. Periodically I passed this bizarre sight on my way from the east side of São Paulo to the industrial suburb of São Bernardo or from downtown São Paulo to Santo André, another industrial suburb. Over time I noticed a slight change in the monstrosity. It had diminished gradually. Reports from local newspapers and rumors propagated by residents confirmed that people were appropriating the metal beams and rods, pieces of copper, and blocks of cement for private use. They were taking back the leftovers of state failure and making additions to their improvised homes.[11] This is *periferia*; this is the contradiction of modernization and modernity.

Reflecting on the trip from the airport, I began to spin out research questions. To what extent does investigation into hip hop culture reveal the particularities of this lingering specter of contradiction in contemporary Brazilian society? How do hip hoppers address the deepening distance of social inequality in Brazil along with the sense of cosmopolitan solidarity through the dynamic fields of technology and diaspora identification? The importance of hip hop lies here, I thought, as one can take bearings on the histories and current interpretations of contradictions vis-à-vis the sociocultural themes and categories of race, class, gender, citizenship, property, and cityscape.

> Straighten out the smoove and keywords get blurred
> Recite without a groove and it ain't cultured
> Hip hop is the repeat, the backbeat, the life of the street
> The salvation of a war-torn people
> Ticket out?
> The rep?
> But don't forget
> "It's not about a salary, it's all about reality"
> Lift, replace, push it, create
> I am the stereotype
> Monotone on the page
> Multilevel in the word
> The message, massage the brain
> It is the wax and wane
> Jump frame

Você Você
Say Boom Pá Boom Pá
Você Você
Say Boom Pá Boom Pá
No futuro
Já era
No presente, quem é contente?
É o seguinte:
Mano, mana
a união cigana
Escondida
Difícil de encontrar
Tanto nas quebradas quanto no ar
A mensagem que eu peço para vocês ouvirem:
Mantras repetidas não salvam as vidas
De ninguém
Sou eu
Estrangeiro ligeiro, olheiro
Nas coisas que eu quero
Priveligiado mas vigiado
Com responsa de representar os dado
Falo mais
A voz é sua, não vacila
Entregá-la jamais
jamais jamais (inspired by Mos Def and *Os Alquimistas*)

Translation of Portuguese text:

In the future
it's already past
in the present, who is content?
it's like this: brotha, sistah
the gypsy unity
hidden
hard to find
[as difficult] in the shanties as on the air
the message I ask you to hear:
repeated mantras don't save lives
of no one
It is I
the quick foreigner, the onlooker
attentive to the things I want
privileged but watched
with the responsibility to represent the facts
I say more

the voice is yours, don't trip
never give it up
never never

My own position in the field, not surprisingly, has had a great influence on the kinds of experience and knowledge I am now able to represent. When the subject is hip hop, even the most cocky Brazilian will usually give space to a voice from the land of gringos (Unites States). Other than my nationality, I represent almost nothing particularly valuable in the hip hop scene. I am not a rapper, graffiti artist, or a B-boy. I have very limited DJ skills. I am not of any recognizable African descent. I am not a producer, an NGO, or a state representative, nor a member of the Zulu Nation. I do not "dress to the T"; I am not in style. I am much older than the overwhelming majority of hip hop participants. Yet, Brazilian hip hoppers, for the most part, gave me space to speak. Unfortunately, I often sensed a certain embarrassment among local hip hoppers in our conversations. Entrée was made simple, but extended relationships were more difficult. Age proximity played a large role in forging meaningful relationships during fieldwork. In retrospect, most hip hop participants point to their experience in hip hop events as fundamental to becoming an adult and gaining self-confidence. I had more success engaging with those who already felt comfortable speaking to someone different. These differences speak to what Tobias Hecht in his ethnography of street kids in Recife, Brazil called the "oxymoron" of cultural anthropology's fieldwork tenet of "participant observation" (Hecht 1998, 12). Such basic social and cultural differences sometimes made it impossible for me to participate in a meaningful way in local hip hop activities. Yet, it was precisely because of these differences that attracted some youth to engage me in conversation and debate.

In this text I ask the reader to flip through different screens. Ethnography is a kind of screening, a mediated presentation of experience and purported knowledge about something. Following graphic designer and critic Jessica Helfland, I use "screen" as a metaphor to articulate the material presence of vision, that is, "the screen" or the "text," and as the dynamic act of (re)presentation, that is, "to screen" or "to write" culture. As both noun and verb, "screen" refers to the ubiquitous yet empowered "gaze" always inculcated in representation, that is, the "viewing" and "being viewed" of culture. In addition, screens occlude information in the practice of selection within authorship.[12] In screening myself, I expose my voice and provide an essential bit of narrative context.

In some ways, I fall into the description Tricia Rose posits as "white rap fan" practices by "listening in on black culture" (Rose 1994, 5). "Blackness" in this context refers to recognized forms of expression that foreground race and more specifically some sort of Africanity or African American-ness. As Frantz Fanon explained, drawing on the work of Cesaire, Damás, and others, blackness or *negritude* is about "becoming black." Never finished, blackness is a process; however, such a process includes production.

Of course, phenotype does not constitute cultural knowledge and performance style. The "new racial order" in the United States, as hip hop journalist and scholar Bakari Kitwana describes, is about inclusion and porous boundaries within contemporary cultural practices. As Kitwana rightly points out, the foundational institution of the Zulu Nation has always preached inclusion in its articulation of hip hop (Kitwana 2005, 44–45). Just as Miles Davis, so the story goes, could not discern the race of a trumpeter from simply listening to a recording, one cannot simply assert that due to "real experience" African Americans or Nuyoricans necessarily bring more insight to a discussion regarding hip hop. Yet, race and racial identification continue to structure positions of authority and power, that is, who can or should represent cultural practices, rooted in black, Latino/a, and Asian performance. Due to the legacy of race and racialization in the United States, this sort of contextual information is significant.

As I discuss in Chapter 2, the structures of authority and discursive power in Brazil do not follow the same logic. In the case of hip hop, my engagement is more as a representative of the middle-class bourgeoisie "listening in on" marginal culture. The articulation of race, particularly blackness or *negritude*, as discussed in Chapter 4, shifts in and out of focal awareness. What makes Brazilian hip hop "Brazilian" is, in part, this very obligation of how one addresses hip hop in the first place. Again, hip hop is a global, or at least translocal, form, but the way in which performers and analysts position themselves to it varies.

Before outlining the main ideas of each chapter, I dedicate some introductory space to frame Brazilian hip hop as an ideology. This is not to say that hip hop is false or that it lacks grounding in material and life experience. Rather, I argue that when understood as an ideology, hip hop comes into focus as a power that persuades and orients persons in their struggle to understand and explain the world around them. As the vignette below shows, hip hoppers mobilize themselves strategically (at times in essentialist ways) and construe hip hop sounds, images, and texts as cohesive and thus a useful pedagogic tool.

Hip Hop as Ideology

Periferia youth have appropriated, relocated, and recreated hip hop as a set of expressive practices and an overarching cluster of life guidelines. Hip hoppers express ideologies about "reality" and what constitutes "reality" vis-à-vis "truth" narratives and codes of morality and ethics. I use the term "ideology" in a broader sense than what would be called a "standard Marxist" argument. Ideology is not confined to the ideational realm of psychological imagination. Rather, it is grounded in intersubjective discourses and material practices (Eagleton 1991).

Brazilian hip hoppers' conceptualization of reality is slightly different than in the United States. Since the 1990s, U.S. reality, indexed in the hip hop mantra of "keep it real," has come to signal a concern about the disassociation of hip hop from, as Perry describes, the "organic relationship with the communities creating it" (Perry 2005, 87). This sort of co-optation, which is part of any sort of large-scale process of cultural commodification, certainly exists in Brazilian hip hop, but not the extent to which it represents one of the main connotations of "reality." Hip hop is a "marginal" culture made by and for marginalized populations for the most part. While the disconnect between narration, representation, and consumption has not developed to the point that it has in the United States, some Brazilian hip hoppers see this as a potential future. André, one of the creators of the popular hip hop Web site http://www.bocada-forte.com.br explained, "If the *playboizada* [male bourgeois class] ever learn any skills, the *periferia's* hold on hip hop will be over. It'll all change. The already limited opportunities for *periferia* hip hoppers would be reduced to almost zero. Any decent [in terms of hip hop skills] *burguês* [male bourgeois member] can easily generate lots of press, money, and attention. That's the reality." (André, pers. comm.).

That aside, presently hip hop is a "reality" discourse from the perspective of marginalized populations of the *periferia*. It is *periferia*-centric; therefore, everyone and most socio-cultural practices associated with the middle and elite classes are part of *o sistema*. The system includes police brutality; police corruption (especially with regard to drug trafficking activity in the *periferia*); and scarcity of schools, libraries, cultural centers, hospitals, sanitations services, and paved roads. The system's shaping of "reality" also includes histories of racism, domestic labor migration and urbanization (from the northeast of Brazil to the industrial southeast), social class prejudice based on speech patterns (incorrect Portuguese), and appearance (discourses of uncleanliness and general unseemliness).

Brazilian hip hoppers articulate an ideology of *marginalidade* with the objective of making a new system. To this end, hip hoppers repeat the following keywords as mantras of belief and social action. Hip hop is about *transformação* and *união*. Occasionally, hip hoppers give specificity to this solidarity in the form of *nação* or nationhood. Hip hoppers propose that cultural practice should strive toward creating alternative histories of *periferia* communities. Informed by the discourses of Afro-centric and early U.S. hip hop organizations such as the Zulu Nation, hip hoppers claim that self-knowledge is an empowering point from which one can write such alternative histories. They often signal this practice in terms of *informação*, or information, instead of history (*história*) or story (*estória*). In addition to narratives of collective solidarity, Brazilian hip hoppers employ *denúncia* as a rhetorical strategy to portray reality (*realidade*) as lacking and in need of change.

Over the past several years, with the increasing recognition of *a rede* (the "net" or Internet) as part of *periferia* cosmologies, a growing number of hip hoppers have become explicit in linking *tranformação* with technology and globalization. These so-called "positivists" construe globalization as a breakthrough in exposure—an opportunity to articulate *realidade* to "universal" aspects of humanity. At the forefront of this movement are the "evangelical" hip hoppers who highlight the "unlimited frontiers" of religious universalism as a viable answer (*resposta*) to the persistent hardships of *periferia* marginality.

Brazilian hip hoppers differ on how to articulate an ideology of reality, marginality, and change. In terms of production and performance, virtually all Brazilian hip hoppers agree on a methodology of "do-it-yourself" independence. Hip hoppers consistently claim a status of "underground" as a way of indexing individual creativity, entrepreneurship, and difference. However, in practice, hip hoppers in São Paulo significantly depend on state agencies for financial sponsorship and material resources.[13] Discursively, hip hoppers take pleasure in "flipping" or inverting traditional categories of prejudice such as criminal (*ladrão*), as they embrace the term linguistically in forms of everyday address (*e aí ladrão* [hey there, criminal]). Perhaps most impressive to those from prior generations in the *periferia*, Brazilian hip hoppers have organized themselves in posses and politicocultural collectives. They negotiate with local community leaders and state agencies for access to public buildings and open-air spaces to hold meetings, manage workshops drawing on hip hop's four elements, and vote on various projects.

Veteran and novice hip hop practitioners conceive of hip hop as a doctrine that illuminates the existing order of things and as an empowering vehicle through which they are able to join a cosmopolitan formation referred to as *a nação hip hop*. They are *crentes* in hip hop as a project of personhood and collectivity through narratives of mythology and cosmology. Hip hop is a discourse that offers scripts regarding how "I" (individual) and "we" (group) arrived at this point of marginality and what the current situation is (i.e., reality).[14] Furthermore, hip hop is a complex ritual of doctrinarian practice through which performers reinforce the "naturalness" of such relations as sound and language to identity.

For example, hip hoppers assert "natural" correlations between certain bass drum timbres and "blackness," narratives of violence and neighborhood solidarity, and focal vocabulary of brother (*mano*) and masculinity. This process is what Roland Barthes called the "naturalization of the symbolic order" (1957)—an unreflected tension in which we erase the processes and mechanism of articulation in favor of direct, unmediated correspondence. It thus becomes "fact" that a James Brown horn sample *speaks for itself*; it *is* blackness and hip hop, and we (Brazilian hip hoppers) are part of this community (nation) and historical formation (*negritude*). Part of the task at hand is to demonstrate how Brazilian hip hoppers make these "facts" speak for themselves and what forms of representation (sound, image) do they use to achieve this discursive feat.

Hip hop's status as an ideology is complex, because its power of persuasion depends on the belief and representation of hip hop performance (the practicing of its "elements") as a radical break from a dominant logic, that is, *o sistema*. In this manner, hip hop is a discourse of hegemonic critique. Hip hop's efficacy also relies on practices of signification (music, text, image) that highlight hip hop as a continuation of "tradition"—a historically inscribed reality. In Chapter 3, I demonstrate how hip hoppers in the very critique of *periferia* as a suburban space and sociopsychological category, which itself is heterogeneous in practice and intent, frequently reify *o sistema* in the process of articulating hip hop as idea (social transformation) to hip hop as market industry (ideological apparatus of commodity fetishism). Brazilian hip hoppers, even those who call themselves "positive" and argue for a retreat from the *periferia*, often employ dominant representations of the *periferia* to garner recognition from audiences and construct their escape (*fuga*) from the *periferia*.

Such reification or "naturalization" is part of any ideology and speaks to the relative status of hip hop's coherence. The following brief ethnographic vignette demonstrates hip hop ideological practices as part of cultural pedagogy.

It was his first professional hip hop job. After performing with a rap group for seven years, always *na correria* but never formally paid for any performance, Fantasma was hired to teach DJ skills at a cultural center in Diadema, part of the greater São Paulo metro area. He and his childhood friends had disbanded the group, and the members had gone their separate ways. No hard feelings—it was not worth it anymore (*simplesmente não dava mais*). From November 2001 to April 2002 every Tuesday, Thursday, and Saturday morning, DJ Fantasma loaded up his 1986 Ford Monza with two Technics 1200 turntables and a hard-cased box full of vinyl records. Worried about theft, he disconnected the spark plugs every time he arrived home as a precautionary measure.

After waiting for a more than eighteen months on a list, Fantasma had recently moved to a state-subsidized housing project (COHAB) on the south side of São Paulo. The Lego-style building complex sat directly across the street from a relatively small *favela*, independently constructed shantytown, with approximately two thousand residents. Fantasma shook his head when asked if he knew many of the kids on the other side of the street: "You know, there are some who I know and who even go over to the *casa* [cultural center] from time to time, but honestly many of them who I've met they just don't care about anything or anyone. *Eles não prestam e nada presta para eles* [They are worthless and nothing matters to them]."

Fantasma periodically arrives late to his classes: "*Maldita Monza! Também não presta* [Damned Monza! It's also worthless]." He explained the importance of what he calls theory (*teoria*) in DJ classes. Fantasma begins all his classes with at least ten minutes of theory. He slaps a funk record or a soul, jazz, reggae, or blues record on one of the turntables and passes around the album cover to the dozen or so students. Fantasma introduces the sound as "black" and part of hip hop: "This *som* [sound] [in this case a bass line from the 1970s U.S. funk band the Ohio Players], is part of your toolkit as a DJ. You have to know this sound and be able to use it to show that you are *consciente* [conscious]. Knowing this *som* is knowing yourself. Knowing yourself is knowing that we are part of '*cultura black*' ["black" left untranslated]."

Theory for Fantasma is history and identification. In his classes he tries to provoke students to associate sounds with social groups. The Ohio Players bass line is "black" and is hip hop. This kind of *informação* is what hip hoppers claim to "traffick." The sounds and images of 1970s funk all-stars becomes the material of hip hop culture, and Fantasma teaches theory as a process of reification—the sounds stand in for culture and personhood. In the remainder of the class, Fantasma teaches what he calls practice (*a prática*), which involves conventional methods of arranging the sound material. Fantasma refers to this as the process by which those who are *consciente* develop creativity (*criatividade*).

In his work as an educator, Fantasma takes short cuts in his explanation and representation of, in this case, the Ohio Players and funk in general as necessarily "black." There are a number of important contextual details such as the cultural and geographical particularities of Dayton, Ohio in the early 1970s as a place of various funk styles, many of which developed in "softer" ways not useful for later rap DJs and producers (Glen et al. 2004). With that said, Fantasma employs theory as an instrument of persuasion; he simplifies to attract and provoke the kids that these sounds are part of their identities. Furthermore, in practice, they cannot just know the sounds and themselves but use the sounds, flip them around, and cut-n-scratch them to offer their own contribution.

In this book I use ethnography and theory to test and track hip hop ideologies. Virtually all Brazilian hip hoppers profess an essential truth value as basic to hip hop practice, that is, hip hop is all about the truth (*hip hop é tudo verdade*). This phrase stands as a ubiquitous introductory remark in contexts of performance and posse organizational meetings. "Hip hop is all truth" and "all about reality" are commonplace phrases and saving graces as revealed in the initial vignette above. However, it is not with regard to hip hop's "truth" that I direct my analysis, but rather I focus on the construction of ideology in its materiality and the determinations of ideology as an index of certain social situations. For example, in Chapter 4 I contextualize the keyword of *negritude* and historicize hip hoppers' articulation of this concept to the ideology of "reality" and "change." I discuss this relationship in terms of dynamic "moments" of blackness.

Chapter Summaries

In the United States, current hip hop performers, entrepreneurs, and scholars have popularized the concept of a "hip hop generation." This catch phrase is more than a sales pitch; it signifies an expansion of set pop culture skills and attitude into a foundation for a contemporary, youth worldview. The following substantive chapters constitute a comparable claim, namely, that close attention to ideologies of marginality not only affords one insight into Brazilian hip hop but also into contemporary urban Brazil as a social field of historicity, territorial marking, and identity formation. In the next chapter, I expand my introductory statements on position to include a survey of major trends within hip hop research in Brazil. Furthermore, I historicize hip hop in Brazil and introduce arguments concerning the significance of Brazil as a site of research.

In the third chapter, "Making Territorial Claims," I discuss locality as a set of practices. I historicize the category of *periferia* within local literatures of urban planning. My analysis of fieldwork interviews with representatives of housing departments in the city governments of São Paulo, Santo André, São Bernardo, and Diadema reveals undocumented (or lost) narratives of huge populations. Through stories of regional migration, temporary construction projects, shifting cartographies, and locally organized crime syndicates, I trace the formation of *periferia* as clusters of unnamed, unmapped communities and surreptitious land practices. *Periferia* embodies home, and hip hoppers use it as a primary source of *informação* and *transformação*.

In Chapters 4 and 5, I discuss how hip hop performance and consumption work to make and remake (i.e., socially design) current perspectives on race and gender. For example, I demonstrate through my interpretations of ethnographic events that hip hoppers often reinforce the hegemonic force of "racial democracy" discourses and practices even as they rejuvenate a lost fervor of "black movements" from the late 1970s and early 1980s. Curiously, there is a correspondence between the gradual popularization of rap music "made in Brazil" and the relative wane of blackness on rappers' and graffiti artists' rhetorical agenda. In Brazil, this disappearing act makes little noise as hip hop discourse easily slips back to conventional methods of smuggling in race under terms of class. This has traditionally been a collateral effect of the hold "racial democracy" has had on Brazilians.

What is relatively "new" in São Paulo hip hop is a focus on gender. Under attacks from community activists, feminists, and popular culture critics, hip hoppers are attempting to discuss the concept of gender and why it has been absent historically in hip hop narratives and debates. In Chapter 5, I offer my interpretations of such organized debates and how they represent local notions of gender. Similar to the dynamics of race, the performance of gender in Brazilian hip hop reveals contradictory practices. My frustrations in fieldwork around the issue of actually conversing with young women performers or enthusiasts spoke to fundamental aspects of the structure of hip hop, which maintains practices of conventional wisdom regarding legitimate feminine and masculine activities.

In the final chapter, "*Fechou?* (I'm Out / The End?)," I revisit the integrated theoretical and ethnographic threads of hip hop as ideology to assess polemical issues such as Brazilian hip hop's authenticity as "Brazilian" and as "black." More generally, I give my opinion on to what extent hip hop culture is producing any meaningful change in the millions of lives and places hip hop representatives claim as our people (*nosso povo*) and the neighborhoods (*as quebradas*).

Brazilian hip hoppers constantly refer to the state of hip hop as a crisis (*crise*), as they are acutely concerned about cultural representation (identity and history) and political rhetoric (ideology). Yet, *periferia* teenagers and young adults continue to participate in hip hop, for they see it as a viable opportunity to make a living, achieve respect as a person, become a "conscious" adult, and educate others about the importance of knowing who you are and where you are from.

CHAPTER 2

ASSEMBLING BRAZILIAN
HIP HOP HISTORIES

HIP HOP HISTORIOGRAPHY IN BRAZIL:
THE SETTING

In recent years, the project of hip hop historiography has become *en vogue* for students in journalism and social sciences in Brazil. The "shouts from the periphery" (a popular phrase and the name of popular book [see Rocha, Domenich, and Casseano 2001]) are reaching a group of interested middle-class students. Presentations and discussions about hip hop as culture for the first time are legitimate debates. These histories focus on hip hop skills, genres, and cultural elements (Lodi 2005; Assef 2004; Rocha, Domenich, and Casseano 2001); political activism and Marxist ideology (Félix 2005; Pimentel 1997); musicology and industry (Silva 1998); national musical style (Guimarães 1998); alternative education (Ferreira 2005; Andrade 1996; Nascimento 1995); and periphery experience (Rodrigues 2003; Scandiucci 2005; Guasco 2001).

I approach Brazilian hip hop history from the perspective of practice and context so that one can better appreciate the force of hip hop as a set of ideologies. I use the following questions as points of departure: From what tradition or cultural practice does hip hop emerge? What, if any, are the elements of cohesion that allow a historical development? How do practitioners establish and maintain such continuity? In this chapter, I discuss historical cohesion in terms of working-class organizing, political shifts, and an "opening up" to globalized forms of blackness. Practitioners achieve cultural development, in this case hip hop, in a dynamic fashion, which includes the techniques and technologies of various forms of media, state and NGO (nongovernmental organization) bureaucracy, and institution building (radio stations, posses, *galeria* commerce centers). In short, hip hop as a movement of identity politics and artistic expression has depended on the circulation of empowering ideologies of self and group (referred to below as "information") and the occupation of space.

SCHOLARLY DELAYS AND IDEOLOGICAL ISOLATIONISM

Hip hop studies in Brazil are late in coming when one considers that hip hop has enjoyed more than two decades of life and practice. This delay reveals, in part, the relative marginal status of urban popular culture in the Brazilian academy. One could forcefully argue that such paucity represents the skewed concerns of Brazilian academics; that is, "otherness" is relegated to indigenous and Afro-Brazilian groups in rural spaces. Scholarship on Brazilian youth culture in general was scarce until the 1980s, and those few sociological studies actually carried out tended to reduce youth culture to students,[1] which in itself reveals a class dimension to the process of topic selection in the social sciences in Brazil.

Another factor that contributed to scholars' (and the society at large) late arrival to hip hop was that for the first decade of existence, hip hop itself was not particularly visible. Hip hop production manifested itself in live events of B-boy crews, clandestine graffiti activity, and underground dance parties. Informal and formal meetings of neighborhood groups, a practice that would later develop into Brazil's first hip hop posses, were even more underground in nature.[2]

In addition to the underground nature of early Brazilian hip hop, participants have been understandably suspicious of outside researchers, who are usually equated with journalists. Many hip hoppers see journalists as part of *o sistema* and thus perceive them as complicit in the negative representations the *periferia* receives daily in newspapers, on the radio, and on television.

It is only since the turn of the century that local hip hoppers have been able to articulate authenticity to outside exposure. Prior, performers such as Gabriel O Pensador (Gabriel the Thinker), *Câmbio Negro* (in their post-1994 formation), and Claúdio and Buchecha used rap as one element among others (rock, hard rock, and R&B, respectively) in their attempts at recognition. Most hip hoppers interpret this sort of musical hybridity—already common and successful in the

United States over the past two decades if we consider the recordings and styles of the Beastie Boys, Run-DMC, and then later bands such as Jodeci, Rage Against the Machine, and Limp Bizkit—as a betrayal to the "truth" of hip hop in São Paulo. Even with regard to national music with an obvious link to rap, such as *repente*, a griot-style of shouting out the local news in a complex rhyme scheme accompanied by a strummed steel-string guitar, rappers have been slow to appreciate and incorporate such influences as potentially "authentic."[3]

Furthermore, it is only since approximately 2000 that groups from places outside of São Paulo and Brasília have received any respect as part of Brazilian hip hop. Most notable are the southern cities of Porto Alegre (Rio Grande do Sul State), Curitiba (Paraná State), Riberão Preto (São Paulo State), Joinville (Santa Catarina State), and Campinas (São Paulo State). Until 1998, "rap" and "hip hop" in Rio de Janeiro were basically indistinguishable from "funk." São Paulo hip hoppers generally excluded Rio de Janeiro from any sort of hip hop *imago mundi*, because for them, Rio "rap" or "funk" was completely alienated (*alienado*) from any notion of social transformation or reality. In addition, an adaptation of Miami bass sound dominated Rio rap music and thus turned off most São Paulo hip hoppers aesthetically as well. The presence of MV Bill, Marcelo D2, as well as artists such as Black Alien, Speed, and Quinto Andar (Fifth Floor) has put Rio de Janeiro in a different light and has inspired greater contact between the two metropolitan areas. In addition, groups such as Faces do Subúrbio (Suburban Faces) and the early efforts of Chico Science and Nação Zumbi (Zumbi Nation) during the mid-1990s represent the northeastern city of Recife, Pernambuco State.[4]

Brazilian Hip Hop: A Brief Genealogy

In Brazil, hip hop emerged in the mid-1980s as an extension of two areas of cultural activity: B-boy (street dance) crews' public performances and nightclub entertainment contests. The history of hip hop's connection with state government agencies can be traced through the B-boy crews, while the trajectory of rap commercialization is historically tied to nightclub contests.

B-boy crews drew attention because of their occupation of public spaces and their strong sense of group organization. Throughout the 1980s and 1990s, thousands of teenagers—the overwhelming majority of whom are male, *periferia* residents of African descent with little formal education—organized themselves into groups called posses. Through the experience of participating in posses, hip hoppers learned, among other things, how to negotiate with state representatives so that they could organize events, hold collective meetings in public buildings, and occasionally work in state-sponsored social work projects.[5]

The emergence of posses was not an unprecedented act of working-class agency articulating popular culture to state bureaucracy. In fact, hip hoppers drew on either prior experience or advice from older kin on how to procure resources from state departments of culture and social services (i.e., urbanization initiatives) and maintain neighborhood organizations. *Periferia* organizers have successfully lobbied for resources (infrastructure for events, meeting places, a percentage of culture budgets) so that expressive art from the various genres from samba to soul to funk to hip hop's "elements" become integral to what defines "popular culture."

The Brazilian state apparatus organizes and promotes popular culture as a series of nonlabor forums for the majority of the population to build community and feel that they are practicing their citizenship. The contribution of hip hoppers to this long trajectory of working-class state negotiation is that for the first time, the "popular" is essentially an ideology of social change and education. Hip hoppers' negotiation with the state has moved from event-based moments of party pleasure to contract-based programs of sustained and remunerated work. This trajectory is the most common for Brazilians who stay with hip hop and make it their profession.[6]

For its part, the commercialization of rap was a result of the developing nightclub circuit. Nightclub contests depend on sound crews, and *Chic Show* was the first crew to explicitly incorporate a time slot for rap during the dance parties called the rap club (*clube do rap*). As part of a tradition *baile black* dating back to the late 1960s, *Chic Show* itself started in 1967 as a not-for-profit outfit. By the mid-1970s, they, along with sound crews such as Black Mad, Zimbabwe, and later Kaskatas (1981), dominated the dance party production scene.[7]

During the 1980s these production crews developed an infrastructure capable of not only coordinating events but also producing sound recordings. With the exception of the important compilation album *Hip Hop Cultura de Rua* (Eldorado), all rap recordings from the early years (1986–90) were engineered by a handful of dance party sound crews. These include *Ousadia do Rap* (1987, Kaskatas), *O Som das Ruas* (1988, Chic Show), *Hip Rap Hop* (1988, Região Abissal), *Situation Rap* (1988, FAT Records), *The Best Beat of Rap* (1989,

Kaskatas), *The Culture of Rap* (1989, Kaskatas), *Consciência Black* (1989, Zimbabwe), and *Equipe Gallote* (1990, FAT Records). In retrospect, the most important compilation to emerge was *Consciência Black* (Zimbabwe Records, 1989) simply because it introduced *Racionais MCs*, undoubtedly the most influential rap group ever in Brazil.

Hip hop in Brazil began first with dance. The persona of B-boy, or later B-girl, is one who understands and is able to perform various styles of street dance. These include electric boogaloo, poppin', lockin', and break dance. According to hip hop pioneer DJ Hum (known then just as Humberto), B-boys did not know anything about rap. It was just about the break beats and dance. Break beats refer to the segments of music that establish a "groove." They are the sonic highlights or the "hooks" of a particular song. The innovation of early disc jockeys was to isolate these sound segments and weave one to another through the use of two turntables. These were the early methods of musical composition before the advent of rap as a commodity (Toop 1984; Rose 1994).

In general, Brazilian hip hoppers who consider themselves "conscious" and thus reflective about hip hop history and fundamental ethics hold the "element" of street dance in a special place. It is where it all started, and according to many hip hoppers, there continues to be a particular connection between B-boys and B-girls and the true spirit of hip hop competition and camaraderie. I was struck by this sentiment during a conversation with DJ Erry-G in May of 2007.

At twenty-eight years old, DJ Erry-G stands as a veteran but too young to have really experienced the initial wave of hip hop. His first connection was hearing the early *periferia* hit songs of the rap group *Racionais MCs* during the summers of 1992 and 1993. In July of 2007, Erry-G was hired to be a DJ for a regional B-boy/B-girl contest in Joinville, an industrial city in the southern state of Santa Catarina. Erry-G and I met some days afterward in his new home precariously located on the south side of São Paulo near the Billings Reservoir. On a miserable, chilly, rainy morning in late July we ate Passa Tempo brand chocolate cookies as Erry-G recounted his adventure in Joinville. After several narrative detours into the politics of event organization and economics, Erry-G arrived at telling me what he was excited about: the B-boy/B-girl event itself: "Just telling you now, some days later, I get like goose bumps. I can't express to you, Derek, but I was up there working the beats to the ups and downs of the [dance] battles. You know, there's a timing to it. You can't just play the break beats; you've got to really follow what's going out there on the dance floor. Anyway, the whole spirit of the dancers, the incredible camaraderie beforehand and the fierce competition with the "freezes" and postures, the one-ups-man-ship—I remember thinking that this is the real hip hop energy. The breakers know what it's all about. I had forgotten that during the last year or so."[8] Epiphanies such as that of Erry-G were important in the early years of Brazilian hip hop, as street dance pioneers became inspired to organize themselves and emphasize the link between the dance move and the word.

São Bento metro subway station became a place reference for activity starting in 1983. A couple of years later, the popular commercial promenade streets of 24 de Maio in downtown São Paulo, including the malls (*galerias*) and Dom José de Barros Municipal Theater would also become important stages for B-boy performance (see Figure 2.1). Starting in 1987, B-boys at São Bento also began to talk about rap composition. This was the start of Thaíde e DJ Hum as well as early rappers like MC Jack and breakers/rappers Balanço Negro. Nelsão Trinufo, perhaps the first Brazilian to perform and advocate hip hop publicly, and his group *Funk CIA* (reunited in 2001) are foundational to any history of the transition from B-boy dance to rap and DJ performance. Along with Thaíde e DJ Hum, Nelsão succeeded in recording break beats with rap. Unlike in the United States, where the first rap recording (1979, Sugar Hill Gang) is generally remembered as an unfortunate incident of misrepresentation, in Brazil the first rap recording artists were indeed the pioneers of the movement.[9] Prior to 1987 there were groups such as Black Juniors who recorded albums in 1984 (CBS). The closest comparison in the United States would be the recordings of New Edition in 1983–85, in which teenage singers, such as Bobby Brown and later members of Bell Biv Devoe, spiced up romantic ballads and pop songs with intermittent rap verses.

IDENTITY FORMATION AND POLITICAL MOBILIZATION

The history of hip hop in Brazil is part of an overall story of "information" access among marginalized youth in urban Brazil. According to São Paulo DJs, music producers, rappers, and pop music critics, "to be informed" is a valuable asset that speaks to culture, business, history, and ideology.[10] The term *informação* penetrated almost every conversation I had with hip hoppers. Brazilian hip hoppers are always in search of more; they represent an understanding of it in performance, and they divulge it in spaces of education and media communication. It is particularly with regard to exchanging information that consultants exercised demands of reciprocity. Over the past several years, consultants and I have traded copious amounts of information in the form of recorded material; U.S. magazine interview translations; translations of U.S. rap, funk, and soul lyrics; and informal local histories. As I checked my ideas and analyses during the writing of this text against opinions of Brazilian consultants online, we maintained a relationship of "information exchange." In short, hip hoppers explicitly link information to who they are.

Of course, we all are like this to some degree—that is, we *are* what we *know*. However, in the case of the millions of shantytown residents around urban Brazil, identity is seemingly always represented as a lack of or tardiness in access to modernity and citizenship. If not expressed in terms of paucity, *periferia* identity normally signifies a set of negative attributes. As targets of daily yet tacit prejudice within a social system deeply saturated in practices of racism, sexism, classism, and regional-based markers of status, *periferia* residents accumulate countless moments of dehumanizing experiences. Their worth to society is service, enacted in the quotidian gesture of the submissive head nod done in silence. As Brazilian sociologist Luiz Eduardo Soares (2000, 2002) has cogently argued, many young, poor, (sub)urban, black (*negro, preto, pardo*, etc.) kids and adults do not exist *socially*. There is a "social invisibility" that shrouds Brazilian cities.

Brazilian youth who are serious (*sério*) use hip hop to combat what Jose Limón in his description of young workers in south Texas called a "growing depthlessness" (1994, 111–12) related to a flattening of historicity and an increasing proclivity to view culture as disposable. In fact, hip hoppers organize themselves in groups called posses and invest time in developing *consciência*. This process is akin to what Fredric Jameson has described as part of the objective of literary analysis that is tracing the "repressed and buried reality" in a manner that explicitly links to a "master narrative" (Jameson 1981) such as Marxism or, in the case of Brazilian hip hoppers, *o sistema*. Hip hoppers explicitly associate "consciousness" vis-à-vis a recognition of the system to identity formation. In his description of the foundation of *Posse Hausa*, a hip hop organization located in the São Paulo industrial periphery city of São Bernardo do Campo, Nino Brown states, "The intention was to bring together more people, give support to the graffiti artists, the breakers, the rappers, all of whom could go there wherever and be able to say that they were from the *Posse Hausa*; they would have an identity" (pers. comm.).

"*HUMILDADE ACIMA DE TUDO*" (ABOVE ALL ELSE IS HUMILITY): "BLACK" MUSIC, *NORDESTINOS*, AND BECOMING "CONSCIOUS"

As hip hoppers traffic information, they accrue social value and develop a sense of identity. To assess themselves and others in such a process, hip hoppers employ the terms "attitude" and "consciousness." As one gets a stronger attitude and one becomes more conscious (as judged autonomously and by various sociocultural groups), one gains respect as a "real" hip hopper. Hip hop cuts on two, interlocking levels: sociopsychological (respect) and performative-aesthetic (skills in one or more of the "elements"). The developmental trajectory is highly competitive and tends to generate strong sensibilities of achievement and rapid innovation. In urban Brazil, hip hoppers work through a number of concepts in order to achieve respect, a notion hardly ascribed to the typical *periferia* dweller. Again, this is a large part of the power of hip hop, a point often misunderstood by bourgeois Brazilians who take so much of their everyday self-confidence for granted.

One way hip hoppers talk about "consciousness" is to acknowledge that each individual is but one person within a larger collective and that for change to occur, it must be a group effort. "I have come to be a part of something" is an awkward translation of the common hip hop phrase *vim para somar*. According to most hip hoppers, to "sum" or contribute requires an "attitude" (see detailed discussion in Chapter 5) of "humility" (*humildade*), a delicate process of balancing self-esteem and confidence with a sense of not only the group but also the past.[11] The concept of *consciência* in Brazilian hip hop is similar to what Kitwana classifies as "conscious rap" in that the lyrical content "is either Black conscious and/or politically conscious . . . the emphasis is more on the collective rather than the individual" (Kitwana 1994, 32).

Humility is recognizing the local histories of migration glossed in the term *nordestino*, which officially refers to a person from the northeast of Brazil but pragmatically indexes a host of social markers, all of which conjure "tradition," "informality," lack of education and taste (*sem cultura* and *brega*, respectively), and "dark" racial categories (*escuro*). The *nordestino* is a fundamental figure in the modernization of São Paulo during the mid-twentieth century as well as a main character in the concurrent emergence of the *periferia* as a sociogeographical phenomenon in southeastern Brazil. I discuss this dynamic in more detail later in this chapter and in Chapter 3. Humility as a complex process of social status recognition can become productive fodder for hip hoppers in their quest for knowledge of self and community formation. The following vignette centers on a particular *nordestino* who embodies *humildade* and its articulation to hip hop in an orthodox manner. Marquinhos Funky Soul's story is also one of family and migration—a coming of age and intellectual maturity, which he describes as *consciência*.

In September of 2001, I visited DJ Marquinhos in his new home in Parque São Rafael on the extreme southeast side of São Paulo. In 2000 most of Marquinhos's family (parents, four brothers, three sisters, two nephews, and three nieces) decided to return to the northeastern state of Pernambuco and the outlying areas of its capital city Recife. They left their house and property in Parque Santa Madalena in limbo, partially constructed and precariously deeded—a common state of affairs in the *periferia*. Marquinhos decided to stay behind and move into a rented room in a *cortiço*, a housing compound where residents share common toilets, showers, and wash areas, in the nearby neighborhood of Parque São Rafael. He kept up his post office box in Santo André, and his aunt looked in from time to time on their abandoned house. Parque São Rafael and Parque Santa Madalena joined with Jardim Elba stand as a triangle of drug trafficking, violence, and poverty as one traverses a series of peaks and valleys moving in between the municipalities of São Paulo and Santo André.

When I arrived, Marquinhos was preparing a street banner to advertise a dance party he was throwing in honor of the upcoming first day of spring and coincidentally his birthday. In addition, he was selling T-shirts and distributing business cards advertising his show at a newly founded community radio station. The catch phrase on the banner was *"humildade acima de tudo"* (above all else, humility). I ordered a T-shirt, and as he looked around for a pen to write himself a note, I asked Marquinhos what humility had to do with his radio show. He replied that *humildade* is what *nordestinos* know all about.

With a heavy heart, Marquinhos lamented the departure of his mother, especially, and all of his immediate family and began to recount the difficult period during the 1970s when they first arrived in São Paulo. Marquinhos reassured me that they were happy to come to São Paulo and had made the three-day journey by bus without too many problems (thank God, *graças a Deus*). However, soon it became nearly impossible to make ends meet, and there was a time when Marquinhos went hungry, without food (*passou fome*):

No big deal, it's commonplace [*normal*]. I headed downtown to find work [at fourteen years old]. I helped out as much as I could at home and with whatever was left over, I began to buy vinyl records. One of my best friends got into a local dance group and we used to go to the *baile blacks* [black music dance parties]. I started collecting records, especially funk and soul, and I learned a lot [about music and history]. I became "conscious" [*me tornei consciente*]. We talked about *"negros"* and *"afro"* and James Brown, and I started collecting information about all this stuff. This is why I used to act as a consultant for *Posse Hausa*. [This is where Marquinhos and I had initially met in 1996.] I had knowledge and experience they didn't have.

There were a lot of people going to those parties [*baile blacks*], and most of the time, people got along. We all had certain humility, because we had all passed through hard times. We were all from the *quebradas* [neighborhoods in the periferia], and many of us were *nordestinos*. It was hard sometimes just to get to and from the parties themselves. At that time [during the military dictatorship, 1964–85] the [police] men [*os homi*] always gave us a once over [*os gambá sempre tava aí pra dar um geral na gente*]. There was a sense of community and a sense of equality. Above all else humility, because God is everything. Funk and soul really touched me [*mexeu comigo*], and so I collect these vinyl records. I don't like CDs so much, but nowadays I buy them every once in a while. This party on September 22 is going to be great; it'll be right near where we met the other day, near the McDonalds near the bus terminal in the center of São Mateus [name of residential district].

Marquinhos'a choice of the term "humility" as part of his banner, T-shirt, and business card mottos is not aleatory. "Humility" embodies the complex experience of domestic migration, family dispersal, and daily violence. Humility is also the knowledge that inspires collectivity—a respect for others that many remaining participants of the *baile blacks* during the '70s and '80s, such as Marquinhos, try to pass down to those of the hip hop generation. Humility is part of the process that hip hoppers call "becoming conscious."

OUTSIDE CULTURE INDUSTRIES AND DOMESTIC SOCIAL MOVEMENTS

The two forces of U.S.-centered media and entertainment industries, in addition to the second wave of Brazilian urbanization, greatly influenced hip hoppers' consciousness. The former includes most directly the Civil Rights Movement and the Black Cultural Revolution in the United States, and the latter refers to the formation of the contemporary *periferia*.

The contemporary currency of *consciência* within Brazilian hip hop is in part due to hip hop's roots in popular social movements organized in response to the military dictatorship (1964–85) in urban Brazil. Political scientist Sonia Alvarez explains that in Brazil, the military dictatorship employed a development model that, in fact, while promoting capital accumulation, resulted in expanding the structural base of the opposition to the government. Many hip hoppers refer to this period and their active extended family members a generation before as part of the overall working-class process to develop an "oppositional consciousness." Such organizational practices laid the groundwork for what would later become the "political openings" during the so-called "transition" to representative democracy during the mid-1980s (Alvarez 1990, 37–43).

Hip hoppers' contact with consciousness discourses and social activists exposed them to a number of social issues concerning class but also race, ethnicity, feminism, and ecology. The result is that there exists a latent expectation that hip hoppers are conversant with pertinent debates, active leaders, and prominent social institutions including the state. To a significant extent, this is true as hip hoppers work closely with the MNU (United Black Movement); the PT (Labor Party), PV (Green Party), and other official political parties; NGOs associated with the women's and black women's movements such as *Fala Preta!* and *Geledés*; and state departments of culture, education, labor, and health. Again, this dimension of hip hop responsibility distinguishes Brazil from the general characterization of U.S. hip hop, which dictates a responsibility to know styles and skills primarily and politics and social context secondarily, if at all. With that said, it is important to note that Brazilian hip hop *consciência* is an uneven phenomenon and one skewed by limited interests. This causes a host of internal contradictions. I investigate these in greater detail in Chapters 4 and 5 with regard to *negritude* and gender, respectively.

Following Brazilian sociologist Helena Abramo, it is the focus on expressive culture, attitude, and general stance, articulated through the culture industry that sets the hip hop and punk youth cultures of the 1980s and 1990s apart from the prior youth movements (Abramo 1994, xi–xv). Ethnomusicologists such as Averill (1997), Waxer (1999), Manuel (1993), Keil (1984), and Rose (1994) have discussed the importance of cassettes as material evidence of the appropriation of media culture in local musical practice and creativity. Of course, the Internet has changed the substantive structure, but the dynamic exchange and creativity has carried through. In Brazil since 2004, Internet technology has become significantly more accessible, and thus the role of sound (MP3, etc.), still image, and video shareware Web sites such as MySpace and Orkut has become increasingly important. These processes are part of what Brazilian hip hoppers include under the term "trafficking information." As Waxer explains, these practices represent notions of historicity, scene making, and musical creativity (1999, 249). With regard to artistic forms highlighting music (text and sound production), dance, and fashion, there is a trajectory moving from samba-rock,[12] soul, funk, and finally hip hop.

Hip hop in Brazil is part of a longer tradition of "consciousness" mobilized through *periferia* contact with the happenings of black popular culture in the United States. Local hip hop intellectuals, such as Nino Brown and Marcelinho Back Spin, often cite their initial moments of consciousness as part of information access[13]: a neighborhood party in 1976, discussions over a film from 1983, a comment about James Brown in 1975, an uncle's purchase of a pop culture magazine in 1990. In his memoirs, the legendary rapper Thaíde recalls the television program *Comando da Madrugada* (literally, Late Night Command). Thaíde describes what happened on one particular night in 1982:

> It was in the wee hours of the morning [*madrugada*]. I slept in a bunk bed, the top part; my mother slept in the bottom bunk. I lived in a shack with three families, lots of children and various dogs. They were playing "The Big Throw Down" and Goulard de Andrade (the TV show presenter) said it like this: "And we're here at the Chic Show dancehall—a typical sound system get up—and you'll never guess what these niggers [*crioulos*] are doing down here. Come with me, let's find out!" And, so, the camera went down and the sound got louder. It's when they showed Nelson Triunfo and these other guys dancing break. . . . I knew one thing for sure: I had to learn how to dance that way. I saw those guys [*neguinhos*] spinning around, doing the robot. Total insanity. It was that, that's what I wanted. I think I can mark that as my first contact with hip hop. (Alves 2004, 24–25)

Probably the most cited example of early cultural "information" is film. In particular, the Hollywood films *Style Wars* (1983), *Wild Style* (1982), and *Beat Street* (1984) continue to be important in São Paulo, and local hip hoppers often cite them in stories of "consciousness." Legendary street dancer Marcelinho Back Spin explained the importance of *Beat Street* in the following manner: "We had seen some moves here and there, but nothing like that. It was like the film was talking directly to me" (pers. comm.).

Emergence of *Música Black*

Brazilian hip hop's ideologies of self-worth and "attitude" involve becoming conscious of race and, more specifically, blackness. The dissemination of the struggles and victories of civil rights participants in the United States inspired *periferia* residents to make such connections between personal expression and group organization in the hope for social change. This was particularly true during the early to mid-1970s when the Black Power Movement in the United States, although in organizational demise, was at it highest point of national and international exposure. In 1978, the MNU (Unified Black Movement) was officially founded in response to an explicit, violent act of racial prejudice directed at a black taxi driver. During the late 1980s and early 1990s, the MNU established significant partnerships with various posses throughout the São Paulo area. In fact, my first contacts came through attending an MNU meeting in São Bernardo do Campo with a sociology graduate student from USP (University of São Paulo). It was there in August 1995 where I met members of the *Posse Hausa.* While MNU representatives saw the emergent hip hop culture as an important channel into youth communities of African descent, hip hop organizations perceived the MNU as an important organization with which they could "traffic information." (I discuss this research entrée in more detail in Chapter 4.):

> [The appropriation of forms, styles, and histories of struggle] was facilitated by a common fund of urban experiences, by the effect of similar but by no means identical forms of racial segregation, as well as by the memory of slavery, a legacy of Africanisms, and a stock of religious experiences defined by them both. Dislocated from their original conditions of existence, the sound tracks of this African-American cultural broadcast fed a new metaphysics of blackness elaborated and enacted in Europe and elsewhere within the underground, alternative, public spaces constituted around an expressive culture that was dominated by music. (Gilroy 1993, 83)

Urban Brazil, and especially São Paulo and Rio de Janeiro, in the late 1970s and early 1980s became an empowering site of what Gilroy describes as "a new metaphysics of blackness." The emergence of the Black Rio Movement in Rio de Janeiro and Brazilian funk and soul in both cities was more than compelling post-tropicalia grooves. Artists such as Sandra Sá, Gilberto Gil, Tim Maia, Tony Tornado, and Banda Black Rio, internationalized Brazilian *negritude* by creating a hybridity of "traditional" Africanity, contemporary Brazilian social commentary (some artists, of course, more than others) influenced by "roots" reggae, and globalized black pop of James Brown and others. This "new metaphysics of blackness" in urban Brazil was distinctively a youth movement, as these new sounds, images, and narratives attracted a new generation of Brazilians looking for alternatives to "roots" samba.[14] One can listen to the recordings of Trio Mocotó or Gerson King Combo, peruse the extraterrestrial lyrics of Tim Maia's *Racional* album, but these products do not translate the full impact of Brazilian funk and soul.

Similar to any other phenomenon of popular culture, it is the practice, the complexities of production, consumption, and distribution at all levels that brings one closer to the meaning. In the case of funk and soul, young Brazilians such as Beto, Tito, and Marcão (older colleagues of Nino Brown I met in 1997 at a cultural center in São Bernardo do Campo) practiced networking, organizing, and reflecting beyond artistic and social dimensions, thus creating a nexus of what would later be recognized as an example of popular citizenship (Dagnino 1998; Pardue 2008). Figures such as DJ Marquinhos, Zulu King Nino Brown, and Nelsão Triunfo became transitional agents of "information" and helped provide coherence among Brazilian samba-rock, funk, soul, and hip hop.

In hindsight, local hip hoppers see music history as a trajectory of *música black*. This term is an actual market category in record stores. Under this label, one will not find samba, bossa nova, candomblé, or music associated with *capoeira*. Instead, the category of *música black* includes everything from Marvin Gaye to Public Enemy to *Racionais MCs*, Thaíde e DJ Hum, and national soul stars such as Toni Tornado, Tim Maia, Jorge Ben(jor), Gilberto Gil, Lady Zu, Cassiano, Banda Black Rio, and Sandra Sá. This term captures the syncretic nature of hip hop culture in Brazil, one inspired by Africanity from the United States and also Jamaica, England, and South Africa, and then "reterritorialized" in the local milieu of *periferia* reality.[15]

Christopher Dunn has termed the "black" movement *blackitude brasileira*—an insightful neologism capturing the cultural capital of "black," the identity politics of *negritude*, and the local specificity of Brazil (Dunn 2002: 82–84). The value of "black" refers to the opening up of Brazilian media and the rise of the English language replacing the former dominance of French. Brazilian youth in Rio de Janeiro and later in São Paulo, Salvador, and the new nation's capital Brasília also associated "black" and *negritude* with a new politics of racial pride. Unlike the idea of black culture (*cultura negra*), "black" represents a challenge to traditional Brazilian conceptualizations of race and most specifically the national ideology of Brazil as a "racial democracy." The concept of "racial democracy" refers to the idea that the Brazilian nation was founded on principles of equality and that this is represented in all institutions of civil society. Created, in part, as a nationalist discourse in distinction to the United States during the Jim Crow period, "racial democracy" defined Brazilian society as a harmonious mixture of European reason, indigenous spirit and local knowledge, and African creativity as Dionysian fanfare.

"Black" and *música black* are challenges to this ongoing Brazilian convention, because for the first time, Brazilian urban youth have articulated race to identity not in a fashion of African retentions or nostalgia but in a pragmatic sense of affirmation. Brazilian soul star Jorge Ben in his song "O Negro é Lindo" (Black is Beautiful), and later rapper Rappin' Hood in his hip hop anthem "Sou Negão" ("I'm Very Black"), indexed James Brown's famous phrase, "We are black and proud (say it loud)."

Hip Hop Historicity Emerges from Brazilian Urbanization

The ideologies of empowerment of hip hop historically based in working-class-community organizing and "information" of globalized "blackness" contain a spatial dimension as well. It is important to note that the two historical centers of Brazilian hip hop culture, São Paulo and Brasília, became the homes of huge shantytown areas in earnest during the 1970s, the period of samba-rock, soul, funk, and the transition to hip hop. In this section, I briefly outline the contemporary histories of São Paulo and Brasília as they relate to the interconnections of demography and expressive culture. In the following chapter, I focus more closely on the ideologies and practices of *periferia* and "marginal" in the context of São Paulo.

From the beginning of the Brazilian Republic (1889) to the "New State" (*Estado Novo*) under dictator Getúlio Vargas (1937–45), a shift of regional power occurred placing the southeast, including the states of Rio de Janeiro, São Paulo, Rio Grande do Sul, Minas Gerais, and Paraná, as more powerful and influential than the northeast, represented by the traditional aristocracy of the states of Bahia and Pernambuco. The second "boom" of domestic migration in the 1950s and 1960s, from the northeast to the southeast, represents a continuation of this general trend. Migrants headed for São Paulo, Rio de Janeiro, and the new capital city of Brasília in search of employment and a better standard of living. They would become the first generation of the contemporary *periferia*.

Before the first major wave of Brazilian industrialization (ca. 1900), São Paulo was a small town, a leftover missionary station from the mid-sixteenth century. The famous Brazilian modernist author Mário de Andrade (1893–1945) wrote as late as the 1940s of his neighborhood Barra Funda as the outer ring of São Paulo, where track housing sheltered low-wage laborers. Barra Funda by anyone's estimations today stands as part of the urban center. It is a mere five metro stations from the center and founding point of Sé Cathedral. As late as the 1960s, Maria Carolina de Jesús wrote of everyday life in the shantytowns constructed along the river Tietê. *Paulistanos* commonly refer to this area as the "marginal," for it once served as a city limit. Until the 1960s, the two rivers, Tietê and Tamanduatei, did function as margins. However, during the late 1950s and early 1960s, Brazil underwent economic transformations leading to a greater emphasis on mechanized industry, especially around metalwork including automobiles, airplanes, and tractors.

For its part, Brasilía as a city did not exist until 1960.[16] Planners Lúcio da Costa and Oscar Niemeyer envisioned Brasília as a modernist architectural dream combining a Bauhaus aesthetic with socialist ideals of equality. The great experiment of aligning spatial engineering with social organization quickly deteriorated into the bureaucratic management of a bourgeois mall (Brasília proper) serviced by the *candango*[17] residents of the surrounding impoverished "satellite" cities. "Airplane" is a better word choice instead of "mall." The blueprints of Niemeyer and Costa show Brasília as a city shaped like an airplane. As Brazil's new capital city, Brasília would presumably lift the country out of the Third World and jet-propel Brazil into modernity and into the leading global position it has always "deserved." By the same token, the symmetry embodied in the architectural design would ensure a balanced distribution of Brazil's future success and progress. Brasília thus became the new manifestation of the national flag's insignia— "Order and Progress," bolstered by the modernist aesthetic of "form as function."

The redistribution of social capital, perhaps an ignorant illusion of the Brazilian bourgeois architects, never had a chance and was never a great concern of President Juscelino Kubitschek. The so-called *bossa nova* president reckoned Brasília as an innovative launching pad for his economic plans of accelerated industrial growth featuring a mixture of neoliberal negotiations with multinational corporations and ISI (Import Substitution Industrialization) nationalism. Persons from places like Guará and Ceilândia considered the necessary workforce depositories of the new capital city, travel upwards of eighty miles roundtrip daily for employment. Gog (Genival Oliveira Gonçalves), the most famous rapper from Brasília's satellite cities, has dedicated his efforts to describing such travels as a point of mobilization—*baú sempre lotado, vida dura* ([bus] bench always crowded, [it's a] hard life). Similar to ex-members of legendary *Câmbio Negro* (Black Change), Gog recently relocated to the nearby city of Campinas in the São Paulo area.

In Brasília, rock music has been the most influential force on local rap. U.S. and UK punk rock and new wave bands of the late 1970s were popular among much of the middle-class youth. The 1980s was the decade of Brazilian rock, and Brasília was its center with groups like *Paralamas do Sucesso*, *Legião Urbana*, and *Capital Inicial*.[18] In the satellite cities, residents gravitated toward "heavier" rock and new sounds of rap. Long before U.S. groups such as Limp Bizkit, Kid Rock, and even Rage Against the Machine, groups such as *Câmbio Negro* and *Baseado nas Ruas* fused hard rock with rap. Relocated in São Paulo, rapper X of the group *Câmbio Negro* explained in a public debate held at SESC[19] that rock music was part of the local hip hop culture in so far as rock bands often opened for rappers and vice versa: "Musicians frequently participated in both kinds of groups" (public presentation by X, 2001).

Popular Media: Distribution Practices and Informal Institutions

Since the late 1990s rap music and DJ practice has become gradually more accessible and a safer bet for financial investment. There are more nightclubs willing to give up primetime spots for rap. Hip hop has produced a wider audience on Yo! MTV Rap Brasil, more revenue in CD sales at the *galerias*, and a limited market space in upscale shopping spaces in chic commercial neighborhoods. For example, the French corporate establishment FNAC created a section in their CD collection for "national" hip hop. In addition, hip hoppers have produced video clips and have participated ever increasingly in Web sites, YouTube, MySpace, chat rooms, and other interactive and expository virtual communities (e.g., MSN Messenger, Orkut).

However, as all B-boys and graffiti artists know and any rapper/DJ pair with any sense of *humildade* recognizes, the community base of hip hop is limited in its access and connection to these spaces of consumption and distribution. While virtually all households have TVs, some are not able to receive MTV, and relatively few possess even the most modest personal computer, much less have the wherewithal to afford private Internet connection.

In Brazil the years 1998 through 2000 marked a "boom" in dial-up Internet technology access. Some local hip hoppers took advantage of São Paulo's relative position as Brazil's leading economic and technological center by investing in an array of affordable desktop computers and software as well as the newly abundant options for Internet service providers and financial payment plans. It is important to note that this "boom" does not mean that the "digital divide" or the issue of "digital exclusion" (*exclusão digital*), as it is often termed in Brazil, has been resolved. In a study published by IBGE (Brazilian Institute of Geographic Statistics) in November of 2005, the report concluded that 68 percent of Brazilians have never used the Internet and only 9.6 percent use the Internet on a daily basis.[20] For their part, hip hoppers such as Oswaldo, who has made his profession on Internet and image design support for rappers and hip hop groups, explained that it is only recently in 2004 that monthly costs for wideband Internet connection have dipped below 50 percent of a full minimum-wage salary. In short, while the Internet and other information technology have expanded, it remains a struggle and a considerable investment for most hip hoppers and other *periferia* dwellers to establish and maintain consistent contact with translocal image schemes and communities. Many working-class Brazilians circumvent these problems, at least in a limited fashion, by using computers at their place of work and patronizing local Internet cafes.[21]

Historically, one of the most important forums of hip hop distribution has been the local community radio station. During the 1990s large wattage FM radio stations such as FM 105, Transcontinental, and Joven Pan established a touch-and-go relationship with rap music. Personalities ranging from rappers such as Ice Blue (*Racionais MCs*) and Rappin' Hood (*Posse Mente Zulu*), nightclub entrepreneurs such as Natanael Valença (Kaskatas sound crew), hip hop producers such as Milton Salles (radio station owner and early producer of *Racionais MCs*), and popular activists such as Paulo Brown (participant in Black Movement, one-time Yo! MTV Raps VJ, emcee for various *baile blacks*, and frequent interpreter on visits by prominent U.S. rappers such as Ice-T in 1996 and Public Enemy in 1991) all occupied the airwaves with the newest in "international" rap and R&B. They played songs from the United States and occasionally from Jamaica, England, and France, in addition to the hottest jams of São Paulo's own hip hop scene. The radio emcees did their part in trafficking information about upcoming shows, debates, and expositions and periodically opened up the phone lines to discuss current events within the local and international scene. These shows continue to be a Friday and Saturday night highlight for the thousands of teenagers with nowhere to go and little means for entertainment.

However, historically, the "real" hip hopper, the participant who goes beyond the "old news warmed up" every weekend on the big FM radio stations and the kid who wants to engage with hip hop everyday, tunes into his or her neighborhood community radio station. Classified as illegal by the mainstream media,[22] community radio stations are necessarily clandestine as they struggle to stay on the air.

I observed and participated in thirty broadcasts in five different community radio stations on the south and east side of São Paulo as well as the neighboring municipality of Santo André. What is evident is that these stations do not struggle for lack of interest or audience participation. Despite a limited broadcasting radius (average of five hundred meters) and frequent interference from other community radio stations, local DJs work nonstop answering the phone, entertaining guests in the studio, and broadcasting music and news. DJs Jair, Marquinhos Funky Soul, Cleber and so many others conduct live interviews with visiting artists, report the play lists, give shout outs to friends, do limited promotions of neighboring businesses (ice cream parlors, butcher shops, bakeries), and repeat station call letters and phone numbers.

As implicit above, the community radio station is not just an interface between local DJs and listening audiences; it is also an important place where performers, usually rap groups, set up interviews and expose their ideas to different listening communities. As rapper/producer Jamal said repeatedly in our conversations, it is one thing to be known in your *quebrada* (neighborhood), but it is quite another to get respect and recognition in someone else's *quebrada*. The stories of well-known rap groups *RZO, N Dee Naldinho, Facção Central*, and *SNJ* are ones of remarkable success and respect all over the São Paulo area and beyond. As noted by the members of these groups, their "blow up" was due primarily to the power of the "microphones of the poor" (Pimentel 1998, 9) located inside the community radio stations throughout the São Paulo metropolitan area. Although this scenario has changed somewhat since 2004 due to the increased partnership between Anatel (National Agency of Telecommunications) and the federal police in the prosecution of such radio stations and the gradual increased access to hip hop on the Internet, the community radio, or "pirate" radio, remains a significant institution within the Brazilian hip hop topography and, at the very least, a key reference in the reigning ideology of hip hop as a "spatial conquest." I will expand on this concept in the following chapter.[23]

Expansion of Place and Purview: Hip Hop Posses, the *Galerias*, NGOs, and State Agencies

The formation of posses, a grassroots style of hip hop organization, was fundamental for the establishment and longevity of Brazilian hip hop. In addition to providing support systems and networks for interested hip hop participants, posses are negotiating bodies whose members lobby for state and NGO aid to have the wherewithal to organize performance events, provide access to computers, and obtain grants to study studio production among other projects. Posse members educate themselves in the art of proposal writing and bureaucratic loopholes. With city government agencies as problematic but functional assets, hip hoppers most often negotiate for space in the form of a building to hold regular meetings, a neighborhood park to hold performance events, or wall space to create a public graffiti mural and provide "community education."

Toward the end of the 1980s, centers of hip hop organization expanded. During most of the 1980s, hip hop claimed one space—metro station São Bento (as mentioned above with regard to street dance). At first, network expansion stayed close to the city center. Remaining in the old downtown area of Consolação near a strip of whore houses (*putarias*) overlooking a historic Catholic cathedral, hip hoppers, now interested in integrating B-boy dance with rap and DJ performance, organized in Praça Roosevelt. The first posses including Black Syndicate (*Sindicato Negro*) were instrumental in bringing together the Black Movement and hip hop.

The disseminating process of hip hop "information" rapidly increased, and the tone of Brazilian hip hop "information" became more political and social and less oriented toward leisure. Hip hoppers often refer to this moment as the real beginning of hip hop as a "movement." By 1990 hip hoppers moved posse organizations to the *periferia*. Some important examples include Street Concepts (*Conceitos de Rua*) in Capão Redondo (south side São Paulo) and Black Alliance (*Aliança Negra*) and Active Force (*Força Ativa*) in Cidade Tiradentes (east side São Paulo).

Figure 2.1 Images from inside the 24 de Maio *galeria* malls in downtown São Paulo, April 2002.

The directional flows of hip hop organization are important to track and provide another useful point of contrast with the United States. In the United States, more specifically in New York City, the initial flows of dissemination ran from uptown (Bronx) to downtown Manhattan and the pop club scene. This is the story of Fab Five Freddy and his connections with pop star Debby Harry from Blondie, for example. In Brazil, due to the lack of public infrastructure and decent meeting places in the periphery, the flows of dissemination ran from downtown (*centro*) out to the periphery neighborhoods. The everyday work of posses and the weekend showcases became events solely of the periphery. It is only within the last few years that downtown clubs, frequented by the young bourgeoisie, have begun to make significant investment in "respected" rappers and DJs and reproduce the New York story.

By the early 1990s São Paulo hip hoppers and local entrepreneurs had established downtown rap stores as what Paul Gilroy terms a "black cultural institution" (1993, 252). Visual signs and sonic booms of Brazilian hip hoppers' notions of blackness blanket the first two floors of the *24 de Maio galerias*. These signs dovetail with icons and indices of *periferia*. Similar to Gilroy's description of black record shops of the 1980s in urban England and the United States, Brazilian *galeria* music stores are incredibly small. Workers, often themselves aspiring hip hop artists, tape or otherwise post every square inch of the store with posters, album and CD covers, and flyers, including the ceiling and sections of the floor to advertise hip hop, in general, and blackness and *periferia*, more specifically. For the outsider, the *galerias* are almost suffocating and would make many claustrophobic. For the typical hip hopper, they are comfortably hegemonic in the sense that they are both trivial and empowering. They are *normal* (meaning commonplace), and *galeria* regulars exude a palpable confidence in knowing intimately all the products not only of their store but all the other stores as well. There is no doubt that the *galerias* are what hip hoppers term a "spatial conquest" (*conquistar espaço*).

Commercially and ideologically, the establishment of music stores dedicated to rap music, DJ equipment, hip hop clothing fashion, and "black" hair styles represented a spatial conquest. In fact, before becoming part of the hip hop business world, the *galerias* of 24 de Maio were home to many informal gatherings of "black power" groups during the 1970s and early '80s. These "gallery malls" stand as two ten-story towers located downtown in between the landmarks the Republic Plaza (*Praça da República*) and the Municipal Theater (*Teatro Municipal*). Most of the surrounding streets including 24 de Maio are pedestrian thoroughfares and are off limits to cars except for the occasional police wagon conducting street vendor stings (see Figure 2.1).

Designed in 1957 and built toward the turn of the decade, the downtown gallery malls stand as an alternative to shopping on Augusta Avenue in the super chic Jardim neighborhood near São Paulo's "Wall Street" avenue—Avenida Paulista. According to local union leader Antônio Netto, there was a decadent period in the late 1980s before the emergence of rap commerce. There are presently over forty stores located on the bottom two floors that stock solely domestic rap music and hip hop apparel. In the east tower there are ten stores that sell only imported rap music and hip hop apparel.

In addition to the organization of posses and the establishment of market spaces, Brazilian hip hop has benefited from a sustained effort of NGO partnership. In my visits to the various *periferia* communities, it became evident that NGOs are integral parts of shantytown landscapes. With greater infrastructure and operating budgets than posses, NGOs are reference points for *periferia* youth. From weekend events to mundane food drives, NGOs are important landmarks.

Unlike posses, most NGOs are general in focus. Faced with fundamental problems of violence (police and drug traffickers), shortage of basic public services (sanitation, water, health, education, pavement, transportation), and general social stigma, *periferia* residents frequently welcome the opportunity to work with NGO organizers. They use hip hop as a cultural vehicle for residents' general awareness or "consciousness" of living conditions and a motivational force toward social activism. Organizations such as *Projeto Monte Azul*, CEDECA (Center for the Defense of Children and Adolescents), *Aldeia de Futuro* (Future Village), and *Ação Educativa* (Educational Action) have been instrumental in providing financial support for hip hop as part of neighborhood life on an everyday basis. In my conversations with program coordinators, they considered hip hop an effective conceptual and methodological approach to education and vocation for *periferia* youth. Hip hop is then a popular and attractive means to an end.

Many hip hoppers themselves have also realized that hip hop as a sphere of knowledge and citizenship works more effectively when articulated to issues outside of the "four elements." By the time I conducted my formal dissertation research (2001–2), hip hop posses had all but vanished. Posses such as *Posse Hausa* in São Bernardo do Campo broke up into various performing groups invested in both commercial performance and smaller scale projects with state agencies such as the Department of Education. Many posse members began to invest more time in making a name for themselves financed by part-time appointments with a handful of community groups and NGOs around the metro area.

Of those posses that stayed relatively intact, most groups, such as *Força Ativa* and *Aliança Negra* from Cidade Tiradentes in the extreme periphery area of east side São Paulo, identified themselves not as "posses" but as a "cultural organizations" interested in exploring the opportunities afforded by international human rights, education, and social work NGOs. The expansion of posse work and hip hop knowledge does not solely depend on NGOs; state agencies at district, city, state, and federal levels over the past decade have established significant relations with hip hop groups.

Força Ativa is an interesting case in this regard. On December 16, 2001, during the inaugural event commemorating the opening of a community library, group members, community activists, and neighborhood kids wandered in and out of the concrete block building.

Nestled in between a typical street bar (*boteco*) and an abandoned, semi-vandalized store space, the new library was a rare sight. The library consisted of a couple of folding tables, chairs, and six bookshelves filled with hundreds of tattered paperbacks (history, political science, sociology, geography), didactic material (grammar exercises, English-language books), and magazines. Friends and other community organizations donated all the material.

A Força Ativa Biblioteca Comunitária is a place filled with "information" in the middle of dozens of square miles containing housing projects, improvised domiciles, street bars, and "evangelical" churches. In a round of speeches, various group members referred to their negotiations with the city government, in particular COHAB (Coordinating Committee of Habitation) and Departamento do Patrimônio (City Patrimony Department), as part of the process to obtain this simple building space for the purposes of establishing a library. When asked about connections with NGOs, long-time *Força Ativa* member Gois explained that while sometimes necessary, *Força Ativa* greatly preferred to utilize *poder público* (public policy channels or civil society) rather than rely on NGO aid. This decision is explicitly political, for members believe that it is the government's obligation to provide such services, and to negotiate solely with nongovernmental organization results in essentially letting the state off the hook.

Summary

In this chapter I have attempted to integrate a number of histories ranging from urbanization, media, and identity politics to provide the framework to understand the emergence and development of Brazilian hip hop. Local hip hoppers link the cosmopolitan aspects of "blackness" and socioeconomic class with neighborhood traditions of community organizing and bureaucratic negotiation. They regenerate the concept and place of *periferia* and in so doing reposition themselves not as victims (*vítimas*) but as authoritative subjects on what *realidade* signifies to the majority of the people (*o povo*).

In the following chapters, I ask the reader to revisit these places (*galerias;* community radio stations; posse, NGO, and cultural organization meetings) as I contribute to local hip hoppers' retelling of marginality and *periferia*. The messiness of coordinating popular music events that adhere to "reality reports" and social transformation (ideology and hegemonic formations) finds a parallel in the messiness of writing culture and producing ethnographies (argumentation and explanation).

The desire to represent more forcefully the *periferia* and mark *self* as a humble prophet motivates hip hoppers to rework the musicocultural elements of the past and reshape the public spaces of the present into recognizable hip hop places. However, reality is crooked, and while hip hoppers preach mantras of "*união*" and "responsibility" (colloquially referred to as *responsa*) in the understanding and representation of "information" about "reality," differences emerge and reveal discrepancies and even contradictions within the hip hop movement and what is intended by *periferia* and *marginal*. Are the voices of hip hop ultimately reinforcing the persistent contradictions of Brazilian society, so fresh in my mind as I remember early arrivals in São Paulo airports and neighborhoods? Or does hip hop culture mark a significant shift in Brazilian social relations?

CHAPTER 3

MAKING TERRITORIAL CLAIMS

SÃO PAULO HIP HOP AND THE SOCIO-GEOGRAPHICAL DYNAMICS OF *PERIFERIA*

São Paulo is not a humane city. It resembles more an improvised machine, constructed from scrap iron and barbed wire connecting one piece to another, switched around to fulfill the immediate necessity . . . here there is no possibility of playing around, of joking. Everything is very serious. Violence provides the dominant tone. Violence is present in our experiences with the city itself and its spaces, through the difficulties we face in simply moving about.

—Amaral 2001, 86

We are the periphery / We are the majority
Take from the lyrics and / Use your wisdom.

—Ieda Hills 2001

In April of 1997 I traveled to the home of Nino Brown in São Bernardo do Campo. Nino, who is one of the most respected members of the Brazilian hip hop community, has always prided himself on his collection of music, literature, and other material related to *cultura black*. He refers to himself as a "researcher" and "archivist," and it was in this spirit that we scheduled my visit.

Nino has been married for over twenty years and has two daughters who are now young adults. His personality is reflected in his home— simple and humble (*simples e humilde*). These are both honorable characteristics as part of an ethical code in the *periferia*, one that hip hoppers emphasize in public performances. As we flipped through photo albums spanning back to the late '70s, Nino expressed a tension in remembering the old school (*velha guarda*) and back in the day (*naquela época*):

> You see, we were all tight [close friends]. We went out to *bailes* [dance parties] as much as possible. The neighborhood associations (*Amigos do Bairro*) were pretty open and let us organize dance parties. I had an uncle, who was influential with the administration, and one Saturday night when I was thirteen he snuck me in. I wasn't supposed to be there, but he got me in. I remember hearing the emcee (I would later understand what an emcee was) shouting out "James Brown" and "Tim Maia," but I had no idea who or what he was talking about. But, I was so excited. This is what I wanted to do.
>
> But, as I grew up and we went out, I realized quickly that the road to the *baile* was not so easy. We got used to body searches (*batida* or *tomando geral*) by random police sweeps. You had to have your RG (identification card) at all times. This was during the dictatorship, OK. We dressed different, we had afros, we were different. This made it [life] more complicated. There were always patrols that we had to deal with on our way to any *baile* or whatever. This [treatment] became totally normal. We felt safe only inside our homes and inside the dance halls once we got there. The rest was always risky (*arriscado*).
>
> It's different now with hip hop. I think hip hop has conquered (*tem conquistado*) more space. There are a lot of factors and it continues to be a struggle (*luta*) for recognition, but hip hop, I think, really has a chance to make it so these stories of my youth don't become those of this generation and the generations to come (pers. comm.).

Nino's story demonstrates a perception of space grounded in practices of restriction, violence, and surveillance. In his remembering of his youth during the late '70s and early '80s, Nino repeatedly made connections between his and others' personal experiences of persecution to the "conquests" of contemporary hip hoppers. While Nino is generally upbeat about hip hop's future as an expansive "movement" (*movimento*), which legitimizes and potentially empowers youth as more in control of the *periferia*, many hip hoppers worry about whether they will ever achieve such "conquests." The sketchy locales of train and bus terminals, street corners, abandoned parks, and other public places continue to dominate hip hop narration. They are contested sites; the terrain is up for grabs between the two ideological "systems" of hip hop and conventional Brazilian society, respectively.

Just as with culture, space is never simply given; rather, it is, as Lefebvre (1991) argued, a "social product," a negotiation between what he called "representations of space" and "spaces of representations" (1991: 33). Dominant social relations are materially inscribed, yet there are always underground practices of difference rooted in everyday life.

Similar to "information," as discussed in the previous chapter, "space" is a valuable commodity in Brazilian hip hop. In São Paulo hip hoppers use these terms in their general evaluation of an event or the movement as a whole. The hip hop event is good or bad to the extent to which it represents a conquest in space (*conquistar mais espaço*), to borrow from local terminology. Through performance and commodification, hip hoppers strive to mark a larger area as "hip hop" and engage in wider exchanges of information, thus affecting an increase in hip hop knowledge and strength. The keywords of information and space derive their power from conquest, because agents of social inequality (police forces, policy makers, crime syndicates, etc.) have historically limited and regulated access to them for the overwhelming majority of the São Paulo working-class population.

The act of "spacing out" the *periferia* is both geographically expansive and aesthetically creative. Hip hoppers work "the system" (i.e., state agencies and discourses) to gain resources and cover new ground. In addition, hip hoppers oppose the system and commodify their spaces through the contested tropes of violence, death, danger, and crime. In this chapter, I discuss *periferia* as place and ideology and *marginal* as a resident and empowered protagonist within hip hop culture. I argue that hip hoppers, through their cultural work, attempt to restructure the periphery spaces in São Paulo not only through metaphorical refashioning in rap lyrics but also and perhaps more importantly through a heightened sense of "occupation."

In the following, I historicize São Paulo as a twentieth-century urban phenomenon and give particular attention to the emergence of *periferia* as one result of national socioeconomic policies. The process of autoconstruction (*autoconstrução*) in local housing acts as an important metaphor for an understanding of hip hoppers in their articulations of *periferia* as a place of identification (see Figure 3.1). In São Paulo, hip hop is the first organized effort to represent the *periferia* as a distinct symbol of aesthetics and ethics. In this chapter, I delineate the spatial nature of hip hop cultural work through a discussion of event-oriented travel, the opening of a community library, and operating epistemologies under the rubric of hip hop as street culture (*cultura de rua*). I begin with a rumination.

PERIFERIA: THE "WAY DOWN" OF HIP HOP IN SÃO PAULO

With cities, it is as with dreams: everything imaginable can be dreamed, but even the most unexpected dream is a rebus that conceals a desire or, its reverse, a fear. Cities, like dreams, are made of desires and fears, even if the thread of their discourse is secret, their rule absurd, their perspectives deceitful, and everything conceals something else.

—Calvino 1974, 44

Although I have willingly come back to report to you sire, so many voyagers out there in your kingdom are hardly in control of their travels. In hard fact, I am confident that I may err in my description of the next city.

One elderly inhabitant of *Peri Peri* shared a secret with me. He first arrived in *Peri Peri* by mistake he claimed. Unfamiliar with the terrain and illiterate in the language, Phulano had memorized his friend's instructions. He was told to wait for the third stop and then step off the train. Unfortunately, the train made an unexpected stop in Valdrada, the mirror city of Baucis. Held in permanent formal opposition to Baucis, Valdrada exerted a magnificent gravitational force. For its part, Baucis was a lofty place whose inhabitants were fascinated by their own mundane absence. Baucis residents spent the days musing on conditional situations of actually inhabiting the earth and walking its grounds, subject to its laws.

The force brought the train to a halt and accommodations were made. A common hindrance is Valdrada, so banal as not to be considered. Unaware of such trivialities, Phulano indeed counted the stop as one of his three. Phulano proceeded to exit the train, his destination altered forever.

Once inside *Peri Peri* the traveler must put away any maps or guides. The glossy graphics of urban contours pale into line drawings and paint can spray. The belief that generates hope in this city is that at night the city is erased and subsequently made anew the next morning. And yet, although *Peri Peri* is always under construction, it is never renewed. It only expands catching more and more wayward travelers unsure of where to get off.

This fictitious passage emerged as I reviewed my field notes from São Paulo alongside reading Italo Calvino's *Invisible cities*. It is a rumination—a mulling over of experience "regurgitated" in the cannibalistic spirit of Brazil's early twentieth-century modernist movement of

Figure 3.1 A typical *periferia* house in the intermediate stages of *autoconstrução*. I took this photograph during an afternoon lunch in June of 1999 with the family of my long-time friend and consultant Marquinhos Funky Soul.

antropofagia. The short story is based on historical narratives from late nineteenth-century immigrants en route to Montevideo, Uruguay, who mistakenly landed in the port city of Santos and then later relocated to São Paulo.

The periphery (*Peri Peri*) is both a material place and a contested ideology. In general terms, it is one of the most expansive projects in global history. In Brazil, the *periferia* is a place of autoconstruction[1], state abandonment, and strongly marked social prejudice. It is in the way down (*no fundão*)[2] and literally and conceptually "out of the way." Periphery as a socio-geographical manifestation of marginality is "nominally part of the system, but to the extent that it is divested of any real decision-making power, the system also loses any real control over it" (Lomnitz 1977, 11).

Brazilians consider the *periferia* a dangerous place, because it represents the outlaw backlands within the metropolitan spaces of modernity and progress.[3] It is the socio-geographical manifestation of the necessary difference for Brazilian bourgeois identity formation. The dialectics of shoreline culture and countryside tradition have generated a great deal of what is gingerly negotiated as Brazilian national history.[4] The *periferia* is, in effect, out of place. Yet, it is the point of

Figure 3.2 This favela is part of the recent housing developments around the Billings Reservoir on the south side. It was taken in April of 2002 during a weekday visit with Zulu Nation Brasil DJ Érry-G.

address (*ponto que eu peço*), unmistakably the discursive fodder for hip hop culture.[5]

The *periferia* is a field of contestation around issues of semiotic and geographical control with representatives on all sides riffing off of historical key terms held in common. Violence, marginality, criminality, citizenship, and illegality are among the discursive tropes interlocutors invest in as they claim higher knowledge and exercise politics over São Paulo's most polemic spaces. Whether expressed in terms of public policy, educational programs, crime statistics, environmental disasters (e.g., mudslides, massive flooding) or in hip hop cultural practices, the *periferia* is a problematic place that generates debates focused on human value and territorial management. The central presence of violence and criminality in São Paulo hip hop and mainstream depictions of the *periferia* speak to the inherent ambiguity in metaphorical discourse.

"Violence" as a Nervous Category

Popular opinion spatializes violence as a natural part of the periphery or suburban landscape. The general association of violence to discourses of social inequalities in the form of place designation is common around the world.[6] Hip hop has been an important vehicle for marginalized persons to speak to and thus deconstruct such reifications.[7] Hip hop is a global phenomenon in this regard. In the United States, such associations of space and society are part of the "moral panic" pattern, which has remained relatively constant since the 1970s and the beginning of what is termed "deindustrialization" (Lipsitz 1994, 18–19; Forman 2002, 294–301).

In the early 1990s, *Racionais MCs* recorded the song "Pânico na Zona Sul" (Panic on the South Side). This was the first recorded rap song in which Brazilian rappers explicitly linked bourgeois panic to *periferia* activism. The double entendre is one of the most common and productive discursive strategies in Brazilian hip hop. Members Edi Rock, Ice Blue, and Mano Brown of *Racionais MCs* explore the two sides of "panic": fear and agitation.

For hip hoppers, "panic" is a product of bourgeois or "systematic" ignorance structured in practices of racialization and discourses of social class. In their song, *Racionais MCs* commodified a story that I have heard many times, one that details the emergent tension when there is proximity between members of distinct social classes. Rappers spin out narratives about what *periferia* youth think when they hear ubiquitous commentary such as, "Did you see that huge black guy (*cê vui aquele negão*)? Watch out for the poor kid (*Cuidado com aquele pobre / favelado*)." Rappers dramatize and give retorts. "Are you nervous, stressed, worried," asks the street kid to the middle class teenager on the subway, on the bus, or on the sidewalk.

"Panic" also indexes control. It is not just about nervous middle-class youth and adults scared of aggressive and boisterous *periferia* youth. In addition, the *periferia* is under a collective feeling of panic, as police brutality and organized crime take countless lives. Local hip hoppers Miltinho and Horácio, from the east side, quoted Racionais front man Mano Brown's lyrics from "Panic on the South Side" as they related their stories to me about daily struggles and survival: "If I were to list all the names of those who are gone, I wouldn't have time to say anything else" (Racionais 1993).

"Panic" is also a discourse of agitation and activism. As long-time hip hop organizer and community radio station DJ, Marcão frequently stated as a way of concluding his comments, "*por isso mesmo que a gente tá aqui* [it's exactly due to this; that's why we're here]." Hip hoppers utilize panic to try to get people to reflect (and theoretically transform) socioeconomic conditions of poverty, penetrating discourses of fear, and daily practices of violence into a set of aesthetic commodities in which territorial claims constitute a substantial portion of content and form. Hip hoppers explore a wide range of opportunities to playback the *periferia* over and over. In so doing they comment on the idea and structure of São Paulo as a contemporary city.

SÃO PAULO URBANIZATION

São Paulo city administrators and spokesmen during the first half of the twentieth century boasted that their city was the great Brazilian metropolis without *favelas* (see Figure 3.2). The term *favela* almost exclusively refers to city spaces rented to squatters. The residents do not own the land, although they usually own the house. If not rented, then the occupation is part of an "invasion," the term most widely used by popular media.[8] The forementioned claim by São Paulo administrators was part of the general competition among Brazilian cities, especially between São Paulo and Rio de Janeiro. In Rio, the *favela* has been part of the landscape for approximately a century. Even in 1971, according to a study conducted by Sebes (Secretary of Social Well-Being), researchers reported a mere 163 *favelas* in São Paulo with 8,552 shacks (*barracos*) and 41,100 residents, or 0.75 percent of the urban population. In just thirteen years, a similar study conducted by Sempla (Municipal Secretary of Planning) reported over one million *favelados* (shantytown residents) distributed in 1,200 *favelas*.[9]

Favelas are spaces of drastic socioeconomic measures. In fact, most performing hip hoppers do not live in *favelas*; they rather reside in surrounding neighborhoods characterized by more conventional architecture featuring houses (*casas*) over shacks or shanties (*barracos*). Again, to participate actively in hip hop requires a certain material investment. The primary goal of "exchanging information" demands expenditure in the process of becoming "conscious." Purchasing recorded music, clothes, equipment, paint supplies, bus passes, photocopying services (e.g., zines and flyers), and computer and Internet services are difficult but potentially manageable for the typical *periferia* dweller and next to impossible for the typical *favelado*.

Despite this gap, which theoretically divides *periferia* communities, hip hoppers explicitly include the *favela* as an originary point of narration and sociocultural activity through their work in posses and other organizations. The point is that the *periferia* is a heterogeneous space, which nevertheless hip hoppers seek to unite through discursive protagonists such as the "marginal" and rhetorical tropes such as violence and crime in order to establish a new and different "system."

With that said, some hip hoppers certainly do live in *favelas* and over time accumulate information material, develop their abilities to articulate (*trocar uma idéia*), and accrue positive hip hop value. The story of Rappin' Hood, one of the founders of *Posse Mente Zulu* during the early '90s, is well known by Brazilian hip hoppers. He is from one of the largest *favelas* in Latin America, Heliópolis, located on the southeast side of São Paulo municipality. Since 2000 he has been one of the most visible hip hoppers in Brazil appearing constantly on television, radio, and in well-advertised public performances, such as the November 20 celebration of Black Pride.

The story of Cafu perhaps one day will be more widely known, as he and his rap group have risen in popularity over the past couple of years. However, as Cafu repeatedly assured me, his daily life in the *favela* is *normal*. We met in a community radio station in December of 2001. A month later I visited him and his family (older sister, brother-in-law, mother, younger sister, two younger brothers) in a *favela* in Santo André near the major metropolitan transportation artery of Avenida do Estado. As is the case with most *favelas*, Cafu's shanty sits on terrain that is difficult to negotiate due to the inconsistent and occasionally severe slopes and natural terraces.

> DP: So, how's the rap group *A Fita da Perifa*?
> C: It's getting better; we recently changed our line up. I think it's better now.
> DP: How did you get involved with hip hop in the first place? Was your father an influence on you?
> C: Well, no, he left the scene (*saiu da cena*) when I was very young. You know, my mother tells me how the neighborhood (*quebrada*) was much more difficult back then. Everything was dirt and mud, no asphalt. Any rain would put our shanty (*barraco*) at risk. She tells the story about one afternoon we all nearly died in a mudslide. You see the slope here, right? You can imagine. We were all little or just babies. It was a miracle. I eternally thank God for his intervention [at that moment].

As we discussed his plans for the rap group and his style of hip hop, I asked Cafu whether or not his father has had any influence on his tastes. In his response he historicized the lay of the land. While he is thankful that now part of the *favela* has asphalt, Cafu realizes that this is quite rare. He knows that most *favelas* continue to be spaces where fatal accidents are just a matter of time. Cafu has become a community activist and frequently participates in local politics in downtown Santo

André. He has successfully argued for hip hop to be included systematically as part of the municipal's definition and program of "youth culture." Cafu repeatedly insisted that he will never leave his *favela*, as he feels an obligation to the place and (most of) the people. Implicitly, Cafu in his stories of his hip hop accomplishments and community activism pinpointed his *barraco* and his *quebrada* as the basis for his knowledge and motivation to pursue hip hop and consequently work for social and material change.

Favelas are only one form of *periferia* landscape. The history of spatialization practices in São Paulo urbanization is best understood under the more general term of *loteamentos* or distribution of property lots. The practice dates back to the 1910s as the city administration adapted lowland properties near the rivers (Tietê and Tamanduateí) into a Brazilian version of "track housing" for the labor classes. In relative parallel fashion, governmental agencies used the English "garden cities" as models for the highland residential areas, what would later be called the Gardens (*Jardins*). What was originally a government project soon became a private industry as the rise of transportation and real estate barons worked outside of any systematic governmental regulation in isolated urbanization projects (Caldeira 2000, 221). The first bus system was established in 1924 and with it the first prototype *periferia* developments. Organization was spotty at best, because expansion depended almost exclusively on individual or small investment group projects. Government intervention was basically nonexistent until the 1970s. In informal interviews with long-time social workers for the city of São Bernardo do Campo, Pedro and Gil explained that only in the late '70s and early '80s did city government start to dedicate any concentrated effort in regulating or "urbanizing" the city territory. This process includes the provision of basic services (water, electricity, sanitation) and, simply, the registering (*cadastramento*) of residents and the implementation of official addresses and street names. In addition, officials standardized lots in five by fifteen square meter plots.

The lack of government regulation fostered a situation in which high levels of corruption ran rampant. Often real estate agents parceled land illegally in order to boost profits. Frequently, they themselves had not registered the land and thus were officially not in position to negotiate the lot.

Autoconstruction and *Periferia* Subjectivity

As with most populist agendas in Brazil, home ownership was originally a project of the administration under the charismatic dictator Getúlio Vargas (1930–45). During the second major twentieth-century military dictatorship in Brazil (1964–85), government projects around housing occupied a significant amount of bureaucracy and administration. Despite grandiose rhetoric and systematic institutionalization of residential programs such as BNH (National Bank of Residential Policies) and SFH (Finance System of Residence), the objective of complete urbanization was quickly transformed into a middle- and upper-class option.[10]

The shift from popular to middle-class financing plans stems, in part, from definitions of "legal" and "illegal" properties. The BNH, through such programs involving collective housing projects (commonly referred to as COHABs) such as Profilurb, Promorar, and João-de-Barro, in addition to direct individual finance, attended less than 3 percent of the housing crisis during the 1960s, '70s, and '80s (Sachs 1999, 69). One of the major differences between Profilurb and Promorar, which substituted Profilurb in 1979, was that periphery urbanization was designed not to dislocate residents. This had proven ineffective in prior projects as displaced residents after a short period of time opted out of COHAB or "project housing" and returned to the *favela* areas (Sachs 1999, 151). Greatly inspired (or interpellated) by the "dream" to own a house, the majority of São Paulo citizens excluded from such policies explored the options of *autoconstrução* in the *periferia*.[11] This process is distinctive because it combines precarious material conditions with marginal circumstances of legality in the hopes to build one's own house "in the urban hinterland," as James Holston (1991a, 447) poignantly describes.[12] Holston emphasizes that autoconstruction in São Paulo is part of an important albeit frequently contradictory process of politicization of daily life in the *periferia*. Namely, Holston claims that autoconstruction is a "particular social production of space in which the need to build a house represents the builder's relations to a set of conditions that we might call peripheral urbanization" (Holston 1991a, 451). This complex of relations is liberating along the lines of what hip hoppers call "consciousness" and the cultivation of the ability "to speak about reality."

In addition, autoconstruction is controlling as residents make connections between domains such as home and behavior based on consumption practices. Autoconstruction thus becomes part of the more general Brazilian discourse of "appearance" as residents evaluate each other based on a hierarchy of building materials. For example, *periferia* dwellers are extremely sensitive to the range of bricks (*tijolos*) as they invest in home improvement. The Bahian brick (*tijolo Baiano*), for instance, ranks as "popular" and thus not of any particular distinction. The very use of *tijolos* for those in the *favela* is usually something out of reach. They can never seem to shake the fact that their home looks like a shanty, it's miserable (*tem cara de barraco, cara de miserável*), because they do not have the means to construct and add on to their home with anything other than plywood, particle board, and metal sheets. In many cases, the presentation of self and family through house appearances inevitably reinforces the strict power relations of class, frequently expressed through judgmental albeit "cordial" phrases of race such as the expansive discourse of filth (*sujeira*) as it relates to blackness (*coisa de crioulo*).

As with any effective policy, the ideology correlating home ownership to modernity was complemented by legislation. Rent freezes, as stipulated by the Renter's Law (*Lei do Inquilinato*) implemented in 1941 under the Vargas regime, New State (*Estado Novo*), stimulated the "dream" of becoming a homeowner and discouraged the development of any real estate into rental property. Recent demographic research shows that the majority of urban and suburban residents continue to own their place.[13] In fact, over the past decade there has been a significant increase of home ownership in São Paulo from 64.2 percent to 70.7 percent. This increase is due primarily to recent initiatives by governmental funding agencies to promote consumption and renew domestic financial confidence after the 1994 *Plano Real* economic plan.

The various practices of autoconstruction dominate the periphery of São Paulo as demonstrated in a number of studies (Rolnik, Kowarick, and Somekh 1991; Maricato 1979; Holston 1991a, 1991b; Caldeira 2000). Owning a home, regardless of size or quality, is the basis for obtaining space (*espaço*) and personality (*personalidade*) in working-class lives. In his work on autoconstruction practices in the *periferia* of São Paulo, Holston relates local narratives of aesthetic distinction and creating "personality" despite the fact that the material used is virtually the same. Patterns are limited due to the sheer practicality of material costs; however, this does not figure into conceived and perceived difference. It is often a lifetime project and one that generates discourses about the future and potentialities (Holston 1991a, 447).

Brazilian hip hoppers work inside out. They approach spatial "conquests" and "occupations" frequently starting with domestic spaces.

In early 2002, Éboni began a new project to construct a graphics studio in a storage space above the modest garage of his parents' home in Parque Santo Antônio on the south side of São Paulo. Éboni saw this project as beyond personal home repairs, because his idea was to transform this storage space into a *periferia* version of a cyber café and professionalization laboratory. He wanted to invest in a few personal desktop computers, a network of high-speed access, and updated graphic design software. Local youth interested in hip hop, Internet design, CD cover graphics, and communication technology would be able to register for classes and computer time in DJ Éboni's attic/studio. Éboni has always been interested in creating hip hop networks and, as he termed it, "connecting my [neighbor]hood to the rest of São Paulo and also the global centers of hip hop" (pers. comm.).

Éboni's dreams depended on his ability to pitch the community technology project to outside investors, principally the Department of Culture in the São Paulo municipality and local NGOs such as *Projeto Monte Azul*. At the time of this writing, Éboni has been unable to procure the funding needed for the overall project, although with the financial aid of a local business and cultural center, he has transformed the storage space and expanded his office, which used to be synonymous with his bedroom. Presently, he recruits friends and *periferia* youth through contacts with neighborhood organizations such as *Monte Azul* to help him with graphic design projects.

Hip hoppers reckon their cultural activities as complementary work in the long-range goals of providing space and distinction to their families. They understand all too well that this process involves difficult negotiations with a host of state institutions and neighborhood individuals and organizations. The experience of hip hop is filled with such negotiation as stage performance itself is something that requires complicated organization and frequent authorization. Working hip hop offers teenagers an introductory education in the art of persuasion and bargaining—skills that they know from observing their parents are valuable for their future or even present immediate families.

FORÇA ATIVA AND PROJECTS OF OCCUPATION

And Polo said: "The inferno of the living is not something that will be; if there is one, it is what is already here, the inferno where we live every day, that we form by being together. There are two ways to escape suffering it. The first is easy for many: accept the inferno and become such a part of it that you can no longer see it. The second is risky and demands constant vigilance and apprehension: seek and learn to recognize who and what, in the midst of the inferno, are not inferno, then make them endure, give them space." (Calvino 1974, 165)

The case of Active Force (*Força Ativa*), a veteran hip hop organization based in the east side of São Paulo, helps illustrate the importance of hip hop in the overall struggle for spatial (and semiotic) control of and in the *periferia*. The "inferno" of *periferia* life is both fodder for nihilism, which at times is creative, and a productive counterpoint to something new or "positive" in life. The following ethnographic piece represents the process of *Força Ativa*'s involvement in the establishment of a community library in December of 2001.

During my earlier stay in São Paulo from 1995 to 1998, I heard many references to *Força Ativa* as one of the few remaining posses from hip hop's so-called "second wave" in the late 1980s. In a phone conversation with Moisés, he characterized *Força Ativa* as a youth organization (*organização juvenil*). *Força Ativa* "*evoluiu*" from a posse into a cultural organization (*núcleo cultural*) in 1995. Moisés explained that the motivation was to take on a wider range of social issues than what hip hop (especially rap music) was capable of. Moisés summarized that hip hop, which focuses on performance, was not succeeding in raising the level of consciousness of neighborhood people about such social issues as gender, racism, sexuality, and politics. The members of *Força Ativa* felt that a profile and structure of "community cultural center" would improve the situation. Moisés explained to me the organizational structure of the group: there are five "commissions"—press, hip hop, culture, *palestra* (public speech), and general. As mentioned in Chapter 2, the first posses were based downtown near the first public spaces of hip hop performance, such as the São Bento subway station and Roosevelt Plaza. Shortly thereafter, hip hoppers began to organize groups in the suburban periphery neighborhoods. This shift from the downtown to the neighborhood, in retrospect, established a stronger sense of *periferia* locality and resulted in garnering more support from long-standing community organizations. For many, this period transformed hip hop in São Paulo into a "movement" as part of a trajectory of working-class social activism.[14]

Força Ativa was founded in 1988 in the neighborhood cluster of Cidade Tiradentes. The district name is revealing in and of itself. When traveling to Cidade Tiradentes it seems as though one has left São Paulo. By way of avenues named after industries, such as Textile and Metallurgy Avenues, one traverses long stretches of roads lined with occasional residential shacks and substantial forests. Over a hill or two, one passes *Negreiros*, a supermarket chain located solely in the extreme regions of the east side. Take a right, and suddenly one faces an immense network of housing projects. Interestingly, the name "*Negreiros*" refers to the Portuguese slave ships. Part of the store's logo contains a longboat icon. I felt very odd when I first saw this emerging from the nowhere just prior. In fact, *negreiros* is an occasional, pejorative nickname for the buses that make the trek out to the extreme neighborhoods of the *periferia*. Conflating racism and class prejudice, *negreiros* is one more example of how Brazilians frequently invoke colonial metaphors of segregation and difference as part of contemporary imaginations. However, the above association is not the official one. "Negreiros" is also the title of one of the most famous poems by Castro Alves, an abolitionist of the late nineteenth century. Further investigation confirms this logic as a cross street is indeed Castro Alves Lane.

City construction under the agency of COHAB (Metropolitan Company of Residence) began in the late 1970s, and in 1980 Cidade Tiradentes had ten thousand residents. Two decades later the population stands at over five hundred thousand (Ponciano 2001, 70–71). In this sense, the district of Cidade Tiradentes is a city (*cidade*), a

Figure 3.3 Photo of young resident of Cidade Tiradentes in attendance for the library opening. The building next to him is the library, December 2001.

separate community boasting over two hundred four-story residential buildings. The center plaza features a statue of Tiradentes, the historical martyr of Brazilian Independence.

The opening of the community library as part of a larger project called "Let's Read a Book: Center of Documentation and Youth Group for Human Rights"[15] was the result of over six years of negotiation between *Força Ativa* and COHAB. The library constitutes the corner section of the building next to the young man in Figure 3.3. According to Edilane, the closest public library to Cidade Tiradentes was in the Penha district, which is located at least forty-five minutes away by bus or car. Because the district area was almost entirely a project of COHAB, they officially control most of the commercial and leisure space. More recently, private church organizations representing a variety of Pentecostal denominations have developed impressive structures and networks in Cidade Tiradentes as well as in most of the *periferia*.

Cidade Tiradentes represents a governmental success for most city planning officials. As outlined above, most financial aid for housing never reached the working classes. Cidade Tiradentes is one of the few large-scale and relatively completed housing projects in the São Paulo metro area. While this history distinguishes the COHAB project from most of the *periferia*, Cidade Tiradentes shares an important socio-spatial characteristic with the other *periferia* locales. There is little or no social, health, or educational infrastructure. Edilane, a community activist who has worked for fifteen years in various districts within the São Paulo public school system, related a story to me that demonstrates a critique of the district's cultural layout. Prior to the inauguration, community residents knew that the library was open only by word of mouth. One Sunday afternoon during a torrential downpour in the middle of all the traditional weekend television variety-show programming, a woman faced dangerous mudslides to check out a book. Edilane recited the woman's words as inspirational and a positive sign for the library's future. The woman said to Edilane, "Thank you so much for not opening a bar (*boteco*) or a church" (pers. comm.).

Various organizations and individuals donated books to the library. The collection includes literature sections on Cuba, citizenship and human rights, and didactic subjects such as Portuguese grammar and world geography. In one of the inaugural speeches, Aldmir, a long-time neighborhood activist and honorary member of *Força Ativa*, stated. "You can't change the world without understanding it. To read is a principal way of understanding" (Public speech by Aldimir, 2001).

While the local hip hoppers sometimes kid the fifty-year-old Aldmir for being so spirited in his activism, all the members of *Força Ativa* support him and ask him for Marxist bibliographic references as well as personal stories. After the speech, hip hoppers repeated the phrase "*leer é o jeito de entender*" (reading is the way to understand) as a performative introduction. In the subsequent performance, *Força Ativa* rappers defined hip hop as an important medium through which Cidade Tiradentes youth can articulate their knowledge (from reading) to social change. The record needle dropped, and *Força Ativa* rapped local stories as they passed around the microphone.

It is significant to note that many of the principal members of *Força Ativa* make a living with hip hop and human rights issues through a wide range of either governmental-organization or community-education programs. Edilane gave the example of the Projeto Férias, which takes place during July (winter break). Marcos Mendonça of São Miguel Paulista School System organized this program for alternative education, and he sought out representatives of hip hop culture. It was a success, and Djalmão (a *Força Ativa* member), at the time of this writing, was living off of a modest salary from these activities. Ice-Ice, a twenty-eight-year-old widower whom I had met at a hip hop organizational meeting of CEDECA (Center for the Defense of Children and Adolescents) back in 1997, received funding in 2002 to participate in an international exchange of groups from Italy, Belgium, Brazil, and Colombia. The meetings were organized around themes of human rights, and hip hop culture was a significant sector of the participants and activities. In our conversation at the library inauguration, Ice-Ice commented on the presence of neofascism in Italy, especially in Italian universities.

Italo Calvino, in his wonderfully imaginative and metaphorical book *Invisible Cities* speaks through the main character Marco Polo and describes the city of Raissa as a city of sadness: "In the morning you wake from one bad dream and another begins" (Calvino 1974, 148). While Cidade Tiradentes nominally extends a sense of infrastructure and national history, for most residents, life there is more like a concentration camp than anything else. Several residents used "concentration camp" as a metaphor in conversation to express their feelings of alienation and ostracism from social groups at work or in the process of obtaining employment. This provides a context to understand the significance of hip hop cultural work by *Força Ativa*.

Spatial Practices and Citizenship

U.S. hip hop scholars such as Forman (2002) and Rose (1994) have argued that the very creation (discourse and performance) and cultivation (markets and dissemination) of hip hop is spatial in nature. In Brazil, this is also true, but in the case of São Paulo hip hop, participants go further. Many practitioners, especially those with past or present experience in posses, articulate space to knowledge and citizenship, looking beyond hip hop itself. This is sometimes referred to as the "fifth element" of hip hop, which comes from Afrika Bambaataa's own warning for U.S. hip hoppers to form social workshops that can give a more permanent structure for youth in the practices of "citizenship consciousness." Afrika Bambaataa founded the Zulu Nation organization in 1974 in the South Bronx, New York City. The "fifth element" perspective was fundamental in the establishment and administration of the Zulu Nation Brazil in 2002.

Borrowing from state discourses of popular culture and education, some hip hop activists have used hip hop as a conduit for a more general debate. As I have discussed elsewhere (Pardue 2004b, 2007), "education" is a discursive category that includes citizenship. Hip hoppers have been relatively successful in making the argument that the *periferia* as a social space needs not only investment in infrastructure but also resources and funding for programs that motivate residents to engage in civil society (*poder público*) and exercise their rights (not just obligations) as Brazilian citizens. The struggle has come in convincing state representatives that citizenship and popular culture, a long-standing pairing within Brazilian populist politics, are more than occasional public events and performances. Rather, they require a program, or what hip hoppers term an "alternative system," that provides a more regularized option for youth in the *periferia*. This helps explain why so many activists have transformed posses into NGOs and "cultural agencies" (e.g., *Força Ativa*, Zulu Nation Brasil, *Posse Hausa*) in order to gain funding as an organization with a wider agenda.

My approach to hip hop as an articulation of Brazilian citizenship is based on the assertion that "the state" in Brazil presently is best characterized, following Gramscian scholars, as an "ethical" state. The function of the ethical state is "to form citizens and to gain consent, the two distinct projects being in fact the same: the subject is to be formed as one who consents to hegemony . . . the work of formation is continuous, taking place not only through pedagogy but through the work of intellectuals in all the spheres of civil society" (Lloyd and Thomas 1998, 21). Culture, then, does not manifest itself only as artifacts of aesthetic production or "objects of knowledge" but rather as a process of "forming an ethical disposition" (7), which articulates to the representational structures of the modern state (17). In essence, the combination of citizenship and hegemony theoretically resolves the historical problem of political democracy and social inclusion within a system of hierarchy.[16] Yet, the situation is more complex, because citizenship is not only an individual practice but also one of association. The associative factor is important, because it highlights participatory citizenship and potentially the weakening of government authority and thus complicates state hegemony.[17] Within such a frame of theory and practice, hip hop as an integral part of contemporary socialization in (sub)urban Brazil becomes potentially part of producing "normal" states through everyday fields of popular activity and imagination (Hansen and Stepputat 2001).

In addition to the philosophy of the state and citizen formation, there are particular factors related to Brazil and Latin America worth review in regards to macro-level structural developments. Throughout Latin America during the late '70s and early '80s, the idea of "citizenship" shifted from one of strict obligations to a growing sense of individual and collective rights. Following the paradigmatic analysis of T. H. Marshall (1950), "rights" include a range of practices and liberties on social, civil, and political levels. In the late twentieth century, "social rights" would encompass "human rights" and "cultural rights." Not surprisingly, much of this change was the result of regime changes (structure) and concurrent collective organizations (agency) as part of the so-called "democratization" of Latin America. As the military dictatorships and other forms of authoritarian rule ceded to more participatory political systems, people, especially those from the poor, working classes, discovered and "conquered" more space to articulate their concerns and enact changes in everyday life in their neighborhoods and workplaces. However, some of these new or adapted institutions of democratic citizenship were co-opted by suspicious state agencies, or they reproduced long-standing corruptive practices of clientelism, also frequently implicating the state (Arias 2006; O'Donnell 1996). In addition, as many Latin American scholars have demonstrated, the triad of social, civil, and political rights rarely existed in an equal fashion from the very beginning of democratic transition. For example, systematic state violence, both physical and symbolic, targeting indigenous groups in Guatemala, Bolivia, and Peru, as well as the intensified privatization of security in places such as Brazil, have complicated the practical meanings of citizenship in these and other Latin American democracies.[18] Some scholars have argued that the problems of effective citizenship in contemporary Latin America are related not to democracy or capitalism *per se*, but rather they are, in part, due to a particular "consumption" of democratic theory by local intellectuals and governmental administrations (Hagopian 2007). Specific to Brazil, this interpretation resonates upon consideration of the prevailing theory of how Brazilians historically have understood "modernity" (Schwarz 1992) and "race" (Schwarcz 1993).

In sum, there is a common theme in the citizenship literature related to Latin America. Namely, as increasingly more heterogeneous groups "conquer" public space and exercise their rights under new and seemingly autonomous purviews of "citizenship rights," the democratic state's job of hegemony and, by extension, control of identity formation becomes strained.[19] In Brazil, hip hoppers' practices as they relate to culture, education, identity politics, and community reflect a multi-leveled approach. Some hip hoppers articulate identity and citizenship to the extreme locality of the *quebrada* and have made alliances, both discursive and infrastructural, with local crime syndicates and thus challenge the essential authority and legitimacy of the state, NGOs, and globalization. Others try to circumvent the state through transnational alliances with distant hip hop organizations such as Zulu Nation or B-boy and B-girl street dance collectives based in Europe. While still others insist that hip hop must be in dialogue with the state in an effort to force the state to dedicate resources to public projects. As I have outlined above and have detailed in greater specificity elsewhere (Pardue, forthcoming), the efforts of the group *Força Ativa* are an attempt to address this final hip hop approach to citizenship.

SPACING OUT *PERIFERIA*

As Forman asserts with regard to the U.S. ghetto, despite or perhaps because of "all its negative complexity, [it] is still heralded as an idealized space for minority teens within rap's cultural discourses precisely because it is considered as being somehow more 'real' than other spaces and places" (Forman 2002, 60). Tricia Rose locates the emergence of U.S. hip hop culture in the "context of deindustrialization"[20] in New York during the 1970s. Her comments about the interface between hip hop culture and U.S. city spaces resonate here: the city "provided the context for creative development among hip hop's earliest innovators, shaped their cultural terrain, access to space, materials, and education" (Rose 1994, 34).

In São Paulo, the persistence of *periferia* as the unifying ideology keeps the dynamics of the perception of rap as a territorial phenomenon in check. Just as popular access to technology expands imaginations and material possibilities, *periferia* as structure and value regulates hip hop's "spatial mobility" (Kirschner 1998, 250). In other words, the centrality of *periferia* as both an ethical and aesthetic focus of hip hop narration and performance limits its spatial expansion. The most obvious ramification of this is the simple fact that, unlike in the United States where over the past fifteen years the hip hop fan base has become increasingly suburban and even rural, Brazilian hip hop remains an urban phenomenon. For example, in contrast to popular music genres such as *música sertaneja, música axé, forró,* and even to some extent *samba pagode,* Brazilian hip hop artists stick to a limited circuit when they leave São Paulo. As mentioned in Chapter 2, there is a fan base and performance infrastructure in southern cities such as Londrina, Curitiba, and Porto Alegre in addition to central cities such as Brasília, Belo Horizonte, and the coastal cities of Santos and Rio de Janeiro. Recently, there have been a few excursions to the northeast cities such as Recife, but this is rare. The cities within and surrounding the Amazon rainforest area, which comprise over one third of the country's territory, are off the hip hop *imago mundi.*

Hip Hop Events as a Series of Occupations

Hip hop events, just as all social events, are formations involving temporal and spatial development. Events are highlights, but as a social phenomenon, they are better thought of as processes. The prelude and *denoument* of an event encompass trajectories of movement as participants and observers travel, in the case of hip hop, across the city. Different notions of São Paulo emerge from activities within different circuits (Magnini 1985, 1992; Santos 1979). The constitution of hip hop spaces involves a particular intersection of location, economy, and sociality, and in the following I analyze a series of examples in this manner ranging from weekend public performances to rap commodification to journalistic material. Through the presentation of these vignettes, I intend to demonstrate the role that space, especially in the idea of taking over space, plays in the hip hop event. From this general notion of space, I transition to a focus on *periferia* and the currency of violence as a valuable hip hop trope, which both "marginal" and "positive" hip hoppers utilize in their attempts to take account of and reconstitute the *periferia* and thus "reality."

Performances rarely occur in downtown areas or in nightclub neighborhoods. Periodically there are special events booked in downtown clubs such as Green Express and Samba Love. Such downtown spaces are located in a circuit of pornography cinemas and cheap hotels and motels.[21] Many places have no apparent name due to high turnover. The following example demonstrates local socio-spatial hierarchies in São Paulo's nightclub circuit.

In November 2001, I attended the finals of a state-sponsored rap contest, O Festival de Rap—*Projeto Cultura na Rua* (Rap Fest—Cultural Project on the Street). With the grand prize being a set of MPC 2000 recording equipment, over five hundred groups from the São Paulo metropolitan area entered the contest. MPC stands for Music Production Center. It is a coveted piece of equipment for sound engineering due to its capabilities in sequencing, sampling, and interface qualities. Such expensive equipment would basically ensure a recording contract by adding the necessary level of quality to the musical production. Thirty groups advanced to the finals, including my friends and consultants *Os Alquimistas* (The Alchemists), *S.T.A.* (acronym for "We Are All Allies"), and *C.O.T. A Fusão* (Fusion of Original Concept in Triplicate). The finals took place on a sweltering Saturday night on November 24, 2001, in a club called *Usina* located at the bottom and the end of Cardeal Arcoverde Avenue in Pinheiros neighborhood. "*Usina*" literally means factory or mill. Such names are somewhat common in the aftermath of the "warehouse" club phenomenon that took São Paulo by storm in the late 1990s. Hardly comparable to the impressive infrastructure of a *galpão* (a more specific "warehouse" reference term) such as in Barra Funda, Mooca, or Tatuapé neighborhoods, *Usina* is an empty signifier as well as literally a bare structure for entertainment. Traveling by car or bus, the club Usina is the last establishment, save a parking lot, before being dumped onto Rebouças Avenue at the intersection with the *marginal* massive expressway system. The *marginal* is akin to the "beltway" or "loop" system in the United States.

I arrived at one thirty in the morning, adding an hour to the reported stage time of *Os Alquimistas*, only to find frustration. *Alquimistas* member Maulana explained that the event had barely started, and organizers had already changed the rules due to scheduling problems. Maulana along with a number of other participants related several narrative variations on a theme: "It's like that. Sometimes we think, like in the case tonight, that it's gonna be different. But it's not. We're [popular culture and hip hop in particular] always last in line for the state and the system" (pers. comm.). Maulana was hot under the collar. Guzman, another *Alquimistas* member, stepped in and explained that the judges had suddenly changed the rules of the contest. They were now not allowing "intros." In São Paulo the "intro" is the conventional space in which band members or one rapper address the audience, often telling a story about the struggle (*luta*) of the group and thanking the judges and promoters for organizing the event. This is also a space for rappers to thank God, shout out to their neighborhood, and incite the crowd to pay attention or to simply show their support by throwing their hands in the air or jumping up and down.

But, in fact, as Guzman intimated this rule change was really just the last in a series of disappointments. He reminded me that the competition had already been marred by delays and switching locales throughout the qualifying and semifinal rounds: "Maybe for those who are just starting out (*pessoal que tá chegando agora*), it's fine. We've been around for a while and we expected more. Derek, go on in, take a look around in there (*Vá lá, cê vai ver*)." I walked in the front door, paid a few bucks, and entered the club. *Usina* was shaped as a square box with two levels, a lower level dance floor and an upper level four-sided balcony area. At two o'clock in the morning with only a third of the groups having performed, the club was barely at half capacity. Nevertheless, the heat was stifling; it seemed as if there was no ventilation. I watched a random group perform. I have no idea who I saw, because the sound system was horrible. It appeared that there was only one functioning microphone. I was driven out of there back to the cement "patio" in front of the club, where I had first run into the members of *Os Alquimistas*. Sweating profusely and thoroughly lost with regard to the event's proceedings, I began to understand Maulana's frustrations.

The dream to claim space (*conquistar um espaço*) means to exercise cultural and political autonomy. This is frequently absent in hip hoppers' negotiations with the state in urban spaces, especially those with higher social capital such as Vila Madalena. The locality corresponds strongly to constructed notions of legal and illegal as discussed above in the historical overview. Multiple reschedulings and multiple modifications regarding the whereabouts of crucial events become "normal." In the process of adaptation to the confines of state-run cultural events, participants seem to lose their voice.

Place identity is "constructed out of movement, communication, social relations which always stretch beyond it" (Massey 1992, 14). The links among travel, knowledge, and recognition are not lost on São Paulo hip hoppers. It is extremely important for hip hop performers to know the various confines of the immense São Paulo *periferia*.

Through live performance venues, rappers, especially, but all hip hoppers cover a great deal of territory going from one live gig to another. Beyond their own performances, hip hoppers make cameo appearances in events across the metropolitan area starting in the afternoon and going into the morning hours of the following day.

The hip hop performer and fan alike are weekend travelers covering up to a hundred miles without ever leaving the São Paulo metropolitan area. Weekend events in *periferia* clubs, radio stations, cultural centers, public parks, and a friend's (*camarada*) birthday party outline significant spatial networks of culture, ones that engender alliances and promote what is optimistically termed *união*.

Caught between Death and Invisibility: Violence, Criminality, and Marginality

Violence is powerful and empowering, because it both structures the daily lives of hip hoppers and the *periferia* population who they claim to represent, and it embodies central tenets of hip hop ideology. Violence is an act of oppositional aggression. Hip hoppers mobilize themselves in opposition to "*o sistema*," and they understand change to be necessarily an activist process. Violence is real, and knowledge about it is empirical in the *periferia*. Violence and crime are graphic acts; they leave behind stark scenes of death full of inerasable memories of loss and temporary moments of conquest.

For example, *Facção Central*, one of the most popular rap groups since 2000 in São Paulo, combines detailed narratives of *periferia* violence with sounds of a small string orchestra. Moving from one verse to the next the melodic dirge modulates ever higher in pitch. Rapper Erick 12 introduces himself as the "blood [resulting from] a robbery on *favela* soil" (Facção Central, 2000). According to Erick 12, the *periferia* is only quiet when "the bullet hits it target" (Facção Central, 2000). Hip hoppers such as *Facção Central* build their reputation by combining "reality" with poetics and aesthetics.

Erick 12's use of personification and actual direct identification with the blood on the ground has certainly affected many rappers and DJs, including DJ Ícaro. DJ Ícaro always has time to talk about *Facção Central*. He inevitably finds a slot to insert one of their songs on his nightly radio show in the southeastern *periferia* district of Vila Prudente: "*Facção* are great. Their lyrics are so real; they attract a lot of attention. I always get several people who call up the station after I play a *Facção* song. They like to discuss this [lyrical] line or that, because they know and feel that the *periferia* is about the reality of violence and crime" (pers. comm.). The two forces of violence and crime are structural and even "institutional," as various hip hoppers have intimated to me. Hip hoppers perceive and "feel" the saturation of violence and crime as essential to *periferia* "reality" and thus use these concepts as generative forces to construct a style of poetics and aesthetics.

According to Brazilian hip hop's most revered ideologues such as Thaíde, King Nino Brown, Nelsão Triunfo, and others, themes of violence and crime narrated by the "marginal" protagonist must connect to knowledge and respect in order for hip hop's ultimate objective of social *transformação* to take place. Eventually, "violence must be exchanged for peace," and hip hop must work from each localized *quebrada* and spread out to other spaces. The successful "bandit" is necessarily humble and must be explicit in representing himself as simply "one of the millions"[22] from the *periferia*.

The ubiquity of talk intersects with social practice. As a proliferating discourse, talk about crime both tries to resolve fear and reproduce it (Caldeira 2000). In São Paulo hip hop, rap's central focus on crime and violence exposes the essential basis for *periferia* reality manifested in crime syndicates, police activity, and the miseducation of the people (*o povo*). Violence and crime are results of living under the "system" in the *periferia*. To change the system requires a kind of violence that disrupts, or in common talk "revolutionizes," normal social relations. Hip hoppers articulate this sentiment both in metaphorical terms by taking on individual or group names with "crime"[23] or "violence"[24] as part of the actual name. The explicit adoption of "criminal" is evident in everyday greetings among hip hoppers. To call someone *ladrão* is not necessarily negative; in fact, it can be construed as positive and inclusive. In this way, Brazilian hip hop's riffs off of *periferia* as a discourse of criminality are similar to U.S. hip hop's rhetorical tradition of recuperating derogatory terms of race, such as "nigga" or "negro." And in relation to the slander of equating African Americans to animals, U.S. hip hoppers have recuperated and popularized the term "dog."

More commonly, Brazilian rap groups and hip hop posses mark their "criminality" nominally in opposition or in relation to "the system."[25] According to Bob Jay of RDM, "the *periferia* is totally affected by the system.... The system hides; the rhyme denounces" (pers. comm.). C.O.T. *Fusão*, a group of so-called "positive rap," frequently refer to themselves as the "squadron of peace" (pers. comm.). Rather than trying to establish distance from discriminatory stereotypes, São Paulo hip hoppers actually embrace them and emphasize an intimacy with criminality.

In 1997 the rap group *RZO* made famous the common phrase "that's the way it is" (*assim que é*) to describe the resilience of the oppressive "system" of Brazilian society. Hip hoppers have repeated this phrase millions of times as a way of introducing the long, detailed reports of everyday life in the *periferia*. "Unfortunately, it's like this . . . the law of the jungle," and so forth seemingly frame complete resistance as ultimately futile. DJ Tanque and Wesley described the *periferia* as a liminal space "between peace and war, good and bad" (pers. comm.). It is not surprising then that hip hoppers refer to residents as always in search of an "answer" or a "way out." It is the "system" that promotes the conditions so that, as one member of rap group *C.O.T. a Fusão* described, "demons produced by smoking crack" shroud the *periferia* (pers. comm.).

In their hit song "Sangue B" (title refers to *sangue bom*), *Visão de Rua* describes the fatal path that awaits drug addicts. Contact with drug traffickers is a common theme utilized by São Paulo rappers. It is through an acute awareness of this sort of violence, where victims "are already digging graves," that *Visão* rappers literally attack: "Ra-ta-ta-ta, I try to give you the certain truth. Ra-ta-ta-ta, before the bullet gets you first. . . . Good blood, that's right, Blood in the eyes, that's right, who hangs with me and my crew, is good blood" (Visão de Rua, 2001)

As signaled above, the discourse of fear and crime is generative. Hip hoppers have reworked the categorizations of periphery pathology into marginality as a productive utterance: "Yes, we are marginal. We come at you *queima-queima* [at point-blank range]." We are Justice (*Somos Nós a Justiça*), a relatively successful rap group since 1999, popularized the phrase *queima-queima* as part of a repertoire of interjections performed in their lyrics. MC Vulto, who works fifty hours a week in the basement of a glass manufacturing plant in São Bernardo do Campo, once compared the ubiquitous cutting of his hands to the general treatment *favelados* (and worse, *negros*) receive in the mainstream media: "It [the glass and daily life] cuts me. In hip hop, yeah, sure, there's aggression. I don't care if they [people outside of the *periferia*] get scared or not. Hip hop is an [act of] opposition" (pers. comm.).

Leaving the *Quebradas* Behind? Positive Rap's Challenge to *Periferia*

Since 2000 groups of rappers and DJs have initiated a more organized response to hip hop as bandit music (*música de bandido*) in the form of "positive rap." Positive rap is ultimately a response from hip hoppers to the critique that rap only reports *periferia* daily life and offers no "solutions." Proponents of positive rap differ in their approach to solving the representational problem.

While most "positive" hip hop has shifted focus to more general levels of community in their efforts to leave the *periferia* particularities behind, some groups such as *Sistema Racional* (Rational System) and *Xis* understand "positive" as a general quality of life where entertainment and independent thought are the keys to restructuring the *periferia* into a harmless and palatable product for outside audiences. *Sistema Racional* reworked the *RZO* mantra ("that's the way it is") into "it should be like this" (*é assim que tem que ser*) and in so doing at least rhetorically offered a "solution." What the *periferia* should be like is a place where one can simply take a stroll around the block (*dar um rolê*) and stand on the corner (*esquina*) in peace. *Xis* had his biggest crossover success with the song "De Esquina." Originally released in 1997 on a compilation produced by legendary DJ Hum (partner of rapper Thaíde), the song garnered much attention. Years later in 2001, the alternative MPB (Brazilian Popular Music) star Cássia Eller included a version of the song with *Xis* on her widely acclaimed acoustic "unplugged" album. The appeal of the song rests on the desire created in the narrative, which combines the street action (*movimento da rua*) with being "deliriously paranoid" (*paranoia delirante*). Yet, there is almost no mention of danger. The scene and the meaning are all under control as seen through the eyes of the *periferia* flâneur in peace (*na paz*).

Sistema Racional, unlike most positive rappers, criticizes openly the control Protestant or *evangélica* churches have on *periferia* life. Both *Xis* and *Sistema Racional* pitch the *periferia* as a distinct entertainment circuit but one essentially conversant with the middle-class and bourgeois circuits of Pinheiros, Itaim Bibi, and Vila Madalena.

In this case. departure from the *periferia* is primarily commercial. However, even less commercially successful "positive" hip hop artists find it difficult to break away from the discursive paradigm of *periferia*. Over the course of 2002, I came to know Manga, a fanzine publisher and rapper from São Bernardo do Campo. We talked several times on his way to and from recording studios, radio stations, and municipal government departments, as he balanced obligations to his rap group RU10 (United Races to the Tenth Degree), to his fanzines *Folhas de Atitude* (*Attitude pages*) and *Mente Poderoso* (*Powerful mind*), and to the organizers of the annual São Bernardo hip hop event.

During one morning on our way to a studio recording session, Manga admitted that he felt pressure to include marginality on his CD, because, as he explained, "people still want to hear these stories" (pers. comm.). Later during the session, Manga discussed with studio producer Gato the song structure of "Mente Poderoso" ("Powerful Mind"), an otherwise "positive" rap about human potential. Interestingly, he stressed the importance of musically highlighting the passage that included the following phrase: "The crime scene is already set" (*A cena do crime está feito*). Manga argued that the description of reality, as if it were a prefabricated crime scene, effectively provokes the listener into positive (re)action. Limited in resources and recording equipment, Manga suggested the direct sampling of the descending keyboard line made famous in U.S. rapper Coolio's version of "Gangsta Paradise" (1995).[26] Ultimately, drama and tragedy of reality's "crime scene" were musically achieved, as Manga felt obliged to include typical *periferia* stories and recognizable sounds of everyday drama. Soon thereafter, Manga succeeded in convincing a leading FM radio DJ, who is also one of the editors of the two major hip hop magazines in São Paulo, to include "Mente Poderoso" on an upcoming compilation sponsored by the magazine *Planeta Hip Hop* (May 2002).

Members of the *Família 7 Taças* (7 Chalices Family) express departure from the *periferia* in explicitly spatial and spiritual terms. *7 Taças* is a recording label, which includes, first and foremost, the evangelical rap group *Apocalipse 16*,[27] solo rappers Lito Atalaia and Professor Pablo, and soul ensemble *Banda Templo Soul*. Pregador Luo (Preacher Luo), *Apocalipse 16* front man and solo artist in his own right, manages *7 Taças*. Their rise to popularity stems from, in part, strategies utilized by *periferia* churches to open up their worship spaces to popular music performance. Various groups from *7 Taças* travel extensively throughout the *periferia* at the invitation of church organizers. Based on biblical interpretation with the objective of personal salvation, *7 Taças* rappers attempt to fade out the *periferia* by reducing the complexity of life to individual choice.

Members approach representation as universal. Narratives rarely mention specific place names, as national landmarks substitute metropolitan neighborhood "shout outs." Graphics (CD covers, posters, flyers, etc.) either show domestic spaces such as living rooms, urban downtown spaces, or abstract spaces based on computer screens.[28] In addition, the banal sounds of the street such as buses, gunshots, television sets, and the he-said, she-said are revealingly absent. In their place, *7 Taças* recordings privilege a mixed bag of U.S.-influenced contemporary R&B musical production, choral singing styles, sampled heavy guitar riffs, and the occasional European art music motif.

"The keys to life [and death] are in your hands" (Apocalipse 16, 2001). The imagination of leaving the *periferia* is more significant than physical departure. During a phone conversation, Pregador Luo emphasized the durability and resilience of imagination over the temporary nature of art and entertainment: "The music passes but ideas stay" (pers. comm.). Lito Atalaia, one of the solo artists in the *Família 7 Taças*, dismisses material and space as ultimately unimportant: "Our hope is not here and not in anyone, [in] who [then]?" (Apocalipse 16, 2001). The constant development of a relationship with Jesus Christ removes the individual out of existing material conditions of violence and crime and into a potentially life-affirming place based on faith. Members of the veteran posse Black Alliance (*Aliança Negra*) from Cidade Tiradentes echoed this perspective. When asked about the rise of positive and evangelical rap, Edivelton replied that other genres have been relatively unsuccessful in "spreading information" and "conquering space." "[This] has made it clearer than ever that God is the solution" (pers. comm.).

As an unarmed revolution, positive rap thus depends on careful life choices—for example, not selling your soul and self-control during the night. The solutions offered by *7 Taças* exist as a set of behavioral warnings set in opposition to conventional marginality. The keyword "to proceed" (*proceder*) prevalent throughout hip hop discourse indexes a host of responsibilities with regard to personal behavior and attitude.

Proponents of positive rap such as Jamal see hip hop as a refuge away from the *periferia*. Over the past four years, Jamal has set up residence in various places in the south side district of Jardim Ademar. According to data collected by Polis (2000), the south side neighborhood Jardim Ademar in 1999 ranked third in the São Paulo municipality in number of homicides, with 163. Growing up in the middle-class neighborhood of Vila Mariana as part of a live-in family, due to his father's job as building supervisor (*zelador*), Jamal came to the *periferia* as a teenager after his father's death. In our conversations about his 2002 solo album, Jamal explained how he finds in hip hop a method of escape from the *perferia*. Annoyed by the parasitic opportunism of *periferia*, Jamal calls himself "crazy," "abstract," and a "fugitive" from the banal violence of *periferia*.

Jamal was a founding member of *Alvos da Lei* (Targets of the Law), a group who publicly stated that negotiations with local crime syndicates can be more effective than with the state in the organization of cultural events and providing basic services to the residential community. In a twisted turn of events, days after the interview with *Alvos da Lei* was published in *Rap Brasil* (April 2002), member Gilmar was brutally murdered outside of his home in the south side neighborhood of Jardim Missionária. Jamal left the group in 2000 and distanced himself from the remaining members. His career thus has traversed the domains of "marginality" to "positive."

Yet, an investigation into Jamal's creative production demonstrates that the borders are significantly fuzzy. Part of a more general argument related to aesthetics and ethics discussed at length in prior chapters, Jamal's dependence on crime, violence, and the *periferia* in his very escape speaks to the problematic position of "positive rap" as an alternative socio-spatial discourse in São Paulo hip hop. Beyond the gratuitous "rat-ta-ta-ta" lyrical and rhythmic connectors, Jamal employs crime and violence as shaping forces of the narrative landscape through which he must navigate. To be "without fear to err" (CD title) one must be particularly agile and confident to avoid the many "asphalt pits" of the *periferia* and the "*favela* bombs that invade your brain" (Jamal 2002). Despite being a "deserter" and one who locates himself "against the beat," Jamal "attacks" as he himself is a "virtual smuggler" with "sonic contraband" (Jamal 2002).

Jamal cannot flee the war-torn and rotten landscape he describes as geographically and psychologically constitutive of *periferia*, for he depends on it for narration. The "criminal game" is undeniably in the present, and the "solutions" offered by "positive rap" seem to exist as only future promises. Representatives of this new school try to persuade the hip hop community that favorable conditions for growth come to those who wait patiently and intelligently. The discourse is commonplace and sounds familiar, because it is what Brazilian politicians have stated since the founding of the republic. Whether part of the "marginal" or "positive" groups, Brazilian hip hop's mediation of *periferia* often reinforces the general disenfranchisement and isolation of *periferia*. While some exceptional hip hop organizations, such as Força Ativa, and state-sponsored groups such as the *Hip Hop House* in Diadema, Ação Educativa, and others exercise what Zulu Nation Brasil, following Afrika Bambaataa, call the "fifth element," hip hop's most dominant design of *periferia*, especially as articulated by rap musicians, does little more than mirror the constitutive forces of its construction, namely the violent, chaotic process of São Paulo urbanization.

Conclusion

The dynamics of socio-spatial formations are most visible in cities. Cities are inherently unstable environments due to the multiple levels of social diversity. The city as spectacle and palimpsest captures the performative and historical nature of urban life. In Brazil as in most countries, the city is the locus of material and social change.

In part, this debate concerning the role of the city in individual and collective representation manifests itself in the current division in Brazilian hip hop between the "positive" and "marginal" camps, respectively. The tradition of hip hop tends to showcase locality and more specifically urban scenes as the essential basis of cultural work. The city and its banal contours are the primary sources for authenticity against a historical escalation of conflict and contestation in governmental policies and civil society.

In this chapter I have worked my way through the multiple histories of São Paulo and, more specifically, the emergence and maintenance of the *periferia*. The *periferia* as a form of residence and social control is under critique in hip hop through a renovated sensibility of occupation. Through a reading of collected material and a careful reflection on experience, I have demonstrated that hip hop as a social circuit involves dynamic spatial practices. Such hip hop "conquests," however, are difficult to maintain and control. Furthermore, investigation into rappers' narrative strategies around *periferia* reveals that while discourses of crime and violence are generative, they can also reinforce historically grounded and systematically enacted structures of domination. To what extent hip hop practitioners are able to design a more empowering *periferia* through and beyond the mediation of marginality is not simply a theoretical issue of academia, but it also constitutes one of the primary pragmatic concerns of local hip hop activists and intellectuals.

CHAPTER 4

PUTTING *MANO*
TO MUSIC

TESTING HIP HOP *NEGRITUDE*

Hip hop in Brazil is a form of politics and pleasure, which reveals the solidarity (*união*) and the conflicts within the making of race and gender among the working class in the *periferia*. In these final two substantive chapters, I discuss how São Paulo hip hoppers do ideological work and strive to articulate dynamic notions of blackness and gender (masculinities and femininities). Again, hip hop is the vehicle of choice (and, at times, necessity) for thousands of youth in their retelling of "reality." Hip hop stands at the center of how black working-class persons apply *negritude* as individual attitude, collective philosophy, diasporic imagination, and political strategy. To "test" *negritude* is to demonstrate hip hop as part of racialization within Brazilian popular society.[1] Part of my objective in this chapter is to take account of *negritude* as Brazilian hip hop style and what is at stake in a race-first approach to ideology. As I argue in this particular chapter, Brazilian hip hoppers differ on how race operates in Brazilian social stratification and diverge in their approaches to address such issues in performances and pedagogic work, for example, workshops, community speeches, and other organizational events.

Race is a highly contested terrain of signification yet undoubtedly constitutive of hip hop's *raison d'être* in São Paulo. Unlike in the United States, where the notion of "whiteness," both encroaching and contributive, has been a significant part of hip hop's racialization process (Kitwana 2005), in Brazil the concept of *branquitude* or "whiteness" is rarely enacted.[2] This reveals a general understanding of "black" and "white" in Brazil; that is, Brazilians are "neither black nor white" (to borrow Carl Degler's famous phrase).[3] The local hip hop critique focuses on "blackness," as practitioners try to claim race as a mark of change. While most hip hoppers utilize the terms "black," "*negro*," "*preto*," and above all "*mano*," some older, more experienced hip hoppers and allies from prior soul and funk movements refer to "*negritude*" as a common objective that bridges generations and musico-cultural genres. Hip hop culture is important as part of the dynamic of contemporary racial formation in Brazil, because its sustained practice has provided experience and material through which thousands of Brazilians rethink the status of race within their own conceptions of self, personhood, and citizenship. Grounded in perceived biological differences, race becomes a vector of power in the continuous human project of social stratification. Race and gender never disappear from sociality; rather, they take on new, creative discourses and practices as persons try to persuade others about profiling and surveillance, a sense of solidarity, cultural and political constituency building, and a code of aesthetics in artistic performance.

The "making of race" in hip hop involves the politics and pleasures of becoming *consciente* and enjoying togetherness. It is part of hip hop "information," as discussed in Chapter 2, and hip hop spaces, as analyzed in Chapter 3. While in the U.S. scholars and rappers alike have argued that hip hop's rearticulation of the "ghetto" is a central and essential factor in the identity formation of "nigga" (Kelley 1994; McLaren 2000; Dyson 1993; Ice-T 1991; Spice-1 1993; Dead Prez 2000), in Brazil, the centrality of *periferia* has influenced the currency of *preto, negro* (both meaning "black"), and more recently, *mano* ("brother") and *mana* ("sister") as alternatives to traditional notions of blackness and femininity in Brazil. As will be discussed in Chapter 5, hip hoppers reckon the *periferia* as a public, masculine place and see metaphors and structures of family and *negritude* as potentially empowering for all hip hoppers. However, this combination of a limited view of Afro-centricity and "family" has produced little in the way of a progressive feminism at any sort of popular level.

Reflecting Race

As a white male from the United States, my representation of Brazilian blackness is necessarily problematic. Writing *preto* draws on power-laden trajectories of academic careerism (Moura 1988; Ramos 1959; Nascimento 1980) historically evident in the business of cultural representation. These dangers are unavoidable and must be not only acknowledged but also reflected.

I met Batista in September of 1995. Batista was working on his masters degree in sociology at the University of São Paulo. A *negro*[4] from the north side of São Paulo in his late thirties, Batista was indeed a rare person within the Brazilian university student community.[5] I had met prior with a professor in anthropology and succeeded in conveying in my *macarrão* ("spaghetti") Portuguese my idea of studying São Paulo hip hop. She recommended that I seek out Batista. His work centered on the *movimento negro* (black movement) and its involvement in the Chic Show soul/funk dance party production during the '80s and early '90s in São Paulo.[6] Over a beer in the *centro*, he introduced me to a number of activist colleagues. They related stories that these semi-abandoned downtown *galerias* have served the soul, funk, and hip hop communities in addition to the black political groups. I got by enough to elicit an invitation to a meeting in São Bernardo do Campo later that month sponsored by the MNU (United Black Movement), a political organization with an explicitly Afrocentric agenda. This sort of elicitation, I thought at the time, was more a function of racial cordiality than any sort of refined skills of negotiation on my part. I had already grown to enjoy this seemingly relaxed racial atmosphere in my time thus far in Brazil. I was excited about the upcoming MNU meeting.

I took the trolley bus to the final stop in Ferrazópolis a little south of downtown São Bernardo. I walked up the hill and met Batista outside the meeting place. The meeting occurred in a historic building, the place where Luis Inácio Lula da Silva, or now more commonly known as "Lula," the current Brazilian president, started labor union organizing back in the '70s. In 1995 the building still housed the official periodical of the metal worker's union (Sindicato dos Metalúrgicos) of the ABC (Santo André, São Bernardo, São Caetano, and Diadema), part of the industry network of metro São Paulo. We all walked up to a small auditorium on the third floor. Batista had promised that there would be members of a local hip hop posse there in attendance. I was happy to be there and content to observe and try to understand the meeting's proceedings.

Unbeknownst to me, Batista had included me in the meeting's agenda. What I later understood to be some sort of test or experiment related to my integrity and personality, or my perspective on race and power, the trying experience in that MNU meeting would influence my understandings of race in Brazil in addition to the dynamics of my entrée in to the research field. After a spell of bureaucratic discussion around issues of organization for an upcoming event and the "cultural performance" involving a few members of the *Posse Hausa* hip hop organization, attention suddenly moved to me. I was under scrutiny. I felt incredible pressure standing there in front of 150 "*negros conscientes*" with the task of telling a personal story and a word about my proposed research. It was a moment of visceral difference.

Totally unprepared and unequipped linguistically to tell much of a story, I opted for what I thought would be a different and unexpected narrative. I played up my Southern upbringing and Alabama family roots. I hoped to convey a sense of "early recognition" by relating my teenage experiences of imagining what kind of world my relatives a generation or two ago occupied and what indeed their roles might have been. I will never forget the reaction of most of the audience when I uttered the word "Alabama." Well, of course, these MNU members had read about the Civil Rights Movement and the obscene role Alabama government officials and many white residents practiced in fear of losing racist privilege and a so-called "Southern tradition." Many audience members leered at me, and their gaze shredded the veneer of comfort I had donned such a short time ago. What frustrated me, as I would later tell *Posse Hausa* members, was that the MNU representatives could not get past the word "Alabama" and all of its horrible referential power. For the most part, they did not hear the rest of the story. I became obviously nervous and could barely speak a work without stuttering. I wondered what I was doing in this place and how I might be able to turn the story around so that they could understand the spirit of my research and the truth of my intent.

Concerned but more intrigued by my story, a couple of *Posse Hausa* members approached me and asked if there was any hip hop in the South.[7] As I discuss below, while the MNU has had some success in making alliances with local hip hoppers, many "conscious" hip hoppers recognize the limitations of MNU's approach. As DJ Marquinhos would tell me later, "The MNU gets us thinking about race and exploitation and that's important, but they've got too much of a one-track mind. Hip hop is more than that. The *periferia* is more complicated. . . . If we're going to change anything, we need to learn about our *negritude* and create a positive attitude with that knowledge, but we also need to understand that our blackness is not the same as in the United States or Europe. I don't think the MNU understands all this I'm telling you" (pers. comm.).

We talked about Outkast's first album, Miami bass, and the strange ideas about "funk" in Rio de Janeiro. Clumsily and provisionally, I had established rapport and an entrée with the *Posse Hausa*. For many MNU members in attendance that day, I would always be a worthless outsider and, in fact, for a couple of *Hausa* members, those with the strongest connection to the MNU and Islam, our relationship never really developed beyond courtesies. However, despite the awkward tone of our initial contact, some *Hausa* hip hoppers and I saw each other as resources, and we invested in each other as part of the ongoing process of trafficking information (*traficando informação*) and exchanging ideas (*trocando idéia*), so valued in the *periferia* and within hip hop.

Race competes with class and gender for center stage in Brazilian popular solidarity movements. Those Afro-Brazilians who feel race as a fact to be argued and recast struggle against the mythological ideal that race as such tends to pass into the background as part of a unique chameleon society. MNU meetings and hip hop activity demonstrate in different ways how race has become salient as a strategy in political organizing. The curiosity among a few *Posse Hausa* members of a white *gringo* wandering into their social network complemented the example of "whiteness" I provided to many of the MNU activists.

For the first time in Brazil, I felt my race as an unshakable fact. It was held up for inspection and judgment. I became, as Fanon once described, an "object in the midst of other objects" (1967, 109). Like a lab experiment, it was a temporary moment of investigation. It would pass. I would get over it. This is not a story of comparison. How could one compare a moment of whiteness to a "fact of blackness" (again from Fanon)? Rather, this is a story of how persons make race work in the construction of new subjectivities and how race works on personhood as a structural force that "seal[s] [one] into that crushing objecthood."[8] Stories can be defining moments as we reflect on experience. Hip hoppers not only know this but also depend on it as their raison d'être.

I glanced at Batista. He hid his knowing grin and stood up and walked over signaling to wrap up the meeting. We later met, drank beer, and he laughed it all off as he told anyone who stopped by our table, "Have you heard the one about the *gringo* who showed up at a MNU meeting?" Later that night, Batista got us back stage at the Samba Love nightclub, and he introduced me to the members of *Racionais MCs*, São Paulo radical superstars of rap.

My perspective on Brazilian hip hop is not one of upholding black heroes or of lamenting black victims. In the spirit of Lima Barreto, the militant Afro-Brazilian essayist of the early twentieth century, and Carolina Maria de Jesús, the shantytown resident and chronicler of

Figure 4.1 Remnants of slave quarters on a *fazenda* (plantation) (São Carlos, São Paulo State, April 2002).

1960s São Paulo daily life, I take account of (sub)urban blackness as constitutive of hip hop through the voices and experiences of a heterogeneous group of working-class young men and women.

Most Brazilians consider a claim of blackness beyond a notion of African cultural retentions to be anti-Brazilian and, in fact, racist itself.[9] In other words, "blacks, as well as indians, are accepted only as *marks* of Brazilianness, but not as persons" (Guimarães 1999, 27). Early studies of blackness as part of the Brazilian nation proposed that the state and citizenry have a great "debt" to Africans and Afro-Brazilian culture. While certainly true, policy makers and scholars tended to reify blackness as a "mark" of nation—a fixed point of historic atrocity now corrected through national inclusion. It is for this reason that, as Maggie and Rezende (2002) concluded, Brazilians, independent of racial identification, rarely describe other Brazilians of color as "black" *per se*, and instead, utilize a range of focal yet often ambiguous vocabulary terms to depict persons. Since color is above all a "mark," terms such as *escurinho* ("little darky"), *café com leite* ("coffee with milk"), and even *azul* (literally "blue," but used to refer to very dark skin color) make more sense than oppositional and socially loaded terms like "black" and "white."[10]

Putting *Mano* to Music

The word *mano* is a ubiquitous term among hip hoppers. It is the essence of hip hop collectivity, a delicate and often misunderstood process of recuperating marginality into positivity. *Mano* as a concept works to transform the exclusion indexed in the above marker of *senzala* or the ubiquitous directional markers of *periferia* neighborhoods such as Cidade São Mateus into a sense of inclusion and distinction. As foreshadowing, I introduce my argument concerning *negritude* and music making by historicizing one of the basic keywords of hip hop in São Paulo.

The historicity (a collective sense or representation of history) of *mano* begins with the Afro-Brazilian political activist Solano Trindade (1908–74). My inquiry into *mano* emerged from a coincidental meeting with Nino Brown at a neighborhood hip hop event in the São Paulo industrial suburb of Diadema in July of 1999. On that day Nino was wearing a T-shirt with a picture of Solano Trindade on the front. He confessed that he knew little about Trindade other than a couple of his short poems and complained about the difficulties in gaining access to his literature. Nino quickly changed the topic to Eldridge Cleaver, since he had recently finished reading a translation of *Soul on Ice*.

Years before there were soul or funk movements in Brazil and decades before the concept of hip hop proliferated through the *periferias* of São Paulo and Brasília, Solano Trindade talked of *mano* as an achievement marked by difficult and tense negotiation. For Trindade, the Renaissance black activist from the northeastern state of Pernambuco, whose texts cut into the eyes and ears of his audiences through a caustic language of reflection and critique, to circulate *mano* required a labor of forging commonality and not simply assuming it:

> What have you done brother (*mano*) to talk so much like that?
> I planted sugarcane in the Northeast
> And you brother, what have you done?
> I planted cotton in the southern fields
> For the blue-blooded men
> Who paid for my labor
> With whippings and lashings
> That's enough, brother,
> So that I don't cry, and you Ana
> Tell me your life story
> In the *senzala* in the *candomblé* spaces (*terreiro*) . . . [11]
> Whoa black man!

> Who was it who said
> That we are not people?
> Who was this demented soul,
> who has eyes and doesn't see. (Trindade 1961, 40–41)

The tone of Trindade appears forty years later in the voice of pioneering hip hopper Thaíde. Solano Trindade remains virtually unknown in the hip hop community. Apparently, only those hip hoppers who move in activist, scholarly, or literary circles are aware of Trindade's importance. Here I assert a dialogue between Trindade and Thaíde, two leading figures of rhetoric and racialization in popular culture. It is the attitude that comes with knowledge or "information" that both men exude in a spirit of provocation and ultimately positivity:

> I'm right in what I say
> My intention to offend you
> Step off! I'm too black for you. (excerpt from "Sou Negro D+ Pra Você," Thaíde e DJ Hum 2001)

In this section I delineate four moments of rap music with respect to *negritude*. These moments refer to historical moments of discursive trends within rap music. Of course, there is significant overlap, and there are exceptions within each *negritude* moment. Through an informal periodization, I show that *negritude* is dynamic in its formulation, and I provide a more specific tracking of the force of the "racial democracy" ideology. The critical voices of rapper Thaíde and poet Trindade are rare and fall in and out of favor among hip hoppers.

My analysis of the first moment is based exclusively on documents (lyrics and recordings) and consultants' memories. For the other moments, I offer a perspective informed by personal experience in addition to consultants' remarks and documents. In moments 3 and 4, I fold in more detailed explanations of the relationship between *negritude* and *periferia*.

Becoming "Informed": Early Efforts at Rap and *Negritude* (Moment 1)

Today hip hop in Brazil is a form of mass culture with thousands of practitioners and millions of consumers. Hip hop arrived in urban Brazil in the early 1980s. In particular, São Paulo and Brasília were the early centers of Brazilian hip hop. As mentioned above, since the late 1960s diasporic cultural channels widened and intensified as a result of development in informational technology, especially with regard to media sources. These included cassettes, vinyl, magazines, and Hollywood movies. By 1990 Brazilian television established MTV Brasil, and by 1998 Internet access had reached a level of functionality with regard to popular culture dissemination and consumption. The first exclusively hip hop Internet site was established in 1999 (http://www.bocada-forte.com.br).

Consequently, urban Afro-Brazilians reckoned hip hop culture as a contemporary link in the new Brazilian category of black style and culture (*estilo* and *cultura black*). While the first local, commercial recording of rap music in Brazil occurred in 1984 (*Black Juniors*, CBS), it was not until 1987 and 1988 that rappers and DJs joined forces with graffiti artists and B-boys to create a hip hop "movement" with socially oriented objectives. Rappers in Brazil were known as *tagarelas* (babblers, yappers) in the early days, for they elaborated on the basic points of identification—the arrival of Brazilian hip hop as well as "who you are and the place to be."[12]

In addition, the years of 1987 and 1988 were important in national history; 1988 marked the centennial celebration of the abolition of slavery (see Figure 4.1). A great deal of literature, scholarly and popular, was published; and the federal government and state agencies subsidized conferences, symposiums, cultural events, and other public events to take account, at least rhetorically, of the black man in Brazil (*o negro no Brasil*).

Hip hoppers began to establish a working infrastructure of performance venues and commercial production. Just as a decade earlier, when *periferia* nightclub managers hosted weekend parties featuring local funk and soul performance groups and dance troupes, a similar circuit emerged in the late 1980s with regard to hip hop. Club managers employed a common strategy of sponsoring contests, which ultimately resulted in a series of vinyl compilation recordings.

The combination of hip hop "attitude" and general style during this moment of national remembering of abolition inspired some rappers to make their own inquiries into hip hop as a form of *negritude*. Yet, hip hop in Brazil has always upheld an ideal of *união*, and most early hip hoppers, as did most Brazilians, interpreted the centennial discussions as productive with regard to African heritage. The issues of racism or a race-first perspective on identity were overlooked in favor of "racial democracy."

Rapper Thaíde began as a B-boy in the mid-1980s and later joined Humberto, DJ Hum, as one of the pioneering hip hop groups in Brazil. While Thaíde grew up in Cambuci and Vila Missionário, *periferia* neighborhoods on the south side of São Paulo, and DJ Hum came from a more middle-class neighborhood of Mooca, the two came together as a result of a conversation during the dance party My Baby in the Espaço Mambembe, where independently DJ Hum and Thaíde were invited guests (Alves 2004, 48–50).

In particular, Thaíde has consistently discussed Africanity as a constitutive part of hip hop. In the following excerpt, Thaíde includes deities from the Afro-Brazilian religion *candomblé* and refers to his own strength in the *candomblé* terminology of having a "closed body." It is important to note, however, the change in Thaíde's tone as the years progressed. In the early years, Thaíde e DJ Hum were more conciliatory and tended to emphasize community building and syncretism over direct critique as represented in "Sou Negro D+ Pra Você" above.

For their part, *Código 13*, a group included on the first major rap compilation (*Cultura de Rua*, El Dorado Records, 1988) along with Thaíde e DJ Hum and the Neps, a pioneering rap group from São Bernardo do Campo, demonstrates a more conventional perspective on hip hop as a culture that includes the common knowledge of "racial democracy" as integral to *periferia* camaraderie:

> Hip hop style as it is called.
> Blacks (*negros*) and whites on the same side
> [exchanging] ideas around the same topics
> (Excerpt from "Código 13," Código 13 1988)

> I want to live without discrimination, because the black man is a flower
> That emerges from the union of two strands
> What is called *miscegenação* ("racial mixture")
> (Excerpt from "Ritmo Negro," Neps 1991)

In our conversation in September of 1995, graffiti artist and B-boy Talis described Código 13 and the Neps as "commonplace" and "typical" of the early moment of hip hop in Brazil: "The idea of union was very important. The rappers wanted to show that they could work together and were happy to claim that race was not a problem" (pers. comm.). In short, most rappers configured race in urban Brazil as essentially about mixture. Throughout both songs, the legacy of "racial democracy" is reinforced as rappers reduce *negritude* to fate and victim status. *Negritude* thus loses any sort of traction as a self-sufficient discourse; it presumably exists as a temporary problem that *miscegenação* ("racial mixture") ultimately will remedy.

With regard to sound production, the early rap DJs were not yet interested in sampling local or cosmopolitan blackness. Early Brazilian rap contained no references to the great soul or funk stars Tim Maia, Toni Tornado, Black Rio, or even Gilberto Gil, the now world famous MPB (Popular Brazilian Music) artist who had popularized reggae and samba-rock during the late '70s and early '80s. Nor did early DJs and producers utilize much of international funk stars James Brown or Funkadelic and Parliament. Instead, most early rap consisted of stripped-down beats from drum machines, occasional scratch sequences, and unidentifiable bass lines. In rap music, engineering technology influences the range of potential timbres for a particular song. The timbre quality has increased exponentially over the past decade due to increased memory of sampling equipment. In addition, sound producers use software such as Acid, Sound Edit, and Pro Tools to adjust a wide range of levels of the "original" sonic information with regard to pitch, attack, sustain, among other aspects, and finally obtain a distinct sound.

Early Brazilian rap production reveals a gap in what would become a strong musical-ideological connection. By the mid-1990s, hip hop sound engineers explored and fine-tuned the crucial links between sound and idea as performers explicitly "designed" (Pardue, Christman, and Sheehan 2002; Pardue 2005) shantytown identities and diasporic imaginations. Due to a lack of resources and technological knowledge, early Brazilian hip hop producers rarely employed melodic samples, thereby leaving the rapper to provide the primary melodic contours of any particular song through his vocal rhetoric. The result was a limited presence of musical counterpoint and an underdeveloped sense of musico-cultural referencing. DJs in live performances and rap music producers in studio recordings included samples as innocent "hooks." For example, in "Corpo Fechado" a sample of a child's toy acts as the introductory melody from which Thaíde begins his rapping. Hip hop was simply a nascent cultural form, and producers treated it as, in fact, a novelty item. In contrast, in "Sou Negro D+ Pra Você," a sample of a guitar with sound compressor or "wah wah" pedal effect provides the melody juxtaposed with a melodic bass line and an echoing harmonic chord from a keyboard. DJ Hum, the main producer of all of Thaíde e DJ Hum's later releases, demonstrates a sensitive ear for sample counterpoint, historical knowledge of soul and funk, and a rhythmic sensitivity in beat programming.

The first historical moment of hip hop culture in Brazil (1987–92) is characterized by a conventional critique of racism and celebration of racial mixture as part of the overarching discourse of *união*. In the first historical moment of Brazilian rap music, *negritude* only appeared an inescapable fact of self. The very utterance of *negro* was significant as these young men attempted to articulate experiences of marginality to a new sense of collectivity in the form of a new "hip hop movement." Yet, it would take time before local hip hoppers were to become *informados* about what sort of identification processes and performative strategies were possible in hip hop. Thaíde and other older hip hoppers acknowledge the significance of differences in sound sampling, for example, as part of what they call evolution (*evolução*). This process of "improvement" entails a greater knowledge of "black" sounds and history, as well as a gradual recognition that hip hop performance is about becoming serious (*ficar sério*).

Afro-centricity and Moving Away from "Racial Democracy" (Moment 2)

The second historical moment of hip hop development involves an expansion of the term "*black*" (left untranslated in Brazilian Portuguese) to include a greater and more descriptive level of social critique. This moment from 1992 to 1996 marks a relatively high level of consciousness symbolized in more systematic involvement with MNU (United Black Movement) and other black political groups, in addition to a more acute sensibility to diaspora and Pan-Africanism. As mentioned above, the exercise of historical periodization is heuristic in intent. The point is that *negritude* has been significantly dynamic throughout Brazilian hip hop. With that said, it is worth reiterating that the spirit of Afro-centricity in moment 2 is closely related to the notion of hip hop "consciousness" and "attitude" overall and therefore is never absent. Moment 2, in this sense, did not end, but rather the dynamic of Afro-centricity changed toward the end of the 1990s with the relative success of narratives of crime and violence as "reality" told by the "marginal" as a hip hop protagonist. This constitutes what I am calling moment 3.

During moment 2, participants were most active in "roots" discourses. They found "roots" in long-standing narratives of Afro-centricity as well as in more contemporary stories of the members of funk and soul movements during the 1970s and early '80s. Unlike more contemporary "evangelical" practitioners, hip hoppers of the early '90s found strength in cultural history more often than in spiritual devotion. In particular, hip hoppers tapped into the concept of *quilombismo* as a potential epistemological tool for knowledge and black identity formation. The *quilombo* in Brazil stands as the primary symbol of resistance to slavery during the colonial period: "It was through the *quilombo* and not the abolition movement that the black struggle developed against slavery" (Candeia 1978, 7).

What is particular about hip hop is that for the first time in modern Brazil *negros* were articulating Afro-centric perspectives rather than isolated middle-class black intellectuals and activists.[13] When

Figure 4.2 Poster of André Rebouças

hip hoppers in São Paulo make and wear T-shirts with prints of Eldridge Cleaver and Solano Trindade; when they carry around books of Karl Marx and Abdias do Nascimento; when they work their hair like Coolio, Busta Rhymes, and a young Angela Davis; when they circulate pamphlets featuring André Rebouças (Figure 4.2) and Frantz Fanon;[14] and when they tell stories about *quilombos* and *negritude*, they test popular imaginations about Brazilianness (*brasilidade*) and race (*raça*).

Quilombo is a word from the Quimbundo people,[15] a Bantu group located in modern Angola. The Bantu ethnic group was one of the largest populations represented in the Brazilian slave trade. *Quilombo* literally means "capital" or "population," but more specifically refers to communities established by freed Africans in Brazil. There were hundreds if not thousands of *quilombos* during the colonial and republican periods. The most famous quilombo was *quilombos dos Palmares* located in the countryside of Alagoas state in the northeast region of the country. During the seventeenth century, Palmares thrived as a self-sufficient community and resisted repeated attempts by both Portuguese and Dutch colonial forces. This history of resistance and bravery is captured in the figure of Zumbi, the charismatic leader of Palmares during the latter half of the seventeenth century.[16] He died in battle in 1695, supposedly on November 20. In the late 1970s Afro-Brazilians called for a state mandate recognizing this day as a day of black consciousness. Since 1971, due to the organizational work of Abdias do Nascimento, Lélia Gonzalez, poet Oliveira Silveira, among others, the death of Zumbi was made into a memorial.[17]

The prominence of *quilombo* as part of contemporary *negritude* is important. Organizers draw upon the power of *quilombo* when referring to public gatherings or day-long conferences and even regularly scheduled performances. Examples of this kind of *quilombismo*, that is, borrowing from the force of *quilombo* to highlight one's event, is evident in the following events I attended or about which I received pamphlet literature: Sixteenth Festival of Zumbi Community in Araras, São Paulo State (November 1995); Second World Forum in Porto Alegre, Rio Grande do Sul State (Afro Committee Bulletin, January 2002); First State conference of the Black Community in Caxias do Sul, Rio Grande do Sul State (Pamphlet, November 2001); Commission for the March on Brasília (hip hop *Posse Hausa* was part of the commission) in commemoration of three hundred years after the death of Zumbi (newspaper pamphlet in São Bernardo do Campo,

São Paulo State, October 1995); various manifestations with regard to the incarceration of Mumia Abu-Jamal, a black journalist sentenced to death in the United States; "Afro-Brasil," a radio program sponsored by the defunct *Rádio USP*, among others.

MNU

In order to appreciate the second historical moment, one must recognize the significance of the MNU (Unified Black Movement). Brazilians have continuously organized themselves into groups of black militancy and race politics. Throughout the twentieth century groups have invested in a number of projects revolving around the place of Brazil within the larger scope of Africanity and the place of Brazilians of African descent in the Brazilian nation-state. The MNU is important to understand in some detail, because it remains an organization of influence on a sector of the São Paulo hip hop community.

The MNU, originally named MNUCDR (the Unified Black Movement Against Racial Discrimination), was founded on June 18, 1978, in response to a wave of police violence against blacks. In particular, the death of Robson Silveira da Luz, a black taxi driver, on April 28 served as a rally cry for the nascent organization. He was tortured to death in the Forty-fourth District Police Department in Guaianazes on the east side of São Paulo.

MNU members took advantage of the so-called opening up (*abertura*) period of Brazilian politics (1979–85) to organize "black consciousness" groups at the local level. According to Damasceno (1988), by 1987 there existed 138 organizations that identified themselves as part of the *movimento negro* in the state of São Paulo. However, the overwhelming majority of these groups was short lived and suffered from an inability to connect with the black, working-class masses, whose interests they purported to represent. Especially in terms of providing popular forums of culture and community, the black political movement has had its difficulties in demonstrating any considerable amount of capital (Silva 1998, 107). As Andrews (1992, 169) summarizes, the "gap" between the middle-class militants and the poor and working-class blacks has been a common problem of "black consciousness" since the First Republic in Brazil.[18]

The dispersal of black militancy into isolated pockets of the São Paulo *periferia* did not spell a disappearance or an end to activism by the mid-1990s. Hip hop posses in the São Paulo neighborhood of

Cidade Tiradentes have had a tradition of Marxist reading and organizational practices. In field conversations with Ice-Ice, a member of Força Ativa and CEDECA hip hop advocacy groups, he explained to me that a number of rappers and DJs read Marx in order to grasp the class struggle (*luta de classe*). Interestingly, Ice-Ice made a point in our conversation that Marx's own knowledge of class came from readings about African histories and forms of social organization. In this way, Ice-Ice attempted to link class with race as foundational to "consciousness" and to avoid the pitfalls of what the rap group *Sistema Negro* (Black System) called the "mistake of sociologists who forget us," that is, that class explains all social difference and power relations, and race is a derivative (Sistema Negro, 1997).

Similarly, in São Bernardo do Campo, there has been a tradition of community-based activism and labor union organization. These include the organization of the Highway Department (Departamento de Rodoviário [DDR]) highway labor camps, Lula and the metal workers unions of the 1970s, and important community leaders in neighborhoods like Jardim Beatriz near the center square. This area is where Nino Brown's father-in-law and grandfather-in-law combined community mobilization with issues of race and racial discrimination. In conversations about his neighborhood, Nino showed great pride in pointing out these facts and directing my attention to his collection of media snippets about his in-laws' activism. Such an environment proved hospitable to the MNU and hip hop and created a rare moment of working-class blackness engaged in political militancy, local community, and diasporic aesthetics.

Posse Hausa

In São Bernardo do Campo, the *Posse Hausa* emerged from the events sponsored by the municipal department of culture during the early 1990s. The above excerpt from the Neps rap group (moment 1) comes from *ABC Rap*, a collection of rap lyrics published by a group of department officials and researchers. Activists circulated this book around São Bernardo, and *Posse Hausa* members repeatedly recalled the importance of *ABC Rap* events in the conception and realization of *Posse Hausa*.

Posse Hausa was founded in April of 1993. In 1995, it consisted of twenty members, including performers from four rap groups, two graffiti artists, and one B-boy. Nino Brown and Marquinhos Funky

Figure 4.3 Afrika Bambaataa with King Nino Brown at Zulu Nation Brasil Headquarters. (Diego Pereira, 2007)

Soul presided over meetings, occasionally offering historical information about musical references and personal experience regarding negotiations with government agencies. Both Nino and Marquinhos were born in the state of Pernambuco in the northeast of Brazil in the early 1960s and migrated to the suburbs of São Paulo in the early 1970s. As discussed in Chapter 2, they exemplify a small but important sector of hip hoppers who represent the transition from earlier funk and soul musico-cultural movements in São Paulo to the present era of hip hop.

When I first attended a *Posse Hausa* general meeting in December of 1995, I realized that there were multiple interests present among posse members. In part, these differences were cultivated through relations between members and the state, local community radio stations, and the local chapter of the MNU. Such alliances would eventually lead to the fragmentation of *Posse Hausa* along ideological lines of representation and administration; however, for a few years *Hausa* hip hoppers organized events jointly and articulated a more radical perspective on *negritude* together (see Figure 4.3).[19]

An important ally of *Posse Hausa* was the São Paulo–based rap group *Posse Mente Zulu* (Zulu Mind), featuring Rappin' Hood. The name "Zulu" refers to the organization founded by Afrika Bambaataa in 1974 in the South Bronx of New York City. The Zulu Nation would later be regarded as one of the foundational organizations of hip hop. According to both Nino Brown and Rappin' Hood, "Zulu" connotes a "warrior attitude" on which black and other subaltern resistance depends. *Posse Mente Zulu* was rare in that they were able to produce a CD recording with songs that emphasized diaspora, blackness, and the trope of *quilombo*.[20] The following lyrical examples represent *negritude* in São Paulo rap. Most importantly, the song "Sou Negão" ("I'm Super Black") by *Posse Mente Zulu* would later be remixed and released by Rappin' Hood (2001) with a greater emphasis on hip hop as part of a national canon along with samba and soccer.

Most importantly, rappers from *Mira Direta* ("Direct Aim"), members of *Posse Hausa*, actively question racial unity as a problem, not as an assumed position of fact. This marks a significant conceptual difference between historical moments 1 and 2. Mira Direta never recorded any of their music beyond a demo tape format; however, they did perform quite extensively throughout São Bernardo do Campo and Diadema during the mid-1990s. During a commemoration event for the *Posse Hausa* organization in April of 1996, I caught their act.

Mira Direta's performance was effective and appreciated, because they demonstrated an important hip hop style of the period. As Brazilian hip hoppers considered themselves more "informed" about what knowledge and performance entailed, they began to explore more hip hop aesthetics. By the mid-1990s many Brazilian rappers experimented with the high-speed rhetorical delivery akin to Das EFX, or even early Busta Rhymes in the United States, balanced with an authoritative voice modeled on Chuck D from Public Enemy. The explosive and fast-paced sound production of the Bomb Squad (the production team of Public Enemy) inspired mid-'90s hip hoppers in São Paulo to become more animated in performance and assume (*assumir*) a didactic posture of relating experience and showcasing knowledge. *Mira Direta* embodied this spirit as they screamed at the audience on that day in April to "stop, think, wake up, and act . . . with a strongwill, we can change all of this" (Mira Direta, 1996).

For their part, *Posse Mente Zulu* recorded the song "Sou Negão" ("I'm Super Black"). They garnered important attention, but it would not be until 2001 when Rappin' Hood remixed and rereleased the song as part of his first solo album that the song's popularity would contribute to a recent move to incorporate hip hop into the national cultural canon along with samba and soccer.

> Blacks!! We are black!!
> You can call me whatever you want, I don't care
> I'm not a rebel racist and I know that.
> (Excerpt from "Sou Negão," Posse Mente Zulu, 1994, Rappin' Hood, 2001)

While he maintained the words in the two versions of "Sou Negão," Rappin' Hood, the leader and main rapper of *Posse Mente Zulu*, changed significantly the tone and context of the song. The more recent recording is part of a solo effort in which Rappin' Hood attempts to link his stories to not only São Paulo but also to Brazil as a unified nation. He calls out places and people from many states of the republic; Rappin' Hood includes various musical genres such as samba, MPB,[21] reggae,[22] and *embolada*.[23] He has continued this spirit of emblematic inclusion on his most recent recording "Sujeito Homem 2" (2005) by inviting the likes of MPB and samba artists Caetano Veloso, Dudu Nobre, Jair Rodrigues, and Martinho da Vila.

In addition, Rappin' Hood consistently works soccer (*futebol*) as a metaphorical mine for introductory sound bites and sing-a-long refrains. *Futebol* is not the only national frame involved in "Sou Negão." As part of the 2001 version, respected *sambista* Leci Brandão from Rio de Janeiro introduced rap as a new "*partido*" and Rappin' Hood as a new "*partideiro*." These terms relate directly to *samba de partido*, an informal style of samba made famous by Bezerra da Silva and the group *Fundo de Quintal* in the early 1980s. The instrumentation of "Sou Negão" is typical of *samba de partido alto* with the *cavaquinho* providing melodic, harmonic, and rhythmic support for the battery of percussion including *pandeiro, tan tan*, and *repique de mão*.[24] Rappin' Hood, in fact, begins the song with a tribute to samba from Rio de Janeiro with a few verses of sung rhymes directed to the "the hustlers and the little schemers in the shantytown hillsides" (*malandros e pivetada dos morro*) with intermittent chanting by the instrumentalists of "rap ah, rap ah."

All of this samba fanfare stands in significant contrast to the original version from 1994. *Posse Mente Zulu* engineered a sparse "jazzy" groove with a sample of repeated piano chords moving from tonic to dominant, providing both rhythm and a general pulse. There is also a sense of counterpoint in the strategic placement of the bass line and the bass drum pattern against the hi-hat pattern and 1970s soul brass samples used during the refrain sections.

Posse Mente Zulu's original sound production for "Sou Negão" reflects a general trend during the second historical moment. Hip hop producers began to experiment more with the distinct timbre of *capoeira*, the Afro-Brazilian form of martial art, dance, and ritual. In an unprecedented moment of Brazilian hip hop, Thaíde e DJ Hum produced the song "Afro-Brasileiro" (1996). In their attempts to articulate hip hop identity to a complex set of histories and cultures indexed in the term "afro," Thaíde e DJ Hum acknowledged both the fairly recent *negritude* of the Rio / São Paulo soul movement (1970s and early '80s) via the brass horn samples and the long-standing *negritude* of Brazilian slavery resistance by sampling the distinct sound of the *berimbau*, the characteristic instrument involved in *capoeira*. Two years prior, the rap group Potencial 3 from Diadema (another suburban city within the São Paulo metropolitan area) produced an album using the *berimbau*. The introductory cut, "In3dução," frames the album and the group's ideas as a proposed ritual experience.

Violence and Marginality (Moment 3)

The third historical moment (1996–99) emerged as part of the rising prominence of *Racionais MCs*, a group of three rappers and one DJ. The group first appeared during moment 1 on the compilation vinyl release *Consciência Black* in 1988 with two songs, "Pânico na Zona Sul" ("Panic on the South Side") and "Tempos Difíceis" ("Hard Times"). *Racionais* members have historically emphasized their loyalty to the south and north sides of São Paulo, respectively. Their 1990 release *Holocausto Urbano* (*Urban Holocaust*) and 1993 album *Raio X do Brasil* (*X-ray of Brazil*) set the stage for their remarkable commercial success *Sobrevivendo no Inferno* in 1997. The 1997 release, literally translated as "surviving in hell," sold more than one million copies, which is indeed remarkable considering that *Racionais*

MCs refused to appear on any mainstream media and did little formal promotion. Mano Brown, the enigmatic front man, became a *periferia* idol in part because he focused his stories on the extreme locality of shantytowns. He honed his considerable narrative skills to depict the marginal and the *crente*. *Crente* refers to the so-called "evangelical" believer belonging to one of the many contemporary popular, non-Catholic Christian religions in urban Brazil.

In addition, with the decline of posse and NGO influence, the São Paulo hip hop community began to figure race as ultimately secondary to sociogeographical realities of the *periferia*. To some extent, *periferia* and the marginal have always been significant in hip hop, but during these years, the shantytown report of violence and poverty (*denúncia*) became the unshakable paradigm of hip hop narratives. Hip hoppers explained *negritude* as part of the banal nightmare that is "reality" and replaced a focus on Afro-centricity with brief qualifiers of discrimination, thus depicting blackness as a mere side effect of the *sistema* (system).

The dominant faction within São Paulo hip hop uses a "culture of violence" frame to make its concerns visible and recognizable: "Crime offers a language for expressing the feelings related to changes in the neighborhood, the city, and Brazilian society more generally" (Caldeira 2000, 31).[25] As discussed in the previous chapter, such hip hoppers maintain the marginal, the historical figure ascribed to residents of Brazilian urban *periferias*, as the narrative protagonist and the aesthetic style of performance. Curiously, hip hoppers rely on stereotypes of violence and marginality propagated by the mainstream to achieve resistance. In my discussion of moment 4, I analyze this in detail.

Unlike in earlier albums in which *Racionais MCs* invested greater effort in explicating daily life as "black drama," in *Sobrevivendo no Inferno* the term "*negro*" disappears, and "*preto*" is reduced to solely its assumed impoverished banality. In the hit song "Rapaz Comum" ("Common Kid"), Edi Rock tells a story in first person of a young man who experiences elevated anger and violent rage. He realizes that he and his situation of conflict are completely commonplace. Even his imagined death, like so many he has seen, is banal.

> I don't want to admit that I'm just another one . . .
> One more black (*preto*) in the morgue, it's serious . . .
> I can't believe that brother (*mano*) came all the way up here!
> Killed me, [he] wanted to be certain . . .
> (Excerpt from "Rapaz comum," *Racionais MCs*, 1997)

The sound production matches the banality of narrative. In "Rapaz Comum," just as with much of *Racionais MCs'* music, there are no catchy melodies or even attractive, bouncy bass lines. Rather, the group engineers an everyday soundscape through what I call "dramatic" composition. *Periferia* ubiquity is a drama of violence; therefore, many songs contain droning high pitches from synthesizers or repeated closed-voiced piano chords to provide the feel of horror and impending tragedy. "Rapaz Comum" foregrounds a relatively high-pitched piano chord shot through with minor second-pitch intervals, which occasionally and only fleetingly resolves after Edi Rock finishes a verse.

In rap production, the rhythm section (drum and bass patterns) normally is the center of the groove. This is the objective of sound engineering and, along with the rapper's voice, the focus of audience participation. In "Rapaz Comum," it is not the refined timbre that shines through but rather a muddled but "quantized" backdrop plodding through time. Quantization refers to the process used by sound engineers of aligning rhythmic patterns of multiple tracks. This is a basic but debated topic of hip hop production. Quantizing is basic because the sampled or digitally composed tracks must line up rhythmically to produce a cohesive unit. This is a crucial issue because most of the sounds come from a wide range of sources, which vary in meter (e.g., "in 4" or "in 3" as a rhythmic pulse). Quantizing is quite variable and thus becomes part of production style. Too much or too rigid quantizing gives the sound a robotic or overly mechanized quality. If the producer does not quantize at all, the sound appears messy or "off."[26]

One of the major differences between "marginal" and "positive" hip hop in terms of sound engineering is the treatment of quantizing. While "marginal" producers tend to quantize their tracks meticulously so that the resulting groove appears solid and cohesive, many "positive" producers play with quantizing to produce a kind of "swing," or what some producers call a more "human" feel to the beat. Ideologically, this difference translates into an emphasis on *o sistema* within "marginal" aesthetics, in contrast to an "alien" or spiritual aesthetics within "positive" hip hop.[27]

In "Rapaz Comum," the musical orchestration translates the general feeling of urban life within the "system" of Brazilian society. The drum pattern is a basic rock sequence with the bass drum, snare, and hi-hat pattern consistent throughout the song. The bass line is almost indistinguishable by pitch; it rather acts as another line of rhythmic punctuation. The bass line feels like a relentless body blow—systematic and quotidian. Edi Rock accomplishes the main objective of the "marginal" hip hop style in that he calls out the "system" and reveals its everyday innards. *Negritude* is not particularly salient or worthy of specific reference. It is simply an underlying fact of *periferia* misery.

The dominance of *periferia* or the "marginal" aesthetic of São Paulo hip hop limited the space for groups that a few years prior had more influence and community resonance. In the following section, I recall an event held in Diadema during July of 1999 featuring a female soul group, a B-boy crew from the countryside of São Paulo state, and a former *Posse Hausa* Afro-centric rap group *Banzo Bantu*. This piece of ethnography demonstrates the extent to which *negritude*, for many, has been pushed aside within the general hip hop imagination.

Remembering Diadema

I had been to Diadema many times to meet with Nino Brown and others at the Canhema Cultural Center, which later became the Casa da Cultura Hip hop, or simply, "*a casa*." The neighborhood of Canhema is easily accessible by "trolley bus" departing from the southernmost subway station of Jabaquara. Yet on this day, I needed detailed directions to arrive in the right place. Santos, from the rap group *Banzo Bantu*, patiently explained to me over the phone to ask the ticket taker (*cobrador*) on the "inter-urban" bus to notify me when the bus passed the second bakery on the way up the hill. This was the recognized landmark; everyone knows this place (*todo mundo conhece*). I could then yank the chain and signal the bus driver to stop. "Cross the street and walk through the gas station to the other side and look down. Then you'll see it," he told me. Following Santos's directions, I found myself with a bird's eye view of that day's place for hip hop. On this gloomy and blustery Saturday afternoon, many adolescents from Jardim Paineiras and Vila Campanário, two adjacent neighborhoods in the middle of the large periphery area of southeast São Paulo metropolitan area, gathered in the public park. One of the organizers of this particular event, Akan O.A.D.Q. (an acronym meaning "of African origin and directly descendant of the *quilombos*") described at length the profile of Jardim Paineiras. He summarized his depiction by stating that it was a "neighborhood where blood and drugs run freely and often" (pers. comm.). A member of the postal service by trade, Akan has lived almost his entire life in Jardim Paineiras and believes that hip hop culture is a way of self-affirmation and a road to a "caminho procurando o melhor" ("better [life]"). As he prepped the modest crowd for the upcoming group *Banzo Bantu* and the ensuing three-on-three basketball tournament, Akan reminded the audience, "It's like this. We need to transform our community, take on this attitude. Right? Enough complaining. You're unemployed, without a place to stay, look for alternatives. But where are you at? Pay attention to what's coming up next. I'll be out there with ya. Peace." (Akan, 1999).

Levi, a representative of the Municipal Secretary of Culture from the city of São Paulo, who promotes various neighborhood events every weekend throughout the metropolitan area, echoed Akan's sentiments: "Check it. The real deal is the following: peace, lots of peace. Violence for us ain't got nothing going for it. Dig? Without further adieu . . . *Banzo Bantu*." For their part, members Ketu and Honerê of the rap group *Banzo Bantu*[28] introduced themselves as "*caretas*" (squares, not hip) for not "falling prey to drugs"[29] and senseless violence.

Despite the fact that the whole park reeked of marijuana throughout the show by way of seemingly invisible smokers, *Banzo Bantu* and Akan continued to try to mobilize the crowd around keywords of nobility and fortitude within a common racial history, as well as around the presumed benefits of following the path of self-education. DJ Honerê shouted, "Strength comes in our origins not in the stuff the system plants in our neighborhoods." Ketu added, "Look at us, we are *caretas*; but we know where we come from. That is something we will always have. We are *negros*. Look at us and look around you. We are the same and these stories we're about to tell y'all are your stories as well" (*Banzo Bantu*, 1999).

Honerê performed a series of vinyl scratching and concluded his introduction to the song "A Era do Zumbi" ("Zumbi's Era") with bombastic finale reminiscent of the characteristic sounds of the few years prior, at the height of *Posse Hausa* (i.e., moment two). *Banzo Bantu* had hoped to create an atmosphere of power and positive energy against the supposed apathy indicated by the marijuana. Summarizing *Banzo Bantu*'s message: dope makes one a dope and hip hop allows one to rise above and transform the "periphery" into the "center" of black knowledge and subaltern pride.

The roughly one hundred kids and young adults swayed back and forth with mild interest. They milled about the dilapidated playground as the B-boy crew and soul group performed—all in all a chilly reception, which is uncommon in Brazil considering the general high level of applause any performance usually receives. It is not an easy crowd out there for Afro-centricity, as this event made clear. Many hip hoppers complain that the majority of the *periferia*, and even the hip hop community itself, is woefully "uninformed" and "alienated" from "reality." However, as is the case with most if not all cultural groups who utilize popular music in conjunction with social messages, participants of hip hop in São Paulo take up a number of different and sometimes opposing positions with regard to how exactly the "reality" of blackness and periphery should be represented in words, sounds, and visual cues. *Banzo Bantu*'s performance of *negritude* appeared disconnected from the "reality" circulated by *Racionais MCs*. The significant difference lies in the fact that *Racionais* not only directly addresses the drug trafficking scene but also meticulously describes the rise and fall of *os neguinho servindo* (the black pushers serving [the clientele]).

Leaving the *Quebradas* Behind? Positive Rap Revisits Afro-centricity (Moment 4)

Finally, the present moment of hip hop and *negritude* involves a competitive and creative struggle between the aesthetics and ethics of the "marginal" and the "positive" hip hoppers. Differences between these two major tendencies manifest themselves in graphic, sonic, and spatial dimensions. The common ground among "positive" hip hoppers is the belief that denouncements of *periferia* daily life are not enough. They argue that hip hop needs to provide concrete solutions beginning with sharper strategies of collectivity built on education and entertainment. In this section, I discuss the various ways in which "positive" hip hoppers seek to discursively leave the *periferia* behind, but yet seem to depend on the semiotic force of *periferia* for any leverage.

For all their attempts to speak to the general human condition of suffering and enlightenment, "positive rappers" continue to depend on the specifics of São Paulo (sub)urban locality in the *quebradas*. "Positive" hip hoppers configure universalism in different manners, and part of this difference involves the reckoning of *negritude*. *Negritude* has become a point of debate not only between "marginal" and "positive" hip hop camps but also among "positive" hip hoppers. The debate, in great part, revolves around whether *negritude* is central to positivity or if it is simply a new version of "racial democracy."

The emphasis on *união* brings many contemporary "positive" hip hoppers to a position of universalism, which signifies essentially an erasure of race. This is certainly the case with the group *Sistema Racional* (Rational System), whose leader, Fábio Féter, claims to have coined the term *rap positivo*. Fábio and I met during a community radio station interview in February of 2002. DJ Jair from Radio Everest on the east side of São Paulo had invited me to hang out during his Friday night hip hop show. Fábio and I quickly became friends and met several times over the subsequent weeks to discuss his group's upcoming CD release, the Labor Party (PT) in his hometown (the São Paulo suburb Santo André), musical composition, and CD cover design. In fact, Fábio helped me administer the questionnaires used in a fieldwork project related to graphic design. He covered a series of music stores in the *galerias*, and I covered another set. When we met to exchange notes and collect the questionnaires, I noticed that few participants from his stack actually had answered the "social profile" question concerning race. Fábio explained that there is only one race and that the question was bogus.[30] This perspective complements his idea of "positive" rap.

Sistema Racional erases race from their version of hip hop and criticizes sharply popular Christianity as a group filled with opportunistic entrepreneurs. This latter point is explicitly demonstrated in the song "A Igreja do Sal," ("The Salt Church"), which is a play on the Igreja Universal (Universal Church), founded by Edir Macedo, or as satirized by *Sistema Racional*, "Pedir Mais Cedo" (To Ask [for money] Quick and Early).

In some ways, this current sector of hip hoppers revives the musical innocence of the early years of Brazilian rap outlined above under the category of moment 1, but now for different reasons. Gone are the samples of everyday violence and criminality from the *quebradas* of the *periferia* so prevalent in "marginal" hip hop. In their place, producers place occasional children's voices in the case of Xis, and rappers utilize clownish vocal styles for satirical purposes. In the song "Igreja do Sal," *Sistema Racional* couples a vocal imitation of church leaders' authoritarian tones with a strategic use of church bell samples. In the title track to their first CD *É assim que tem que ser*, *Sistema Racional* employs a high-pitched keyboard melody. However, in this context it works not to elicit melodrama but a playfulness of simply *dar um rolê na quebrada com os manos* (to take a swing around the block with the brothers). The significant difference in keyboard use between "marginal" and this brand of "positive" rap is that in the latter, the keyboard is more melodic. Rather than sustained pitches of tension, the keyboard sounds often parallel the melodic contour of the voice or, as is more prevalent in "positive" rap, voices. In terms of composition, the keyboard-voice parallel stands as a common point within the "positive" group as "evangelical" rappers also utilize synthesized keyboards to complement harmonic singing usually during refrain sections.

Another example of a universalist position on spirituality and hip hop comes in the work of *Alternativa C* ("C" stands for Christ). Similar to *Sistema Racional* and *Xis*, *Alternativa C* voids the potential of Afro-centricity and a productive racialization from the keyword *mano*. The following lyrical excerpt comes from the title track of their 2004 the recording "Por que a cor incomoda?" ("Why does race bother you?").

> Why, why does color [read: race] bother you? (2x)
> Is it because you don't realize that we are all equal? . . .
> 100% this, 100% that. You don't admit that we are all mixed here
> In Brazil there is no pure race . . .

The *Alternativa C* rappers preach an ideology of "color blindness" coupled with the Brazilian trope of mixture. Starting with the CD cover, the group chose a paradigmatic image. Namely, the nanny, or *babá*, nursing a young boy is the image *par excellence* of Brazilian social history, a discourse and economic structure of patriarchy and racial mixture. In this case, the members of *Alternativa C* have flipped the image around in terms of race, as the nursing woman (*babá*) is white, and the little boy is black.[31] MC Dom shows his attitude as he claims to "unmask fools, mercenaries, [and] exploiters of those less informed" (*Alternativa C*, 2004). Yet, *Alternativa C*'s narrative does little to subvert traditional vectors of power. Rather, the dominant message is that race-based identity politics is an example of racism; the truth is that all Brazilians are mixed.

There are differences, however, within self-proclaimed "positive" hip hoppers on the place of race and *periferia* in music and collective identity. From a perspective quite different than that of *Sistema Racional*, *Alternativa C*, and *Xis*, other "positive" hip hoppers are, in fact, deeply involved with a number of popular Christian worship organizations. In my experience with hip hoppers from this subgroup, a relatively high percentage of practitioners are of obvious African descent.[32] To simply discount devotees of Pentecostal and neo-Pentecostal religions on the basis of the historical ties between the church and institutions of slavery, or because of religion's tendency to distract worshipers from the recognition of "reality" (i.e., conditions of exploitation), is to talk past a massive potential audience. The emerging school of "positive" hip hoppers, as exemplified by the *7 Taças* crew in São Paulo, attempts to articulate hip hop to *negritude* so as to reach that "lost constituency" (Burdick 1998b).

Narratives rarely mention specific place names, as national landmarks substitute metropolitan neighborhood "shout outs." In addition, the banal sounds of the street such as buses, gunshots, television sets, and neighborhood banter are revealingly absent. In their place, *7 Taças* recordings privilege U.S.-influenced contemporary R&B musical production and choral singing styles. Rappers such as Professor Pablo and Lito Atalaia utilize samples from orchestral European art music coupled with composed electronic music motifs in an effort to bring together the sacred and the secular, the past and the future. The prominent role of orchestral string samples in evangelical rap speaks to an underlying association made by producers and listeners between the sound of violins and cellos with religiosity and spirituality. For its part, the sounds of keyboard melodies, piano or guitar R&B chord progressions, and specific sounds linked to computer use (i.e., error bleeps and boings) work with the lyrics to create an aura of contemporary technology and a movement toward the future and ultimately resolution and salvation. Rather than nostalgia for James Brown, the non-Christian domain of *candomblé*, or even the overtly "African" cluster of *capoeira* and the *berimbau*, these "positive" hip hoppers express *negritude* in a reworking of the sounds of R&B and gospel—a presumably logical point of musical contact between God and Afro-Brazilians.

Unlike *Sistema Racional*, rappers from organizations such as *7 Taças* explicitly link spirituality with *negritude*. In the following lyrical excerpt, Professor Pablo uses a discourse of faith amplified by an interesting mixture of violin and electric rock guitar motifs to relate his version of "reality" as a "black" collective one.

> My people live like this, moved by faith
> (Who's black like me knows the deal)
> We get beat down but stay on our feet
> (Who's black like me knows the deal)
> Whether one is man or woman
> (Who's black like me knows the deal)
> (Refrain from "Quem é preto" ["Who is black"],
> Professor Pablo, 2002)

Whether "moved by faith" or willing to expand *união* into revolution (*revolução*), as other "positivists" such as local group *Afro-Rude* urge, hip hoppers continue to struggle in the position vis-à-vis a now-entrenched tradition of *periferia* narratives. Racionais MCs, Facção Central, along with dozens of other groups codified the popular phrase "*cada um cada um*" (every man for himself) as that which appears inescapable as part of "reality." "Positivists" have reacted by framing hip hop as ultimately race-blind entertainment, in the case of *Sistema Racional*, for example, or linking a more aggressive *negritude*, reminiscent of the mid-1990s, to a spiritual unity. While *Sistema Racional* has enjoyed some commercial success and has garnered state sponsorship through municipal departments of culture, groups like Professor Pablo, *Afro-Rude*, *Banzo Bantu*, and even Thaíde, one of Brazil's hip hop pioneers, struggle for airtime.

I ultimately believe that the one durable legacy of *negritude* as articulated by hip hoppers has been *periferia* youth's ability to strongly associate terms of blackness in and of themselves with social critique. This, in my opinion, is a fundamental part of a productive Afro-centric perspective. The mechanisms of capitalism within the music industry provide a structure, albeit skewed toward hyperbole, for the circulation of social critique. Consequently, *negritude* becomes part of hip hop's cultural capital and thus contains value associated with knowledge and respect.

Conclusion

There are competing ideologies for race-based identities under the rubric of hip hop in Brazil. Hip hoppers have had a mixed relationship with blackness as lyrical theme, as organizational premise, as aesthetic trope, and as political platform. While *negritude* appears in common hip hop parlance, pensive scrutiny reveals that hip hoppers frequently conflate *negritude* with *sangue bom* (literally, "good blood," as mentioned in Chapter 3), and *mano*, as described and historicized in this chapter. However, everyone could be potentially *sangue bom* or *mano*. The idea of consanguinity traditionally associated with race (Stocking 1968, 164) does not hold firmly in the minds of most Brazilians, including presumably "conscious" São Paulo hip hoppers. In effect, the prevailing presence of *sangue bom* replays the national ideology of Brazil's single mixed race. Nino Brown, a transitional figure in the history of Brazilian *black* music bridging the movements of soul and funk to hip hop, has called the sentiment of *negritude* "weak" and a "trace" of the fervor in the past.

In this chapter I have suggested reasons why Brazilian hip hoppers remain somewhat fragmented with regard to *negritude* and its proper place and form within hip hop ideology and identification. Despite the fact that most scholarship produced by Brazilian sociologists and anthropologists has revealed the mythical status of "racial democracy" as a functioning system, the notion that race can ever be primary to one's identity or philosophical outlook continues to be marginalized as un-Brazilian.

Judging from local hip hop scholarship (Andrade 1996, 1999; Pimentel 1997) and my experience with dozens of hip hoppers who, in fact, "get paid," hip hop has been most successful in articulating *negritude* to a politics of identity through what has been categorized as "educational work." In a meeting of the São Paulo Municipal Coordination Committee around "topics concerning the black population," the proposal directly related to hip hop culture (number 7) was classified under "education" rather than "culture," which incidentally only contained two proposals (CEAPN 2003). Proposal 7 argues for a recuperation of the project RAP-pensando a Educação (a play on "rethinking education"), originally operative from 1989 to 1992 during the last Labor Party administration under Luiza Erundina. It is not a coincidence that it was precisely during this period of São Paulo's hip hop history that a great many posses were formed and blackness manifested itself more visibly in hip hop performance.

Despite all of this confusion and ambiguity, hip hoppers such as Thaíde remain philosophically Afro-centric. Through radical critique and creative rhyme and narrative schemes, Thaíde holds up "racial democracy" for popular deconstruction. In addition, some "evangelical" hip hoppers, who predominantly identify themselves as either *preto* or *negro* (black), show signs of incorporating a sense of *negritude* espoused by Solano Trindade. That blackness requires work in the form of individual education and collective solidarity is a concept that potentially emboldens a culture (hip hop) built on the ideologies of "information" and achievement.

Chapter 5

Mano/Mana

The Engendering of the *Periferia*

In both the United States and Brazil, hip hop performers and scholars alike have traditionally understood masculinity as common sense and "natural"—an essence of hardness that requires no reflection beyond statements of class and race predicaments. Thus, "gender" discussions in hip hop, scholarly or otherwise, have usually been about the depiction of women in lyrics and videos.[1] Some scholars such as Gwendolyn Pough (2004) have made more epistemological arguments about black femininity—namely, that the black female voice is not epiphenomenal to hip hop history; rather, it has been a fundamental force to the development of "skill" and "attitude."[2] While scholars of other "alternative" or popular music genres, such as heavy metal and post-punk, recognized early on that artists and fans invest a great deal of energy, pleasure, and ideology in the performance of masculinity and femininity, hip hop scholars are only recently addressing the issue of gender and particularly masculinity as multidimensional.[3]

Gender as the construction of masculinity and femininity is a "nervous" social category. In the case of Brazil, the anxiety around gender does not make hip hoppers timid but rather drives them to perform masculinities and traffic ideologies of power and presumably social change. Hip hop is most influential in periods of "coming of age." Over the past decade, I have seen timid, scrawny teenage boys and girls become confident young men and women, the definition of their physique seemingly moving in parallel with a growing sense of self-knowledge, social position, and relative authority. I have, of course, also witnessed young men and women become disenchanted with hip hop due to its own rules of inclusion and other apparent contradictions. In this chapter, I analyze hip hop masculinity and femininity as a complex system of gendered situations (domestic spheres), language (*mano/mana*), discourses (feminism, violence, and *periferia*), institutions (*Geledés, Fala Preta!*), and musicality (sounds, body images, hip hop "elements"). I believe that the meanings of such dimensions of hip hop gender come into focus only if we ground them in the historical, psychological, and cultural systems of patriarchy, attitude, and *machismo*.

In Chapter 1, I stated that, following scholars such as Robin Kelley (1997) and Marcyliena Morgan (2002, 2005), hip hop is about the politics and pleasures of attitude. Attitude is a complex sociopsychological phenomenon that involves a tension among opinion, behavior, and judgment. Attitude is an acquired trait, a posture, and a demeanor that requires consistent maintenance, especially during adolescence and young adult years. All teenagers construct and perform their attitudes in private and public spaces. What is special about hip hop is that hip hoppers around the world have made attitude into an aesthetic achievement, something to show off. Teenagers are often attracted to hip hop because they are able to employ "back talk"—talk back to attitude labels structured by society (i.e., school, parents, police, and wage employment).

This works differently in the United States as compared with Brazil. In the United States, institutions such as elementary and secondary schools use attitude as a disciplinary category to mark "problem" students and measure "objective" student performance. In practice, attitude frequently means a "bad" attitude, that is, kids with an attitude tend to "get into trouble." As education scholars, psychologists, and sociologists have discussed, the notions of "bad attitude" and "trouble" have historically been structured by race, class, and gender.[4] In the United States this has meant, in general, that attitude is a poor black and Latino "thing" associated with predominantly boys. In Brazil, attitude (*atitude*) is, in general, a positive quality of self-confidence that most teenagers out of the *periferia* lack. Attitude is what middle-class kids are seemingly born with and what eludes so many poor, working-class kids in the *periferia*. One needs to "get an attitude" (*tomar uma atitude*) with respect to some task. Specifically within hip hop, attitude is similar to "information" as described throughout this text, that is, hip hoppers connect attitude to knowledge and thus being "real" hip hoppers. In this chapter, I argue that "common sense" notions of masculinity and femininity significantly structure what counts as attitude among Brazilian hip hoppers. In sum, while U.S. hip hoppers seek to turn the "bad" of "bad attitude" and the notion of "trouble" into an expressive positive and a pleasurable back talk, Brazilian hip hoppers want to prove that they indeed *have* attitude.

Attitude is a key component to one's style. To "check yo'self," or in hip hop *brasileiro*, "to recognize [brother]" (*reconheça, mano*), are often the opening words of a public challenge to "correct" attitude or "come correct." The aesthetics of attitude are made manifest in performative competitions in school, on the street, in the neighborhood park, and on stage during recognized hip hop "performances" including all the "elements."

Hip hop as a complex cultural system provides platforms of expression, potential employment, a wide range of semiotic power, and a general sense of community and modernity; and, as such, it is a testing ground for primarily *periferia* residents in urban Brazil. Young people use hip hop as a forum to test their understandings of self and the world through discourses and performances of "reality." As they come to know themselves, Brazilian hip hoppers "design" notions of masculinity and femininity. Similar to my analysis of class, race, place, time, and spirituality in prior chapters, I interpret hip hoppers' ideologies of gender as not simply about ideas but also manifest in image and sound material.

I use the following fieldwork vignette to begin a discussion about how São Paulo youth perform gender through hip hop. The scene moves back and forth from the highly visible public sphere (neighborhood performances) to more carefully postured scenes in the domestic sphere (home recordings). I follow this with a series of impressionistic and analytical phrases.

On October 21, 2001, I visited what would be the last meeting of the East Side posse organization, *União da Periferia* (Shantytown Unity). They had just put on a show the weekend prior, and apparently it had been a disaster. Someone had sabotaged the power supply and had mixed voltage output frying the already meager amplification equipment. A costly sabotage it was, and accusations flew around the dusty convention hall. Factions seemed to have been forming for some time, and this was the last straw. Before the meeting began, my friend DJ Lâmina introduced me to several members. They apologized in advance for what would become a spiteful meeting. Conversations with posse president Marcão (Ice) and committee members Gilbert, Jota, and others involved dejection and sorrow due to recent events and what they saw as the beginning of an end. However, they expressed an interest in me, the *gringo*, friend of Lâmina, as a chance to talk about future plans and past accomplishments. We discussed plans to make a video and strategies of appearing on MTV Brazil. Momentarily inspired by our daydreaming, Ice ordered a young boy to retrieve a VHS tape, which contained self-recorded interviews with some of the rap groups in the *União da Periferia Posse* along with some live performance footage. In the following, I paraphrase what I saw:

> Teenage boys in the periphery
> look around for symbols
> with which they can express themselves.
> What I know is what is around me.
> Hip hop is an attempt to arrange these things and ideas into a story.
> Posing hard as a façade?
> Performance crumbles cement cells the city government offers as a cultural center.
> Five-second loops repeat
> Microphones give out, short out
> Voices echo and become fragmented.
> Sermons and raps revolve around repetition of mantras
> Marginality, salvation, unity, voice and a hopeful consequence.
> Fierce, piercing rays of sunlight shine through
> The small square opening at the top of the wall
> Overexposure of images and garbled drum tracks
> Melodic tags from terror movies
> Resound as rotating pairs of MCs
> Try to capture a moment of attention.
>
> To appear (*aparecer*) and be recognized is a dream frustrated by Catholic upbringing
> In whatever syncretic form it may manifest itself.
> Impersonating thugs to prove a point?
> Ice told me once, "See, there's a lot of scoundrels (*cobras*) in hip hop"
> Impersonating thugs places the actor standing tall with excess power
> Imaginary, fabricated or desired—
> Directed through objects.
> Whether it's pistols, sawed-off shotguns, extended forearms and fists,
> Video game moves, Karate kicks, dicks and pricks.
> (Applause: everyone was able to have their moment on stage.)

The images on the worn VHS tape were recorded over so-and-so's uncle's amateur pornography film. I am told he's still in the dark, lost in a world of sugarcane alcohol (*pinga*). Most hip hoppers around the world want desperately to display their "skills," to show they are innovative and professional performers. In Brazil, at the level of everyday life and community, this means to "appear" and show that they have something to say and thus are someone. To control a moment in time and a spot on stage is not only about the pleasures of "appearing" and erasing but also, if temporarily, about the "social invisibility" (Soares 2002) that blankets the *periferia*. It is also for many *periferia* youth, especially boys, a step away from institutional correctional facilities such as FEBEM (Foundation for the Well-Being of Minors). *Periferia* youth see hip hop as a way to talk back to conventional notions of marginality. As I have discussed elsewhere (Pardue 2005), most hip hoppers realize that they will likely always be targets (*alvos*) of the "system" in a general sense. They simply want to have more control over how the target is understood, rather than being explained as *"de mal mesmo,"* or "naughty by nature."[5]

The most obvious and often the most nervous issue within hip hop gender dynamics is the role of women hip hoppers within the project of "reality" representation

> The problem [with female hip hoppers] is that you never know if they're really serious about the movement. It's more likely that they will betray you than work for unity (*união*). Sure, they're some great women rappers, B-girls and occasional DJ, but usually, in my opinion, it's too much work. We need to make sure they're OK and comfortable. We brothers (*os mano*) are out there negotiating, making the beats, taking the buses and trains from here to there, we go to the late night radio interviews (*radio comunitário*), because they have other responsibilities. That's how it is; women have great voices; they offer a positive [visual] presence on stage, but they don't have the wherewithal to exchange information (*trocar uma idéia*).

This was the reply of rapper Gordo when asked about the advantages and disadvantages of having women members of a hip hop group. Implicit in Gordo's statement is a set of assumptions about masculinity and femininity related to the routine activities of a rap group within the São Paulo hip hop community. As will be discussed in detail below, femininity is a status of partiality; that is, presumed values and tendencies of womanhood preclude women from fully participating in hip hop. Their link to "reality," indexed above in terms of experiences with urban transportation at night, entrepreneurship, and sound production, is lacking. Hip hop males perceive women as weak providers of "information"; they have difficulties in sustaining a "hardcore" exchange of ideas. As discussed in previous chapters, the latter point is one of the fundamental objectives of Brazilian hip hop, as practitioners connect dialogue and information with identity formation and community-building. Furthermore, since women's value essentially consists of their image, vocal tonalities, and body movement (i.e., "presence"), hip hop males tend to objectify women as relatively beautiful things or assets and thus easily slip into a discourse of "protection." In so doing, male hip hoppers (and many female hip hoppers) confirm a more general notion of Brazilian masculinity within the paradigm of patriarchy.

Configured as male-female relations, public versus private domains, and a set of "natural" affinities, gender is an active discourse and pervades hip hop culture. What differentiates gender mediation from that of race and class in Brazilian hip hop is that hip hoppers appear less committed to radicalizing gender as part of the overall project of social transformation. It is perhaps not a lack of commitment but rather a lack of awareness of how hip hop is gendered in the first place and how this squares with the dominant sociality or *o sistema* against which most hip hoppers claim to work.

For the most part, hip hoppers reckon gender in accordance with the hegemonic discourses and practices of Brazilian machismo. That is to say that while hip hoppers may mediate race and class in relatively unacceptable ways, they generally reproduce typical males and females within the matrix of contemporary urban sociality. In essence, hip hoppers reinforce their culture as a sphere of "homosociality," as Sedgwick termed (1985), by upholding aesthetic and ethical value systems based on national standards of masculinity.[6] Homosociality is a system of relationships configured primarily among men. It is characterized by machismo, an ideology of power and identity formation, which serves to maintain certain sociocultural orthodoxies cutting across race, class, and gender. This configuration is, as discussed below, more of a Latin American design rather than an application of U.S. discourses and counterdiscourses of machismo and patriarchy. Unlike in the United States, Brazilian hip hoppers perform dramas of "hypermasculinity" to talk back to a patriarchy of class inflected by race, not the other way around.[7]

In addition, the emergence of feminism as a guide to social activism involves a considerable history of pragmatic, grassroots organizing. Similar to the historical efforts regarding "racial democracy," the critique of machismo emerged from local and translocal activism. The discourses and institutions of feminism in urban Brazil have provided an infrastructure for interested São Paulo hip hoppers. In this chapter I discuss the importance of *Geledés*, an NGO dedicated to issues affecting Afro-Brazilian women, as an early platform for feminist and *negritude* hip hoppers. *Geledés* was and is still one of the few organizations that articulate race and gender to popular culture and education. In more recent years, the Diadema Cultural Center in Canhema neighborhood has become a locus of hip hop activity. Sensitive to the shortcoming of gender inequalities within hip hop, organizers such as Nino Brown, Marcelinho Back Spin, and DJ Érry G have encouraged the formation of women hip hop groups. To this end, I describe the emergence of the Soul Sisters and their significance to hip hop's mediation of gender in urban Brazil.

Position in the Field

"All knowledge is gendered."[8] In a similar fashion, all researchers are gendered in the field, because positioning is necessarily intersubjective. This came to the fore in many of my conversations with hip hop males and my relative lack of success in establishing long-standing relationships with hip hop females in São Paulo. While marking a person as male or female in and of itself is usually a quick process, the articulation of gender is frequently significant at a more complex level involving a range of discursive activities. Understanding comes with time and intimacy. Establishing rapport with local hip hoppers, which in some cases took a long time considering the significant differences between us, frequently involved an exchange of narratives highlighting a relative sense of achieved masculinity.[9]

Being "married" in Brazil is a social status readily attributed to individuals involved in personal, intimate relationships of any length over a year. The terms couple (*casal*) and married (*casado*) etymologically come from the same root and are much closer in semantics and pragmatics than, for example, their English equivalents. While many relationships do not endure to the point of ritual fruition in the form of a wedding (*casamento*), fiancées (*noivos*) consider the official status as a formality and the ritual just a matter of time and resources. Most hip hop males and females are in relationships as *noivos* or *casados*. Yet, the relative informality of personal relationships coupled with persistent spatio-gender dynamics facilitates young male anxiety.

Confronted with such a set of conditions always more pronounced in the *periferia*, for example, unemployment rates are always higher there than in other urban sectors, young men articulate anxiety and informality through narratives about female cheating and misbehaving. According to such logic, many Brazilian men traffic in women and hold multiple relationships. Similar to the silent racism so common in everyday life, exploitation of women is also part of general tacit knowledge in Brazilian society. Most Brazilians thus recognize, but few explicitly name, female exploitation; and therefore it remains invisible in hip hop public representation. One does not hear or see rap performances, DJ soundscapes, graffiti imagery, or street dance that make women exchange a point of semiotic focus. Rather, the sociality of female "accrual" or male-female relationship exchange is a point of backstage and bus-seat banter.

During February and March of 2002, I met with Giro on a regular basis as we worked on the production of his solo album. He agreed to show me his process of musical production and allowed me to hang around as he negotiated with hip hop store representatives in the *galerias* downtown in exchange for taking photographs and helping with the visual design of the CD cover and insert. We spent a great deal of time inside subways, waiting for buses, and inside my Volkswagen Gol car. It was in these spaces that Giro enjoyed relating his stories of making plays for young women (*jogando charme pras mina*). As we moved through the city and passed dozens of beautiful women, Giro interjected come-ons, remembered scenes during past hip hop performances, and tried to elicit responses from me.

Giro and I already knew each other to the point where he no longer felt it necessary to ask comparative questions such as, "And the girls in Illinois, or in New York or Chicago, what are they like? Like the ones in that Jay-Z video, is that for real?" We had already had those conversations. I had given my stock answers such as, "Those women exist, but you know, I'm an old man. What do I know? It's all a business anyway, those videos." Or, "Sure, there's lots of beautiful women up there, but, you know, I like it down here. I married a Brazilian woman." Giro knew that I had some sense of what it was like in the Brazilian society and how many men stare at women overtly. He repeatedly tried to elicit some "real" story of masculinity from me: "Ok, I know you're married. You are so clean and quiet. Come on now, it's not like that." I had nothing to say other than an apparently unconvincing viewpoint that to look and to take are not the same. I welcomed the noise of the overheated bus engine struggling to carry the load up a steep *periferia* incline leading to Avenida Jabaquara, one of the main arteries linking the subway stations on the south side to the city of Diadema and other points south. We knew that this interaction would end soon as we would go our separate ways until later in the week as we scheduled a meeting to discuss the layout of the CD cover.

It is here where my position of *gringo* and "older man," often an obstacle to in-depth fieldwork, actually helped me. At times I resorted to explaining my relatively unsuccessful performances at masculinity with regard to personal relationship negotiation as "cultural differences." In other situations, accompanying hip hoppers jumped in and explained it in this way *for* me.

Establishing rapport with young women hip hoppers was a significant obstacle for me during fieldwork. In her article, Maria Silva categorizes some women at hip hop events as *já falada* (1995, 521–22). This category of "already spoken for" refers to a woman who is active in hip hop spaces but has already literally "said her peace." This is generally recognized as a sign that these women are more stringently under the control of an accompanying man and are thus not open to much "outside" conversation such as meddling questions from male anthropologists.

Machismo manifests itself to a great degree through a discourse and practice of "protection." I analyze this as it relates to the four "elements" of hip hop later in this chapter, but suffice it to say that hip hop male protection of "their" females (girlfriends, wives, fiancées, sisters, cousins) is a result of an anxiety over masculinity. In short, most of my conversations with young women or girl hip hoppers occurred vis-à-vis a male, who was either present during the conversation or approved it prior.

The gendered nature of my fieldwork experience directly influences the analysis I am able to provide. I was able to have meaningful conversations with a couple of all-women groups and an older, more established woman rapper. Therefore, my insight into feminine agency is limited. For the most part, I understand femininity, as discussed below, as a "remainder" of masculinity in hip hop performance and sociality (cf. Neal 2007, i–iv). Due to my own positioning in the field coupled with hip hop's dominant tropes, the performativity of gender in Brazilian hip hop primarily concerns the making and mediation of masculinity. In hip hop the articulation of femininity is normally a subaltern voice, a position of reaction, if active at all. Expressive femininity is marginalized because it appears unnecessary under the hegemonic rubric of machismo. In this regard, hip hop in Brazil is generally about the process of men delineating masculinities and femininities (as voiceless remainders) and a few women articulating themselves as gendered agents of femininity or semiotic objects of men's narrations and practices of masculinities, both of which often reinforce the paradigms of masculinity espoused by male hip hoppers.

But, what is the structure of hip hop's machismo, and how does it operate simultaneously as overtly visceral and reflexively invisible?

Machismo

In the United States, hip hop scholars have historically constructed their analyses of gender through the perspective of black feminism, understood broadly as a claim for black female subjectivity, and thus not black women as simply victimized objects of hip hop discourse (Keyes 1991; Rose 1994; hooks 2003; Perry 2005; Pough 2006; Pough, Richardson, Durham, and Raimist 2007). These authors have asked the question, how do young black women *use* hip hop to advance a range of agendas? In addition, a smaller cadre of authors has given serious critical reflection on black masculinity as a complex issue within U.S. hip hop (Boyd 2002; Ferguson 2001). Scholars have presented the articulation of blackness to femininity or masculinity as a "natural" development in the case of the United States, based on the particular "cultural design" of U.S. hip hop. In Brazil, this articulation is not so commonsense, because there are other historical and systematic matrices of gender, namely machismo and patriarchy, which have been emphasized in a more explicit fashion as part of a general Latin American way of life. Of course race, particularly blackness in its local expressions, informs contemporary understandings of both machismo and patriarchy. In the case of Brazil, the greatest importer of African slaves in the Americas, blackness has been essential in the very creation and development of machismo. Nevertheless, there is a Latin American distinction that requires specific attention.[10] In the United States, hip hop (and mainstream society) configures machismo and popular patriarchy as "black" and more recently *Latino* "things." Following Rivera, "Puerto Rican women are portrayed [in hip hop] as ghetto-tropical, lighter-skinned variations on black femininity" (2003, 128). In Brazil such social structures of gender are widely considered nationally inclusive, that is, a Brazilian or more generally a Latin American "thing."

Machismo is an ideology practiced by men and women in which gender is naturalized through moral discourses of labor division, public presence, emotion, physicality, and other marks of social value (Gilmore 1990). Machismo is a discourse constructed to resolve one of the basic problems of society—the "problem of order" and distinction. Brusco's definition of masculinity associated with her work on Colombian evangelicalism addresses the issue of order: "Masculinity is viewed as a culturally constructed bundle of roles, and it is the problematic nature of the social reproduction of male domestic roles (e.g., husband and father as actual domestic roles rather than as public statuses) in the Latin American setting that is of special interest" (1995, 84). As Roger Lancaster forcefully argues in his ethnography about everyday life in Nicaragua, machismo is not epiphenomenal to basic sociality and social change (e.g., Sandinista Revolution) but rather sets conditions for people's lives. Machismo is "an organization of social relations that generates ideas. . . . It is more than an 'effect' produced by other material relations. It has its own materiality, its own power to produce effects" (Lancaster 1992, 236).

Ever since the Portuguese colonial project starting in 1500, Brazil has been at the center of European configurations of gender and sexuality. The development of machismo within the Latin American context draws much of its power from the historical narratives pitting the dark savage excess (eroticism and exoticism) of Brazilian indigenous communities and African slaves against the civilizing mores of the Portuguese, Dutch, French, and later the British and the Americans (Parker 1991, 7–29). The emergent, native ruling class codified such "mores" under the paradigm of patriarchy traditionally referred to as the *casa grande* system. I draw upon Heidi Hartmann's definition of patriarchy as used in Sedgwick: "Relations between men, which have a material base, and which, though hierarchical, establish or create interdependence and solidarity among men that enable them to dominate women" (Hartmann 1981, in Sedgwick 1985, 3). The patriarch is the central figure, with the family as the basic social unit through which persons are ascribed categories of identity and to some extent persons achieve levels of social status.[11]

Art as part of popular culture is a powerful mode through which men and women employ machismo to articulate gender, class, and race in the performance of identity. Male hip hoppers utilize machismo as a system of representation to signify on "violence" as a resistant discourse and mark it as an exclusively male domain. With regard to U.S. hip hop, Ebron explains that "because violence against the community is aimed at men, resistance by the community is also conceived as a masculine act. The enemy is feminized, and Black resistance returns a dismissive stereotype of women to put down other men" (1991, 26). Similarly in Brazil, hip hop acts as a complex cultural system that predominately young *periferia* men use to negotiate the dialectical forces of self-doubt and self-confidence. As rapper Gordo confirmed in response to one of my questions about what makes one rapper better than another, "a good rapper or a strong hip hopper is a guy who knows how to take on an attitude [*tomar uma atitude*]" (pers. comm.).

As part of maturation, a reconciliation of these psychological and social aspects of personhood emerges through hip hop performance and spectatorship. Hip hop thus becomes an important part of adolescent and young adult "identity work."

Hip Hop and Domestic Spheres

Fieldwork in São Paulo was most active for me during the weekend as hip hoppers, similar to everybody else in the *periferia*, work long hours either employed or in search of employment. Weekends are usually good opportunities to make meeting times. It is a time when most men spend more time at home, and this facilitates the logistics of scheduling a meeting time and place. After several afternoons talking to hip hoppers from all around the São Paulo metropolitan area, I started to learn something about domestic spaces in Brazil and the gendered division of labor.

In February of 1997 I met DJ and producer Gregório in his home in Vila Carrão on the east side of São Paulo. It was only after some time that I realized that what was, relatively speaking, a banal and seemingly uneventful fieldwork visit was, in fact, quite revealing.

Gregório is infamous for being "confused" (*atrapalhado*) and has a reputation for being late to everything. After weeks of numerous missed connections and playing phone tag, I finally caught him at home. After all, he had insisted several times that he was anxious to hang out and show me a set of Japanese hip hop magazines and mini-CDs. By way of subway, two buses, and some of my own "confusion" (*confusão*), I found my way to Gregório's home. Protected by a low, rusted wrought-iron gate, the house was located in the rear of a small dirt lot. Contrary to most *periferia* residential property, the "yard" (*quintal*) lay in the front rather than in the back (*nos fundos*). I shook the gate chains a bit and yelled out, "Hey, Gregório." Within seconds a band of dogs greeted me with barking, and I heard Gregório's voice. He ordered his younger sister Fabiana to open the gate for me. She obeyed her older brother, quieted the dogs, and unlocked the gate with a brief glance toward me as she mechanically said, "Hello. Gregório is in the living room (*sala*)."

Gregório welcomed me warmly into his home: "It's not much, but it's ours. I've got my equipment and a bed. That's it." After exchanging jokes about the city buses and the band of dogs, Gregório and I got down to business. He had made some initial contacts with some Japanese hip hoppers and music production businesses. He wanted me to help him with translations using English as a mediating language. "This [translation work] is serious stuff. Before this, let's get something to eat and drink. Oh, I forgot. Come here Fabiana and Tais. Come in here! This is Derek; he's from the U.S. and he's helping me out." The sisters, Fabiana, who was younger, and Tais, who was older, said nothing. They simply nodded. Gregório didn't give them much time anyway, as he almost immediately ordered, "OK, bring us a snack [*salgadinho*] and some soda [*refrigerante*]." While we ate, discussed the translation, listened to soul and hip hop music, and perused the Japanese catalogs, the sisters tirelessly cleaned the house.

Regardless of social class, a visit—especially by a *gringo* like me—places substantial demands on various women in the household. Brazilians, even of the most modest of socioeconomic standing, usually offer a guest at least a beverage and sweets, if not an entire meal. On countless occasions, within ten minutes after my entrance into the living room to chat with a male hip hopper, the male would yell out to his sisters and sometimes his mother, who were scurrying about in the kitchen, to come out and meet me. Often the male hip hopper introduced his sisters and mother. The mothers would say little and would usually retreat back to the kitchen only to return to order their daughters to serve us food and drink. These situations were more delineated and authoritarian when the mother was absent, such as in my visit to Gregório's house. It was a sense of expectation by both the males and females that was most impressive to me.

The following fieldwork vignette provides another example of hip hoppers' reinforcement of traditional gender dynamics in domestic spaces. In 1997, a comedian and commercial pop singer named Tiririca released an album marketed as preteen or even children's music. One of the singles released from the album gained notoriety because in the lyrics Tiririca explicitly states that the little black girl stinks (*a neguinha fede*). All too pleased with the publicity, Tiririca appeared on a number of popular weekend variety shows to "discuss" the song and commodify his clownish approach to music and life. Coincidentally, I had scheduled an interview with the rap group *Comando Negro* in São Bernardo do Campo right in the middle of Tiririca's performance on one of these variety shows. Group members eagerly critiqued Tiririca and the networks for giving this clown space on such prime-time television. Our conversation revolved around standard practices of racism in Brazil as normal and part of *o sistema*.

Goa, one of the members of Comando Negro and the host, told his younger sister to turn the TV off. *Chega!*—We had had enough. Suddenly, all four girlfriends of the members of *Comando Negro* arrived and took their places next to their respective boyfriends. I decided to record their presence by asking them to introduce themselves and say something about their relation with hip hop. Roselaine remarked that she had always liked dance music and more recently electronic music. But, when she met Goa and understood hip hop and the "*movimento*," she changed her tastes and habits. Hip hoppers often refer to "*o movimento*" as a way of connecting the MNU (Unified Black Movement) and hip hop in one generic phrase—"the movement." After Roselaine finished her comments, Nepalm made a revealing joke. He created a double entendre on Roselaine's recognition of the "movement" by repeating her words obviating a different reference of "movement"—Goa's penis. Everyone laughed, and Roselaine was immediately embarrassed. The other three young women did not protest or even "turn the table" (*virar a mesa*). I expected a performance of joke telling. The joke and subsequent silence were revealing, because they demonstrated and confirmed a commonly held belief among hip hopper men and women that women only participate in hip hop to find boyfriends and have sexual relationships.

In 2004, seven years later, I met with Nepalm, then almost thirty years old, in his family's house high atop a hill on the south side of São Bernardo do Campo. We sat and chatted perched on a dirt mound overlooking the massive Volkswagen factory below. As we recollected, I worked our conversation back to that Saturday afternoon in 1997. Nepalm dismissed those comments as "you know, boy things." He had become a more visibly complex person since then. Nepalm has participated in several rap groups with varied musical tastes and performed with funk and jazz musicians in upscale "playboy" (i.e., bourgeois) clubs. He has become more "conscious" and "informed," and these changes have affected his views on gender and his direct organization work with hip hop in São Bernardo and Diadema. His lyrics represent what Perry has called a "process of coming to a position" (2005, 144), that is, a demonstration of reflection on masculinity and femininity through, in this case, rap composition and performance. I was struck by the following lyrics at a show as part of *Semana de Cultura Hip hop* (Hip Hop Culture Week) sponsored by the NGO *Ação Educativa* in July of 2005. In response to much of the debate around polemic and progressive terms for women, Nepalm makes a play at respect: "To respect a woman requires one to be very masculine."

Later in the same song Nepalm perhaps appeases other fans with a more conservative approach: "Of course, we all know that there are lots of women who don't deserve respect."

Hip Hop Masculinity and Violence

As I have mentioned elsewhere, the very naming of a hip hop group becomes a space to denounce the "system" using the discourse of oppositional violence. In September of 2001, I met two members of the group *Periferia em Chamas* (*Burning Periphery*) somewhat randomly in a locally organized hip hop event held in Jardim Planalto on the east side of São Paulo. In our conversation about rap music, hip hop style, and the concept of "gangsta," rapper (MC) Jefferson and DJ Canhoto made it clear that the gangsta is the archetype figure of masculinity and productive violence. While other hip hoppers had implied such connections, Jefferson and Canhoto were particularly direct:

DP: What is gangsta to you? What is cool about it?
DJ C: You understand, it's against the system (*anti-sistema*)
J: It's more than that. The gangsta is the man (*o cara*), who uses violence to make a new system, because the one in place now in the *periferia* is not working.
DP: Do you think of yourselves as gangstas? If so, how so?
J: Sure, you see that's what hip hop is about. That is what attitude is about. It's feeling the energy and aggression of being a gangsta in your chest (*sentir no peito*). And you beat on your chest (*bater no peito*), because attitude is about strength. You understand?
DP: Can a woman be a gangsta?
DJ C: Sure, I mean it could happen. There are some women in hip hop who I consider gangstas. I don't really like talking to them though.
J: Yeah, there are some women who have a gangsta attitude, but it just doesn't stick (*não cola*).
DP: What about the name of your group "Periferia em Chamas"? How do you see burning an act of productive violence?
J: The name is posture; it is an extension of attitude. We [in the *periferia*] need to start over again. But to do that, you gotta eliminate the present system.

Machismo is an ideology of empowerment, which generates various types of violence (Soihet 1999). The association of violence to *periferia* narratives in rap music, for example, is part of the recuperation of the *marginal* as protagonist and potentially a positive figure. However, the reinterpretation of violence as resistant or productive has traditionally been the domain of men in Brazil. Alba Zaluar, a leading social chronicler of *favela* ways of life in Rio de Janeiro, introduces an article regarding the division of labor in crime by stating, "Whenever the subject is violent crime where outlaws are in charge, women are not the main protagonists. They are not the bosses, . . . and they don't defend their place in this business through the constant use of guns" (Zaluar 1999, 109). Zaluar demonstrates the various roles women play in crime syndicates but ultimately concludes that women normally figure as possession (*posse*)[12] in the homosociality of *favela* masculinity (112).[13] If women take up arms and pursue conquest, they transgress into masculinity as part of a recognized practice of male rage and *machista* power.

While such "ghetto reality" receives steady airtime in U.S. "gangsta" rap and general so-called "playa" (player) hip hop, the explicit depiction of women as trading material between *periferia* men is rare in Brazilian hip hop. This is not to say that São Paulo hip hoppers offer much of a sustained counter narrative or critique of such materialistic perspectives of women, but rather they elide the issue.

In general, Brazilian hip hoppers feel obliged to, if not criticize the crass materialism of U.S. hip hop, at least avoid such a position. Masculinist discourses evince themselves in rhetorically "softer" machismo, such as the ubiquitous phrase "grab a little body" (*agarrar um corpinho*), which refers to the anonymous place of femininity in everyday life from a hip hop perspective. There are, of course, exceptions to such a characterization. The group *SP Funk* recorded perhaps the most imitative album in the history of Brazilian rap music, in which they actually rap about "bitches," a word left untranslated. In addition, woman rapper Cris attests to a certain influence from U.S. "gangsta" rap on Brazilian rap club performances. In other words, while machismo may be toned down on Brazilian rap recordings, the weekend club performances tend to play up this aspect live on stage.

In my experience, explicit performance of conventional masculine and feminine sexuality depends a great deal on the type of nightclub and the location of the event. For example, occasionally multinational corporations sponsor an event. In recent years, Red Bull has financed an annual hip hop event, which takes place in public outdoor venues around the downtown São Paulo area. In the two events I attended in 2001 and 2002, there were dancing girls off to either side of the stage, and DJs played primarily U.S. hip hop between the local acts. In more neighborhood or *periferia* clubs, women are normally dressed up, but with plenty of clothing, and there is rarely such demonstration of erotic dancing on stage.

Mana and the Engendering of Hip Hop Discourse

The linguistic structure of Portuguese, similar to all Romance languages, is explicitly gendered. All nouns are gendered as either masculine or feminine. Since there is no such word as "it," all third-persons pronouns are gendered as well. Significantly, all plural constructions (e.g., "they"), are conventionally placed in the masculine form *"eles"* unless "they" refers to two or more women or recognized feminine nouns. This cursory knowledge of Portuguese linguistic structure is instructive in understanding recent debates around the term *mana* in Brazilian hip hop.

Created as a counterpart to *mano*, *mana* serves to provide gender balance to the popular hip hop convention of personal address. *Mano*, a version of the Spanish *hermano*, meaning "brother," is a common reference to a person recognized as being part of the hip hop community. Although some Brazilian youth have expanded *mano* to refer to almost anybody, as discussed in the previous chapter, general usage of *mano* remains limited to a relatively positive and "inside" term.

Language is part of human habit and social practices of inclusion and exclusion. To stylize speech and create neologisms for community members and salient parts of "reality" is crucial to identity formation. The fact that *mano* is both highly masculine and systematic with regard to hip hop becomes significant in the codification of hip hop as a social convention. Perry's comments with regard to "nigga" in the United States follow a similar line of thought: "It is a masculinist word. Niggas are men, and even though the word sometimes describes people generally, the referent remains a masculine subject" (Perry 2005, 142). To address female hip hoppers requires resorting to "outside" vocabulary of urban Brazilian Portuguese colloquialisms or conventional speech such as *mina, menina, garota*, or *mulher*.[14] Another option is to simply expand *mano* to encompass women as well. With this background, the importance of the *mana* debate comes into focus.

In the mid-1990s during my first extended stay in São Paulo, the issue of gender and language was not part of public debate. Young women have been part of hip hop culture in Brazil since the beginning; however, this participation has not translated into even basic terms of reference. Since 2000, there has been a gradual insertion of gender, normally articulated as the "role of women" into hip hop discourse and event organization. Municipally funded institutions such as the Centro Cultural de Canhema (Canhema Cultural Center).

The Canhema Cultural Center and NGOs such as *Ação Educativa* and CEDECA promote annual debates for the public to engage with hip hop artists around a dynamic set of polemic issues.

On August 24, 2001, gender and hip hop framed the last set of debates during *Ação Educativa*'s week-long event around hip hop. The politics of style, often glossed in terms of speaking incorrectly (*falar errado*) came to the fore during the debate. Slang (*gíria*) and conversation style are marks of location, and with regard to hip hop that means *periferia*. The debate among rappers and other hip hoppers revolved around the value of speech style—*gíria* versus standard (*padrão*). Inevitably, albeit indirectly, participants' comments hinged upon conflicting notions about what constitutes "education."

The linguistic perspectives of hip hop's two leading groups, *Racionais MCs* and *Thaíde e DJ Hum*, with the former representing an insistence on slang as primary, and the latter representing the more integrated approach, characterized this debate. The issue once again came to a head with respect to the topic of gender when Lady Cris articulated a perspective similar to that of *Racionais*. When questioned about using phrases like "*cachorras loucas*[15]," which translates into "crazy bitches," Cris frowned at suggested alternatives such as "*manas*," "*hermanas*," or simply "*mulheres*." For Nino Brown and those on the side of *Thaíde e DJ Hum*, there exist associations between ungrammatical speech and a more general state of cultural/educational stagnation. *Falar errado* indexes, in the opinion of Nino, a mindset of permanence in the periphery and in misery. From my perspective, I see a great deal of miscommunication here, for, based on conversations with representatives of both sides of the debate, my sense is that most hip hop participants desire a hybrid position in which a person can navigate between *periferia* slang and institutional Portuguese in an effort to carve out places of respect for both modes of speech vis-à-vis dialogue.

The lack of feminine neologisms reveals the problematic inclusion of young women as hip hop participants and the linguistic pull machismo holds in the hip hop perception of "reality." By the same

Figure 5.1 Reprint of images from newsletter produced by Zulu King Nino Brown, member of *Posse Hausa, Hip Hop Yo! Hausa*.

token, my learning of Portuguese through local São Paulo situations and hip hop *gíria* and *periferia* style worked to counteract my substandard performance of masculinity (as discussed above). I had no working knowledge of Portuguese before 1995, and I spent a great deal of the linguistic formative period in the *periferia*. As I

Figure 5.2 Reprint of images from newsletter produced by Zulu King Nino Brown, member of *Posse Hausa*, *Hip Hop Yo! Hausa*.

appropriated this style of discourse, which accompanied other more institutionalized forums of Portuguese (e.g., newspaper, television, relationships with journalists vis-à-vis my wife), I implicitly improved my standing as a masculine interlocutor.

BANZO BANTO TOQUE DE MANO (A BROTHER'S TOUCH)

In his essay "A Family Affair," Paul Gilroy criticizes the "family" as a productive metaphor of black nationalism on the basis that kinship terms often imply a host of patriarchal assumptions, which tend to hinder any sort of progressive black politics, representational or otherwise. The trope of "race as family" by Afro-centric artists and pundits quickly slips into boundary maintenance of "fake niggas" and "real niggas" based on traditional notions of black masculinity (Gilroy 1992, 312). Many Afro-centric hip hop posses in São Paulo, who modeled themselves on a mixture between MNU politics and "black conscious" U.S. rappers, fall into similar traps outlined by Gilroy in his use of "family affair."

Figure 5.1 is a flyer from the fifth anniversary event held for *Posse Hausa* in São Bernardo do Campo in 1996. Figure 5.2 is a reproduction of a typical *Posse Hausa* flyer conjoining the empowering icons of James Brown and MNU as hip hop organizational logos. The position of the hip hop male and female in both images reveals what I found to be the dominant perspective of masculinity and femininity, namely a discourse of power and control exercised through tropes of protection.

With regard to language, some groups articulate *mano* to a sense of masculine authority. Rappers frequently frame themselves as *mano* in a narrative about "wisdom" or "advice" about the ways of the world. Presumably concerned about their *neguinhas* (diminutive form of "black women"),[16] male rappers seek to protect and control women and notions of femininity. The following lyrical excerpt demonstrates such a perspective from one of *Posse Hausa*'s rap groups.

> *Mana*, your attitude is problematic; involvement with whites is out
> This mixture hasn't brought anything only making our children all confused
> Follow the reason of Banzo Banto . . .
> Banzo Banto gives a *toque* (tip), a tip from a *mano* (brother).

Banzo Banto represents a relatively radical element within Brazilian hip hop with regard to race and a conventional majority in terms of hip hop masculinity. However, the conflation of protectionist rhetoric with practices of subordination is all too commonplace.

Engendered Sounds and Bodies

Elements of rock music that had been coded as masculine, such as heavy beats, are negotiable, insofar as female fans are willing to step outside of traditional constrictions of gender identity.

—Walser 1993, 132

Pressures of inclusion and exclusion are difficult to overcome for those young women who "are willing to step outside," because it is dangerous. Groups such as *Visão de Rua* gain audiences through rough beats and hardcore *periferia* narratives, but the two female rappers have periodically lost respect within the hip hop community for not being "real women." They have "sold out" their femininity to imitate hip hop men.[17]

Part of gender authenticity with regards to rap involves vocal timbre. In fact, many listeners who are unfamiliar with *Visão de Rua* recognize the women's voices as male and assume that the group is a conventional *periferia* rap group. The timbre of the two female rappers is rough, and the pitch range is generally low. Beyond this, their voices are full of rage, an anger typical of the "marginal" rapper and typical of masculinity.[18]

In addition to vocal timbre, the dynamics of orchestration and sound production are important in assessing the ideology of gender in Brazilian hip hop. Both in the United States and Brazil, producers have de-emphasized the role of the bass as a melodic instrument. Gone are the days of explicit James Brown and George Clinton samples, when the bass provided the "hook" of the song. Hip hop producers have developed a greater range of percussion timbres and a wider "library" of brass, string, and electronic sounds. In Brazil the obfuscation of the bass has changed the referent set of popular terms of aesthetic evaluation. For example, "heavy" (*pesado*), which once applied to the funk grooves of a recognizable bass loop, now more frequently refers to an engineered soundscape of *periferia* tension. Likewise, what is "*fodido*" or "da bomb" ("cool," for lack of a better translation) is caught up in discourses of violence and danger within the Brazilian hip hop "mainstream." Again, as discussed in prior chapters, the subgenres of "positive" and even "nostalgic" hip hop do provide some alternatives to the "marginal" aesthetics and ethics of *periferia* hip hop. In fact, it is in those spaces that more women, and at least nascent feminism, find more room for maneuver.

Ieda Hills, a protégé and occasional stage partner of Thaíde, is one of the few young women who has succeeded in articulating gender to race, thus making her narrative more recognizable and accessible. Ieda Hills argues that "*som de preto*" or "black sound" necessarily involves "respect," and that includes women as subjects, not objects indexed under popular musical genres of *axé*.[19]

Femininity in hip hop normally manifests itself in the figure of the "back-up" singer. Following the U.S. hit-song formulas of Mary J. Blige and Method Man and Janet Jackson and Busta Rhymes in the late 1990s, the Brazilian hip hop culture industry began to employ more women in this supportive role. As the women sing "give me your hand, trust in me . . . only with you," the male rapper interjects "can I trust you, really?" (Lino Crizz e Gueto Jam 2001). More often than not, R&B vocal styles facilitate a notion that femininity in hip hop provides words of comfort and support through discourses of relationship and an implied domesticity.

An analysis of the song "Rosas" by the group *Atitude Feminina* (Feminine Attitude) reveals that frequently women rappers, even as lead performers, rely on "back-up" singing styles and narratives of support. *Atitude Feminina*, a group from Brasília, what lead rapper Aninha refers to as the "*cerrado*,"[20] tied for first place in the 2005 annual Prêmio Hutúz hip hop award in the category of best "Demo Feminina" (female category of demonstration tape, CD, or other sound file). The song represents a comparable search for a "position" as described above with relation to male rapper Nepalm. "Rosas" tells the story of male violence against women as an everyday occurrence. Structured as a typical "marginal" rap song, "Rosas" consists of extended, detailed lyrics and repetitive musical sequences. The six minutes of narrative are transparent, as Aninha implies in her interview, of the trivial violence against Brazilian women.

What is striking about the song from the point of view of style is that it sounds like a romantic ballad. The tempo is relatively slow, and the beats are "soft." The ethereal and spiritual melody of the refrain holds the tune together as the listener quickly realizes that this story is told as a post-mortem memory. The narrator takes us on a journey as she remembers her tumultuous relationship with "her man," from infatuation to love, family abuse, violence from drug trafficking situations, pregnancy, boyfriend retaliation, to finally her death at the hands of her brutal boyfriend.

"Rosas" begins with a reporter's voice providing the listener with a litany of statistics about domestic violence and ends with the same activist's voice explaining the existent legislation within the Brazilian system to protect female victims. This information acts as bookends to the narrative of "Rosas." The daunting statistics stand in stylistic contrast to the heavy-handed poetics delivered by the protagonist of the story. She recounts the smell of cologne and the warm feeling of having her boyfriend as her protector. She remembers how she thought that pregnancy would "lead to peace" in her life and how she longed for her boyfriend, who was sent to prison for two years. Throughout the song narrative, there is no agency; the protagonist's life is a result of others' actions. While *Atitude Feminina* offers an obviously important story of everyday conditions of Brazilian women, any sort of attitude present in the song emerges as a remainder of men's actions and decisions.

The genre of ballad (*balada romântica* or "romantic ballad") has generated not only femininity as "remainder" but also important forms of masculinity. In the ballad, Brazilian hip hoppers express romanticism as a discourse of longing and separation. This causes the rapper pain and ultimately inspires him to work through his present miserable situation on his way back to his girl and to an empowered sense of self. The group *Sampa Crew* in the early 1990s and 509-E in the late 1990s achieved recognition based on their ability to articulate certain sets of sounds and metaphors to an established subcategory—the masculinity of *saudade*.

In Brazil, the discourse of longing, or *saudade*, has a long and engendered history. Beginning with the first Portuguese colonizers who made their way to the American continent, *saudade* emerged as a discourse of gender. The musical genre of the *fado* in Portugal represents a "tradition" of longing. Sung primarily by women, *fadistas* imply a sense of national femininity as the longing of abandoned women in reflection on exploring men.

Contemporary Brazilians most readily associate *saudade* in musical terms to the internationally popular genre of *bossa nova*. "Chega de Saudade," one of the first recorded *bossa nova* songs, relates a reversed tale from the *fado*—the man pines for his female love to return. But, more importantly, *bossa nova* and "Chega de Saudade" (loosely translated as no more longing, or even no more "blues") were reactions to the highly dramatic *sambas* and crooners of the 1940s and '50s. The gender dynamic of *bossa nova* is one of middle-class bourgeois sublime, where complex harmonies voiced by the *violão* (nylon-stringed guitar) and soft, subtle vocals speak to life's essential simplicity and a detached or "cool" approach to masculinity and femininity. Lyrical descriptions of personal relationships as well as harmonic development are embedded in idyllic poetics and progressions of complex chords (major sevenths, ninths, etc.) often voiced in inversions.

In hip hop, the *baladas* combine what is thought to be the strength of contemporary *samba pagode*, romanticism and melodrama, with a hip hop attitude represented by a sparse drum track. The success of the *balada romântica* is, in part, due to the transnational currency of Tupac Shakur and his rap ballads. Especially since his death in 1996, Tupac Shakur's status as a hip hop icon remains unquestioned. Songs like "Mama" were particularly influential in Brazil as romantic narratives from a "hard" and "hardened" man. Two examples of the hip hop *balada* are *Sampa Crew*'s "Aroma" and "Saudades Mil" (A Thousand Longings) by Dexter from 509-E. Both songs use samples from pop/soul songs from the 1980s as the central melodic figure. In addition, they make references to *samba pagode* by foregrounding the keyboard synthesizer in the mix.

Sampa Crew achieved relative success in the mid-1990s (by some accounts, they were third in record sales after *Racionais MCs* and Thaíde e DJ Hum) with such *baladas* as "Aroma." They filled a void in Brazilian hip hop by focusing on the male-female personal relationship as a topic of melodrama and "reality." In "Aroma," the singer/rapper JC Sampa longs (has *saudade*) for the "smell" (*cheiro*) of women. I had the opportunity to meet the members of *Sampa Crew* as my friend DJ Simplício occasionally worked with their production team at Big Posse Records. When asked about their success, Alam Beat, a member of Sampa Crew, explained that their *baladas* translate well the *saudade* and physical desire that many young men and women experience, especially in the *periferia* where many of the initial dating contacts occur in so-called matinee (*matiné*) dance clubs.

Dexter from the group 509-E extends such physicality and transparency in his *baladas*. Unlike the members of *Sampa Crew*, Dexter and Afro, the cofounder of 509-E, approach the ballad from the side of the "underworld." Both Dexter and Afro were inmates in the infamous Carandiru prison complex, Casa de Detenção Flamínio Fávero, when they formed the group 509-E, named after the cell block in which they resided. In the song "A Thousand Longings," Dexter describes

Figure 5.3 Member of rap group *Alvos da Lei*, July 1999.

in great detail the longing of an inmate. He presents the song as a part of a supposedly long-standing exchange of letters between him and his girlfriend. However, within seconds he begins a laundry list of young women with whom he made mistakes in the past. His girlfriend becomes part of an individual's history of becoming a man—a trajectory of maturation. Dexter expresses the sentiment of longing as part of prison masculinity and the exercise of writing letters as an exercise in moral and psychological fortitude.

Finally, hip hoppers translate the sense of anxiety and daily tension into a set of body images. That is to say that masculinity as a social formation takes on physical proportions as hip hop educates young men into a desire for certain body types or at least specific body expressions. Hip hop masculinity is a discourse of "hardness," not only in personal experience and collective representation through narratives of resistance and social transformation, but also, hip hop masculinity is about fashioning and displaying hard bodies and hardened faces. Most Brazilians call this sort of posturing *"mau encarado"* (one who looks mean). Many ask why hip hoppers don't smile.[21] Facial gestures and upper body shapes are literally the embodiment of "hardness" and "reality" within the discourse of machismo (see Figure 5.3).

Such images continue to be ubiquitous throughout the rap and hip hop scene in São Paulo. From the standpoint of the visual, these sorts of signs place Brazilian hip hop squarely within a black masculinist paradigm that has been the hegemonic force in many global hip hop centers. For authors such as Cheney (2005), this ideological and visual cluster is rooted in a lineage of black nationalism, from which particular U.S. rappers have drawn for activist inspiration. For his part, Todd Boyd (2002) has interpreted visual "hardness" as an effort to "counter the demonization of the black body" in recognition of another historical lineage of resistive power struggles in the United States. As Paul Gilroy stated in his critical analysis of "black" music album covers, "the black body, publicly displayed by the performer, becomes a privileged 'racial' sign" (1992, 246). He quickly articulates race to the aestheticization of gender as he states that "blackness appears in gender-specific forms that allow for the construction of distinctive modes of masculinity and femininity which, though connected by a common 'racial' identity, may be actively antagonistic" (248–49).

As Brazilian rapper Jefferson commented (see earlier in this chapter), hip hop is a "posture," one that is composed of strength, knowledge, and maturity. In fact, similar to their U.S. counterparts, some Brazilian hip hoppers articulate body image to a sense of general hip hop solidarity and less frequently to a back talk against conventional slave narratives, which define blackness as body via physical labor value. However, the majority of hip hoppers connect body performance and presence to a confidence or simply "*atitude.*" Similar to the scene in the United States, women rappers, B-girls, graffiti artists, and DJs from Brazil have tried to expand the notion of body attitude to include a space for various expressions of femininity. The final section of this chapter deals with local conceptions, implementations, and shortcomings of feminism within the hip hop community.

Colorblind Feminism

The anti-feminist character attributed to black Brazilian women results fundamentally from the incapacity of the Feminist Movement to contemplate the issues generated by the effective differences and opportunities between black and white women in all social sectors.

—Carneiro and Santos 1985, 43

Hip hop's mediation of gender in Brazil involves not only the multiplicity of masculinity but also the articulation of *feminismo* to *negritude*. As discussed in the previous chapter, race in Brazil silently pervades all facets of daily life. It is everywhere in the day-to-day and seemingly nowhere in national histories and public policies. Race is an active but officially silent discourse and practice. Such conditions have made race and racism a difficult target against which to mobilize popular concern. Brazil's social movements around issues of class (labor and land distribution) and gender (feminism) have historically kept silent about race (Roland 2000; Caldwell 2000; CNMB 2002). Demographic reports often contribute to this silencing treatment. In the late 1970s as the feminist movement gained momentum in Brazil,[22] statistics gathered by PNAD (National Research of Residential Locations) became instrumental in organizing. Activists such as Edna Roland and others used statistics as "hard" evidence to support their speeches and newspaper editorial essays concerning living conditions and social access of Brazilian women. However, just as the national census of 1970 excluded the entire category of race, the PNAD reports from 1976 provided no comparable variable of race with regard to gender. Instead, these categories were presented as separate and nonassociative spheres of daily life. In 1982, the sample group recorded with the variables of gender and race was so small compared to the sample of 1976 that the results had little comparative significance (Carneiro and Santos 1985, 1–4).

For this reason, as Alvarez observes, an increase in "demand for extragovernmental institutions that could produce specialized information about women's status" occurred (Alvarez 1998, 306). The period of the late 1980s and early '90s marked what Alvarez and others have termed the "NGOization" of Latin American feminism.[23] It is in this context that one must read the importance of *Geledés* in São Paulo and Brazilian hip hop organizations in general.

Many Afro-Brazilian women such as Lélia Gonzalez, Sueli Carneiro, and Edna Roland worked to articulate the rising *consciência* of *negritude* during the late '70s and early '80s with *feminismo* (feminism). Influenced by the early work of black feminists such as bell hooks (1984) and Michelle Wallace (1979), Afro-Brazilian women articulated a new platform of feminism built from difference and distinction (*negritude*) rather than commonality (*mulher*). Carneiro and Santos observed that within the feminist movement, the general denial of race antagonized participants as speakers drew on a wide range of experiences, histories, and theoretical perspectives resulting in frequent contradiction with regard to strategies and proposals (Carneiro and Santos 1985, 48; Roland 2000, 251–53).

Part of this conflict arises from the systematic connection between race and domination. As Gonzalez (1982) explained, more often than not, significant victories for white feminists translated into further subordination of black women. An unwillingness to address race within feminism as well as machismo in the Black Movement[24] has historically hindered both movements' effectiveness and splintered active constituencies. In addition, Silva adds that Brazilian feminist movements are usually "adult-centered" and thus miss the various characteristics and situations held in common between adolescents and adult women (Silva 1995, 524).

The fact that in leading journals of feminism in Brazil (e.g. *Estudos Feministas*), black women rarely find a space has perpetuated a mistrust of conventional feminism among many black women. Furthermore, this lack of discursive production reinforces the general conception that racism, if it exists at all, is individual in nature and not systematic.[25] Therefore, theorization of race is a burden of blacks, of which there are so few in academic circles (Azevêdo 1994).

GELEDÉS AND FALA PRETA!

Geledés—Instituto da Mulher Negra (*Geledés*—Black Woman Institute) was created in 1988 as a splinter group from the prior organization Black Women Collective of São Paulo (*Coletivo de Mulheres Negras de São Paulo*). Organized into three sectors of activity (juridical, health, and education), *Geledés* published important journals throughout the

1990s. In the early '90s members recognized the importance of popular culture as a vehicle of communication and a way to attract young black men and women. With respect to hip hop, *Geledés* is most recognized for its organization of the *Projeto Rappers!* (Project Rappers!) in 1992. This project emerged from a few individuals' initiative based on a public debate in which representatives from *Geledés* explained the details of a new governmental program called *SOS Racismo*. This program ensured legal recourse for victims of racism, and it was this information that inspired young rappers to approach *Geledés* and denounce a group of military police for their participation in the assassination of a young rapper. After the Fourth World Conference on Women in Beijing in 1995, *Geledés* extended the idea of *Projeto Rappers* to more directly engage with issues of gender roles and hip hop and thus created *Femini Rappers* (Silva 1999, 96). According to José da Silva, *Geledés* is important because it represents "the reorganization of the Black Movement" in that women and youth popular culture began to emerge as central objectives for recruitment and informational exchange (1998, 102–7).

Geledés's social and ideological work as described above all occurred before I arrived to São Paulo in 1995. When I first contacted *Geledés*, *Projeto Rappers* still existed, and I thought it would be an excellent opportunity to expand my knowledge of the cultural terrain. Unfortunately, the inflated evaluation of the *real* currency had detrimental effects for NGOs, such as *Geledés*, that depended on international funding sources. In June of 1995 one dollar equaled approximately eighty-five *centavos* (cents). In previous years before the *real*, when the *cruzado* and *cruzado-real* suffered from inflation, there appeared to be an excess of funds for *Geledés*. In late 1995 I found members of *Projeto Rappers* depressed and financially strapped. As a couple employees reminisced about the recent past and debated schemes for domestic funding, most sat in the office to watch the movie *Terminator* as part of the major Brazilian TV network Globo's *sessão da tarde* (afternoon session).

Fala Preta! ("Speak out black women!") is a more recent addition to the organization network of black women social activism in São Paulo. Members of the health sector from *Geledés* founded *Fala Preta!* and started a magazine with the same name. Primarily concerned with issues of AIDS and STDs, *Fala Preta!* has recently branched out into areas of education, and it is here where the most consistent contacts have occurred with hip hop organizations. Beyond sporadic sponsorship of events, *Fala Preta!* has given support to the plethora of new hip hop Internet sites.

Hip Hop and Feminism

The work of Brazilian feminists during the 1970s and '80s was not lost on all hip hoppers. Constantly interrogated about their perspectives on gender and hip hop, Brazilian women rappers have educated themselves on feminism to answer such questions. Part of this education includes an understanding and identification with one or both of the two main categories of outspoken womanhood: "feminism" and "feminine." While these labels are not mutually exclusive, as rapper Cris (Lady Rap) explained in a magazine interview (Costa 1993, 35), they are normally interpreted as contributing to the fragmentation of movements toward gender equality. Cris explains that for her and her social circle, *feminismo* usually translates into "unloved or poorly loved women and homosexuals, etc." (in Silva 1995, 518), or that to be a *feminista* is to claim oneself as a "victim" (Sharylaine in Silva 1995, 519). Cris and others' narrow conceptions of love are just one set of results stemming from the operating paradigm of "complaining" (*reclamação*) as discussed above. Furthermore, Cris along with many other men and women hip hoppers conflate gender with sexuality so that interrogations of one necessarily translate into "problematic" transgression in the other sphere—that is, feminists are lesbians, and lesbians are feminists. Such perspectives on feminism also reveal the hold that the discourse of male "protection" has on many women hip hoppers. To be loved is a significant part of women's expectations of men, that is, it is men's responsibility, under the social system of patriarchy. Under this logic, feminism as a discourse of complaining and questioning is essentially a response to an absence and a general shortcoming of male-female relationships.

In her article about women rappers in São Paulo, Maria Silva demonstrates through the narratives of Sharylaine, MC Regina, and Cris (Lady Rap) how participants utilize the concept of "woman" (*mulher*) in the definition of self and hip hopper. For example, Cris, a self-proclaimed feminist, considers the category of "*mulher*" lacking: "*mulher, sou bem mais*" ("woman, I'm much more [than that]"). In other words, femininity, as it is currently reckoned, is not enough if a woman wants to perform and represent hip hop. By the same token, MC Regina construes hip hop itself as a potential vehicle for such transgression. For MC Regina, rap amplifies her voice; she is able to perform gender as a "*desabafo*" (unburdening). It is a liberating experience for her (Silva 1995, 517). For Lica of La Bela Mafia, from the southern Brazilian state of Rio Grande do Sul, to recognize the value of womanhood requires "knowledge of self as a human being and understand the gamut of existing social roles. This is the first step for a woman to modify the *machista* world of submission and alienation in which we live" (in Gil 2001).

From the perspective of most hip hoppers, the problem with performing femininity, especially as a rapper, is that it conflicts with deeply entrenched notions of discursive ethics and politics. What is feminine is for talk in the home, not on stage. Hip hoppers also do not consider the making of femininity a political issue in its conventional usage, for they associate its very conception with private spaces of home and body and small social units such as the family.

Women rappers find themselves in a paradoxical situation. On the one hand, some women rappers work to expand the notion of politics through narratives of childcare, pregnancy, relationships, and physical appearance. Implicitly, they have joined the efforts of Latin American feminists since the late '70s in overturning the idea that women are politically passive by nature (Brito 2001; Caldeira 1985; Blachman 1976). Furthermore, theoretically, the presence of women in public hip hop performance venues creates what Sonia Alvarez, borrowing from Fraser (1993), has referred to as "subaltern counterpublics" in the construction of new "social movement webs" (Alvarez 1997), or what Spivak termed a "politics of location" (Spivak 1988; see also hooks 1991).

In her essay "Travels in the Postmodern: Making Sense of the Local" (1990), Elspeth Probyn theorizes the gendering of space and time by creating three categories: "locale," "local," and "location." It is this final classification in which the place (e.g., *periferia* home or public park stage) and event (e.g., family, appearance, style, hip hop performance) are "ordered," as Probyn borrows from Foucault, into relations of power through discourses of "human nature" and "truth." In short, a "politics of location" is a struggle over the ontological and epistemological dimensions of knowledge, which, in the case of hip hop as I have argued throughout this text, is at the core of participants' ideology of "reality."

Hip hop as a variegated discourse on everyday life lends itself to such ideological work. It is not a large leap of faith to include the domestic and women's experiences of the *quebrada* as part of hip hop's overarching goal of *periferia* representation. It is not too distant an imagination to conjure the family as a space of violence and part of "*o sistema*" carried out by means of a complex set of technologies of gender. But, what is at stake for a rapper with a feminist attitude?

As mentioned above, for MC Regina, rap is a process of unburdening the ills of daily *periferia* life as a woman, but in the end, in the minds of most, "it's [life] just like that" (pers. comm.). Being a *mulher* is "not enough" as Cris stated, because ultimately "being a woman" is more securely fixed as a set of difficult spaces and obligations, most of which serve the interests of most men in Brazilian society (pers. comm.). Cris's statements suggest that a woman rapper must transgress gender boundaries to find success. This too raises flags and invites scorn from the hip hop community.

One of the most controversial groups to emerge in this decade on the national hip hop scene is *Visão de Rua* (Street Vision). The group is composed of two young women, who are the main rappers, and an Afro-Brazilian male DJ. They are controversial precisely because they reject many categories of Brazilian femininity. The group embraces a hip hop style sometimes referred to as "gangsta," and their narratives follow much of what I have described elsewhere as *periferia* or "marginal" aesthetics.[26] A recent member of the group, Lia, articulates "gangsta" through dress and positions herself as not "imitative" of men but simply this way: "I am gangsta, I wear my pants like this, all wide, this is what I like. I am just like that" (Rebelo 2001, 4).

This approach to femininity certainly has many hip hoppers up in arms. I frequently used the example of *Visão de Rua* to elicit commentary from young male hip hoppers. Most expressed to me that they thought the group was a farce because these male interlocutors did not believe in women's performance as women. Essentially, male hip hoppers questioned these two women's gender as performed through rap music and DJ sound production. However, *Visão de Rua*'s ideas about issues such as abortion fall in line with a more conventional notion of femininity and masculinity in terms of obligation and legal rights. Dina Dee explains, "Everyone for themselves, but, that doesn't make it [abortion] not a crime. You're taking someone's life, and so it is a crime like any other crime" (in Rebelo 2001, 4) These views are shared by the majority of hip hoppers and remain one of the most visible "points of tension," as Silva (1998, 106) described, between hip hop and social rights organizations such as *Geledés*. Are there alternatives? The case of Soul Sisters offers a different but certainly not unproblematic perspective on hip hop and feminism.

Soul Sisters

Flávia and Simara are the two founding members of the hip hop group Soul Sisters. As one of the few all-female groups in São Paulo hip hop, the Soul Sisters have made their fame on their skills as soul dancers.

They are part of a recent turn to nostalgia and a reacquaintance with samba-rock dance forms within hip hop, *cultura black*, and popular dance-club culture in São Paulo.

In 1997, Flávia traveled to the municipal theater of her hometown Diadema to see *Se Liga Mano* (*Check Yourself Brother*), a play produced by long-time community activist, MNU proponent, and freelance journalist Oswaldo Fausto. I was also present that afternoon in Diadema as Nino Brown had invited me to the premier. But it would be four years later when I would meet Flávia and the Soul Sisters in her neighborhood Canhema at the cultural center, a location soon to be home of the Zulu Nation Brazil. Flávia cited that play as pedagogic and the inspirational force in her decision to pursue hip hop culture. In our conversations during December 2001 and January 2002, Flávia explained that her experience in hip hop has provided her with a foundational base in her education as she prepared for the entry exams of leading universities in São Paulo in the field of dance and the performing arts.

Simara is from Cooperativa in the southern *periferia* of São Bernardo do Campo, a neighborhood close to Jardim Silvina where many of the members of *Posse Hausa* reside. In fact, it was Nino Brown, the respected historian of *música black* and president of Zulu Nation Brazil, who encouraged Simara to attend street dance (*dança de rua*) classes at the Canhema cultural center in Diadema. Simara and Flávia met in dance class and joined forces. They both cited the importance of Nino Brown, Nelsão Triunfo, Marcelinho Backspin, and DJ Érry-G in the building of their self-confidence to actually form a group and perform regularly. Flávia reflected on her transformation from "student" to "professional" through hip hop "education" and a sense of becoming "independent" (Soul Sisters, pers. comm.).

As I turned the conversation to issues of gender, all four members of Soul Sisters employed a discourse of "transformation" as part of their distinction from the majority of young women and their reasons for participating in hip hop:

S: Hip hop has been about change for me. I've become more serious. I feel good as I get to know myself. I feel good going up there on stage.
DP: Ok, tell me more about this change (*transformação*). I mean, what's so different? What are you "serious" about?
F: Now we have a hip hop attitude. We are confident. We know something about where our dances come from. Nino Brown has helped us from the beginning.

DP: Do you see yourselves as different from other hip hoppers or other women? Have you made or lost friends along the way?

F: Well, you know, the original formation of Soul Sisters was with two other women. One was a friend of mine from my neighborhood and the other was from a neighborhood near Simara in Cooperativa. They left recently. One because she thought hip hop would give her fame and fortune. The other because she was in hip hop to look for a boyfriend. She found one guy and that was it.

S: You see, that's not attitude. That's not what we want to show as women hip hoppers. I have another friend who was in a group that started around the same time we did. They were all our friends. But, she left the group, or they kicked her out, because she got up there [on stage], didn't know her rap lines, and just shook her ass (*rebolava*). What is that? She became simply an ass (*ela ficou só uma bunda*).

F: All that is bad and has nothing to do with being serious and a conscious hip hopper. We're trying to be professional about all this. We want to do this right with consciousness and attitude.

The members of Soul Sisters implicitly linked professionalization, that is, to be "serious," to a kind of feminism, with which women with attitude are able to articulate technical education (the techniques of performance) to an expanded sense of womanhood and hip hop performativity. In addition, education with attitude provokes female subjects to separate themselves from conventional feminine perspectives on popular culture, which ultimately serve to reinforce *machista* oppression of women. The Soul Sisters cited conventional categories of Brazilian femininity, including desire for relationship and body commodification, in their stories about friends and former hip hop class colleagues. They explained these connections with hip hop as ultimately traps for young women as they end up either silencing themselves due to an overprotective boyfriend or vis-à-vis a dependence on their own bodies.

The Soul Sisters' articulation of *negritude* is less explicit in their lyrics and interviews but emerges through style and articulations of hip hop history. As mentioned above, the Soul Sisters are part of a movement within hip hop of nostalgia and a recuperation of *cultura black*. Flávia explained to me that their style of dress, dance, and voice is an attempt to "show knowledge of the past and create a continuity with the present" (pers. comm.). This "knowledge of the past" is precisely rooted in the lineage of Brazilian versions of funk, soul, and samba-rock central to Afro-Brazilian popular culture during the 1970s and early 1980s in Rio de Janeiro and São Paulo. While many hip hoppers have criticized the Soul Sisters as being too mild in their "black" style and performance, others appreciate the sense of historicity they bring to both the stage and, in particular, the dance workshops held in the "Hip Hop House" (*Casa*) in Diadema city.

In 2005, I crossed paths with Simara again at the *Casa* during one of the Hip Hop In Action events. Now a mother of a toddler boy, Simara and I exchanged baby boy stories and photos. In e-mail conversations during May and June of 2006, I asked Simara to reflect on the *Casa* from her new perspective as "mother" and "older" hip hopper. The *Casa* continues to be the main reference point for "community hip hop," according to Simara. It is the "place we have conquered and I'm glad I could be and continue to be a part of that" (pers. comm.).

While Simara repeatedly stressed the importance of hip hop as something that had "always struck a chord in her" (*sempre mexeu comigo*), her stories and recollections quickly moved away from the individual and focused on the collective imaginary. She expressed that the *Casa* is a place of articulation, a place where

> youth receive information about their history, what it is to be a real citizen, and information about what's out there in the world. The *Casa* is a place of identification. Hip hop is a direct language and kids simply, and sometimes this takes place over a period of time, identify with one element (rap, DJ, graffiti, street dance) and begin to explore and develop. Because the *Casa* professors always try to work in "theory" (*teoria*), youth learn not just skills but also they get an education about language, history, time and rhythm, mathematics and division, and something about other places in the world—the path of hip hop.

Echoing her and Flávia's comments from 2002, hip hop constitutes a medium through which someone from the *periferia* can become a "professional." As Simara explains, however, all hip hop professionals are not the same: "It also varies from artist to artist (*profissional*). Some people in hip hop don't care about these issues, but for me, such concerns are a key point so that you don't become *alienado*. The world is not just hip hop; you have to understand how to deal with all the social forces and understand how to live and claim your rights and not be a puppet manipulated by the system. Well, this is what the *Casa* meant for me since I started out" (pers. comm.).

In contrast to *Visão de Rua*, the Soul Sisters see discourses and imagery of *periferia* violence as masculine domains and thus interpret women who perform *periferia* in this manner as essentially imitative of men. Current debates over accepted dress for women hip hoppers are part of a long-standing trope within Brazilian sociality. "*Boa aparência*," or "good appearance," is a phrase that links ideologies of race and gender in conventionally congenial terms. In the case of Brazilian black women, "appearance" is not simply an aesthetic issue but one that indexes an expectation among women and a perceived obstacle for Brazilians of African descent (Schwarcz 1993, 1996). The Soul Sisters join many male hip hoppers in denouncing *Visão de Rua* precisely because the two women of the group do not put forth a "good appearance" and thus are lacking as women. Although the two women of *Visão* are not of predominantly African descent, their success to some contributes to a "dirty" image of hip hop, one that racist one-hit-wonder acts, such as Tiririca, are able to articulate into marketable forms of popular culture (see earlier discussion).

Herein lies the contradiction. The Soul Sisters in their comments about appropriate narratives and presentation style implicitly reinforce conventional domains of masculine and feminine discourses. In effect, the discourse of "professionalization" as transformational, while part of a transcendence beyond traditional spheres of femininity revolving around domestic spaces and personal relationship dependence, also results in erasing gender as a site of direct contestation. Epistemologically, the Soul Sisters do not interrogate the dominant paradigms of hip hop gender; rather, they interpret "professionalization" and "attitude" as corrective measures to wayward females. It is not surprising that the Soul Sisters almost exclusively perform soul beats, lyrics, and body movement, a semiotic cluster organized around conciliatory themes of a celebratory rather than confrontational *negritude*.

Engendering Hip Hop's Four Elements

Hip hop culture consists of four "elements"—rap, DJ, graffiti, and street dance. While philosophically, all participants recognize a unity in history, aesthetics, and performance, each element involves its own set of techniques, practices, and material. They are separate occupations and similar to other conventional and routinized activities; hip hop's four elements are marked by gender. Of course, convention and routine are dynamic. For example, since I first arrived in São Paulo in 1995, I have witnessed a significant increase in young women's participation in B-boy and B-girl crews. There are more women on stage, although usually they sing "back-up." Young women eager to participate in hip hop have acquainted themselves with the recent trends of rap/R&B crossover performances in the United States and invested in singing classes. During the same interval, I have seen almost no change in the number of female DJs. However, this rate of inclusion does not somehow make one element more or less "gendered" than the other. Gendering practices and discourses adapt as cultures change and persons move in and out of public performance.

Most hip hoppers associate femininity with a "natural" proclivity of women toward body movement. Accepted and celebrated male body movement in hip hop consists of a range of gestures, while women are expected to excel in dance. This social fact reemerges as a valuable commodity within current hip hop perspectives on B-girl participation. The hip hop element of *dança de rua*, or more popularly referred to as "break," has been traditionally more inclusive with respect to women (Rocha, Domenich, and Casseano 2001, 107–13). According to many women rappers I heard in performance or with whom I had the chance to have a conversation, part of the reason for this acceptance as B-girl is that dancing is done with the mouth closed (*com a boca fechada*) and thus poses less of a threat. In a similar fashion to the general male public, hip hoppers tend to see [and not listen to] women as a moving collection of body parts, any one of which may stand in a metonymic relationship to the whole person.

For its part, the gendering of the DJ "element" of hip hop involves the physicality of transportation and the electronic know-how of turntables and sound recording.[27] In Brazil, the conventional perspective that public space is masculine grows more rigid as the sun sets and precludes a general acceptance of traveling women DJs carrying cases of vinyl on city buses to and from events (Silva 1995). This viewpoint on public space also applies to the gendering of graffiti by most hip hoppers. Graffiti is, in fact, usually an illegal act, save sponsored murals by the departments of culture or by local shop owners. Thus, graffiti practice normally occurs during the "informal" hours of late night.

Brazilian hip hop is a discursive community that generates popular dialects and slang. As discussed in prior chapters, much of hip hop style emerges from metaphors of violence, crime, nation, and community related to social class and to a lesser extent race. In addition, some hip hoppers have articulated hip hop technique to gendered divisions of labor. For example, the word "squash" refers to a type of DJ scratch motion. It also indicates the conventional movement involved in the technique of washing clothes at the wash tank (*tanque*). Rapper Cris related stories of being told by male hip hoppers to go "sing at the sink and *squash* at the wash tank" (in Silva 1995, 521). DJ Lica of La Bela Mafia from the southern state of Rio Grande do Sul, among other female DJs, attests that often her most problematic competition are other young women. She recounts stories of other female DJs "stealing her instrumentals, straight up, right in my face" (Gil 2001).

Conclusion

In this chapter, I have retold marginality in Brazilian hip hop by detailing the process of "getting an attitude" (*tomar uma atitude*). My account has centered on the deconstruction of masculinities and femininities as social formations and competing "cultural designs." For the most part, feminism in Brazilian hip hop has been limited to a discourse of "inclusion" rather than one of epistemological "critique."[28] My recollections of fieldwork conversations with various hip hoppers demonstrate that male hip hoppers are concurrently uncritical about their emergent attitudes toward women in the home. Yet, males' lack of reflexivity does not mean that gender is a dead category in hip hop culture. To the contrary, it is quite lively.

Hip hop is a youth culture of primarily teenagers and young adults coming of age and working through the life processes of physical, psychological, and cultural maturation. They are anxious to define themselves as distinct individuals and part of various social collectivities. Hip hop provides *periferia* youth a set of discourses and practices with which they are able to mediate gender as a social category and situate themselves as Brazilian. In recent years, hip hoppers have turned their attention to gender as an issue of debate. However, as I have demonstrated in this chapter, hip hop talk and practice continue to reinforce much of what *o sistema* indexes as conventional gender roles and practices.

Hip hop is, for the most part, a "homosocial" practice, which involves the production of masculinity through male-male interaction. The intersections of machismo and patriarchy figure femininity as a remainder of this practice. In Brazil, hip hop's elements are gendered, as girls and young women seem to find space only as dancers and occasional rappers. As rappers, with few exceptions, women reinforce femininity as passive and imitative in relation to conventional notions of masculinity. In sum, while Brazilian hip hoppers take aim on criticizing and opposing much of what "the system" offers in the way of race, class, socio-geography, national history, and art, they seem to turn the other cheek with regard to gender critique.

Chapter 6

Fechou? (I'm Out / The End?)

Concluding Remarks about a Crisis and an Opportunity

Research Conclusions (Remix)

I began my project with two basic questions: why does hip hop matter, and how does hip hop work? From these two points of inquiry I developed a theory of cultural practice as "design" based on a set of ideologies to explain and narrate Brazilian hip hop. Such a keyword is heuristic; it is the spirit behind the ubiquitous hip hop phrase *é nóis na fita* ("we's on tape"), central to the opening staement of this ethnography. The ideologies of "we" and representation discussed throughout this text have led to, in my opinion, both a crisis and a potential opportunity for local hip hoppers. The case of Brazil resonates in other hip hop locales as well.

Hip hop matters, because it gives voice—a transparent tone of demand. Its participants have developed ideologies and institutions that now have a hold on not only the collective imagination of the *periferia* but Brazil at large. Brazilian hip hop matters, because the bourgeoisie has become irritated that state agencies such as the Ministry of Culture under Gilberto Gil have subsidized a number of hip hop organizations, including the Casa da Cultura de Hip Hop, under the category of "cultural point."[1] As kids become excited about hip hop, they begin to pay attention to issues such as race and education and formulate opinions about pressing issues such as racial "quotas" in Brazil's higher institutions of learning.[2]

While a significant part of Brazilian society continues to write off hip hop as *gringo* imitation and simplistic anti-art, there is an undeniable community of practitioners, fans, and sympathizers who understand how to organize and who have developed the essential skills of expressing (returning for a moment to the opening section of this text) identity. Hip hop matters because it is one of the strongest discourses and practices of contemporary citizenship, especially for those who historically and systematically have been marginalized from empowering discourses.

Hip hop works through a development and articulation ("design") of ideologies concerning value and practices of occupying spaces. This is the work of "attitude," "information," and spatial "takeovers." In terms of popular discourse, hip hoppers' engagement with violence has drawn favorable attention from not only a cadre of educators, community activists, and scholars but also from agents of the state and occasionally from mainstream media outlets such as Globo television channel and *Veja* magazine. In particular, with regard to the latter, journalist Rodrigo Brancatelli has asserted a connection between hip hop workshops and the recent gradual decline in urban violence, such as homicides (Brancatelli 2005).

The nexus of material and ideology is a vehicle for social use. Hip hoppers mediate a wide range of social categories including race, gender, class, sexuality, and spirituality and purport a contemporary social design through cultural practice. This is not only a project of personhood and identity formation, but it also reflects the dynamics of social stratification. This is particularly salient in Brazil, a nation-state whose history has been significantly shaped by the ambiguities of race, the paternalism of *machismo*, the socio-geographical cartographies of class, and the multiple interpretations of Christianity.

As is evident from the competing trends within São Paulo hip hop ("marginal" and "positive"), hip hoppers are hardly unified in their approach to representation. This element of any cultural group both stimulates aesthetic innovation and fragments sentiments of solidarity. Nevertheless, practitioners design experience into performance and periodically a commercial product and make hip hop work as social commentary, aesthetic historicity, and alternative entrepreneurship. Is the commercialization of hip hop a viable opportunity or an emerging crisis for the ideologies of we's on tape (*nóis na fita*) to become more public?

Cultural Commodification

In an article published in the *New York Times*, Lynette Holloway describes new methods U.S. hip hop stars have incorporated into the project of commodifying rhyme and style (Holloway 2002). She explains that U.S. hip hoppers as shrewd entrepreneurs are now demanding a cut of the profit from the sales of a host of products based on the correlation of music sales and explicit product placement in visual and lyrical contexts. Rappers construct their rhymes using the phonetic sounds and shiny images of Hennessy, Courvoisier and other cognacs, Tanqueray and other gins, Gucci fashion accessories, Mountain Dew, the Gap, and Nike sportswear. The signification practice is not new, as Holloway reminds us that Run-DMC made a hit song out of introducing themselves as part of "my Adidas" back in 1987. What is different starting in the last decade is that hip hoppers are beginning to negotiate large dollar figures for their product endorsements.[3]

For most Brazilian hip hoppers, the market is an enigma—a mysterious opportunity for exposure and potential loss of face. While there is a growing scale of commercialization linking hip hop culture to specific consumer products, Brazilian hip hop remains a relatively small market. Hip hop products are isolated, for the most part, to hip hoppers and hip hop fans who venture downtown to the *galerias*, as described in Chapter 2. In short, local hip hoppers would be hard pressed to make similar arguments as their U.S. counterparts. Judging from a range of media, including television, the Internet, magazines, and film, hip hop's force in the generation of consumer product industries beyond the music industry itself is most expressive in the area of clothes and fashion. However, these styles are for the moment only present in independent and local companies limited to large urban areas such as São Paulo, Rio, Brasília, and so on.

As I discussed in Chapters 3 and 4, the commodification and "spacing out" of hip hop in Brazil is a sharply debated issue. The crass merchandising practices of product placement and incorporating brand names in rhymes index general bad taste for most hip hoppers in Brazil. Whether motivated by a political rejection of U.S.-style capitalism or an ideological rejection of hip hop being associated with alcohol and forms of entertainment, many hip hoppers steer away from such connections. In so doing, hip hoppers see their aesthetics as a set of relatively "closed" semiotic systems and thus are not particularly interested in "occupying" such commercial spaces.

One current debate in Brazilian hip hop is the transformation of "positive" ideology (community, citizenship, self-affirmation) into commercial product. For members of Zulu Nation Brasil and those hip hoppers who invest the majority of their energies in social organization, the commercialization of hip hop leads to misunderstanding. Under this perspective, hip hop becomes like any other musical genre that is an expression significantly controlled by market logics rather than critical thinking. U.S. hip hop scholars, such as Imani Perry, have applied the theories of early twentieth-century situationists (Guy Debord and others) to explain or at least warn against the potentially dangerous process of representation within the popular spectacle.[4] Although Brazilian rap music, specifically, and hip hop in general, remains "underdeveloped" within the domestic and international music industry, the transformation of the hip hopper as "cultural worker" to the rapper as "celebrity image" is certainly at work. In São Paulo, local hip hoppers have borrowed the mainstream phenomenon of the "artist" (*artista*) within the reality television boom in the early years of the twenty-first century and "recast" (to borrow from Schloss 2004) the term as a point of critique against hip hoppers who place entertainment above social change.

Maulana, an experienced rapper from São Bernardo do Campo, an industrial satellite city of the São Paulo metro area, worries about the future:

> If hip hop becomes solely a product, there will be less space for people from the *periferia* to perform and participate. They [recording industry] won't need us. The moment that some bourgeois guy (*burguês*) learns some mic [microphone] skills, it's all over. They still need rappers from the *periferia*, because we know what we are doing, what we're saying, and how to perform. I think that soon hip hop will leave the *periferia* and soon have no more relevance. This is frequently what people mean when they talk negatively about the *artist*.

The problem remains: how can local hip hoppers speak to a wider audience? The status of hip hop within both national and global commodity markets deserves particular attention. The fact that hip hoppers have had great difficulty articulating rap music, graffiti, or street dance as any sort of "traditional" expression of Brazilian Africanity is significant. Competing music industries have already reserved such slots for popular cultural forms including *axé* and *samba* and "traditional" expressions of *capoeira* and *candomblé*. The conservative perspective within the national and global imagination of Afro-Brazilian culture reveals not only how race is reckoned by Brazilians and outsiders interested in consuming Brazilian culture, but it also helps explain why Brazilian hip hop has altered its discursive emphases over the past few years to include class and place (*periferia*) at a more prominent level.[5]

CONCLUSIONS AND OPINIONS (NEVER A CAPPELLA)

In this ethnography I have given specificity to what hip hop does in São Paulo neighborhoods and Brazilian conceptions of contemporary urban society. Although I take full responsibility for all the ideas presented in this text, I do not claim this work to be an a cappella cut with instrument tracks faded out leaving only a single voice. Ultimately, as Louise Meintjes (2003) and others have clarified, ethnography is a mediation, and I have tried to bring at least into temporary relief the ideas and expressions of São Paulo hip hoppers, Brazilian scholars, literary figures, popular musicians, community activists, municipal employees, as well as U.S.- and European-based cultural critics and popular performers. By foregrounding local scholarship and community literature, I hope to have contributed to an ethical and political agenda that argues that local knowledge and scholarship not only inform but influence cosmopolitan epistemologies. Returning to my initial comments in Chapter 1 on hip hop as a transnational phenomenon, I reject the notion of U.S. practices as "templates."

The contrived dialogue among recognized scholars, artists, and other local consultants produces knowledge and hope as well as anxiety. Honestly, there are too few Brazilian hip hoppers worried about a potential implosion of hip hop, as "marginal" representations often reinforce a limited purview of *periferia* and concurrent social possibilities. Even local "positivists" in São Paulo appear to rely on daily violence and terror as semiotic material for their narratives of future utopias and diasporic communities. And, while I believe hip hoppers often produce significant value through empowering design strategies out of the raw material of violence, death, and banal despair, an encroaching feeling has emerged as I grow older and compare observations and experiences over time. This final vignette about DJ Q-Suco reflects the constant struggle to beat back and talk back to despair. As time passes, hip hop and its interpellating mantras of "unity" and "attitude" can grow faint.

I met DJ Q-Suco in 1999, and during 2002 we became good friends. His insatiable appetite for "information" fueled our relationship. We read through various hip hop literature, magazines, and Web sites. We debated about potential projects and proposal strategies for funding. Q-Suco's attitude complemented his impressive DJ skills as he rose quickly through the ranks of workshop professors and attracted a large group of local kids in his weekly DJ classes around the metro area. His rap group Kingsize enjoyed some local success. With his agenda increasingly full, Q-Suco needed to invest in a reliable car. On my way out of the field in 2002 I needed to sell our used car, a Volkswagen Gol. Q-Suco and I struck a deal and sat down with the bank representatives in Diadema. Q-Suco smiled as he loaded his turntables and vinyl into the hatchback, already late to a DJ class in downtown São Paulo.

Jorge da Silva, alias DJ Q-Suco, was born in 1979 on the southside of São Paulo. His parents had migrated to São Paulo a few years prior from the state of Bahia. Jorge described his father to me as a "belligerent man, who beat my mother everyday. He taught me nothing but rage" (pers. comm.). Jorge's mother often escaped from her own house with her three children and ran for shelter at night. During the day Jorge and his brother and sisters frequently sold random food items and car parts at stoplights and street fairs to help the family get by. Q-Suco cited this as the main reason why he had less than an eighth-grade education. In fact, he was barely literate upon consideration of his emails. Q-Suco described hip hop as his own form of addressing this reality: "Hip hop showed me a different side of education. I really never had a chance during my childhood to have a 'normal' day and think about learning anything. I remember being always tired from hustling my mom's food and stuff and running from one house to another away from my father. Hip hop gave me a spark—a desire (*vontade*) to find out stuff, to discover music as something serious. I have knowledge and I feel good about that" (pers. comm.).

Since 2005 Q-Suco had gradually isolated himself and become increasingly ostracized by various hip hop organizations. His outspoken views on event organization and funding strategies conflicted with views of others. Groups such as the *Casa de Cultura Hip Hop* in Diadema started to vote him out. In 2006 Q-Suco sent me by e-mail his account or testimony (*depoimento*) about a frustrating night in October. Q-Suco was struggling to make ends meet and decided to use his car as a portable vendor stand. In a sense, he had returned to those childhood days of selling knickknacks. That night Q-Suco had targeted an elite nightclub and was preparing his goods when the police arrived. Unlike many working-class Brazilians, Q-Suco did not simply capitulate. He, in fact, tried to explain to the police officers his intentions and his rights to this space. No such luck. The police officers beat Q-Suco down and arrested him for distribution of goods without a permit. Indeed, this was a low point (*momento baixo*) in Q-Suco's life. He prefaced his email testimony with the following words: We all have our ups and downs. That night was definitely a low point. I continue to be a warrior, a hip hop warrior. I am a true fighter. But, that beating and those officers calling me names and the police station officers telling me that we [people from the *periferia*] are all criminals. All of that has gotten to me. I feel like I have to start all over again.

Let me explain how it all happened.

In July of 2007 I visited Q-Suco's new home on a precarious mudslide lot on the south side of São Paulo. Now in his late twenties, Q-Suco is focused on a series of independent projects and is once again motivated to show his hip hop skills and knowledge. However, he knows that his state of affairs is as precarious as his current dwellings. Q-Suco understands that he has to make hip hop work, because there is little to nothing else. The rest is the quicksand marginality of dangerous criminality or total poverty. The rest is everything that hip hoppers aim to change. From the perspective of hip hop attitude, the rest is a defeat of personhood.

Enthusiasm and empowerment can fade, and agents of more durable structures of domination and power relations are always there to take hold on life and exert control on *periferia* options. Hip hop has always been about achieved, not ascribed, power. Unlike the bourgeoisie, the working classes, which represent the population pool and main point of address for Brazilian hip hoppers, depend on change in order to shape the essential discourses of hierarchy. They need to retell their stories of marginality in hopes that the conversation might change and thus afford greater access to power.

If Brazilian hip hoppers do not continue to investigate and take advantage of intersecting points of "their" ideologies (reality, attitude, information, *periferia*, and *negritude*) and institutional opportunities (meeting places, libraries, schools, radio stations, Internet spaces, nightclubs, etc.), the resonance of hip hop as it relates to Brazilian society and potential social change will change significantly. If hip hoppers cease to link "attitude" and "information" to life chances and citizenship skills, there will be little to stop the general market tendency to "pitch" that which was a sociocultural "design" (*periferia*, marginality, *negritude*, feminism, etc.) into purely a graphic and sonic design. This is my fear and most São Paulo hip hoppers' reality.

Epilogue

Since the first edition of this book, surprisingly little has been published about Brazilian hip hop in the English language. The increasing visibility of Brazil in discussions of global politics (potential permanent UN security council membership, constructive diplomacy with Iran), economics (relative prosperity during recent/current recession, impressive alternative energy resources and technology), and culture (greater penetration of Brazil and the Portuguese language into Hollywood cinema and music through the animated film *Rio*, the Oscar nominee *Wasteland*, and artists such as Seu Jorge) is undeniable. Yet in recent hip hop scholarship, Brazil continues to be relegated to passing remarks on samba, favelas, and Rio de Janeiro dance clubs (Forman and Neal 2004) or celebrations of "new" racial awareness in urban Brazil (Pieterse 2010; Perry 2008; Forman 2010). It is not that these accounts are false, but they simply remind us of the dynamics of research. In my case, the basic research questions around the function and impact of hip hop in Brazil revealed certain coherences but always with accompanying tensions. As is with any hegemonic formation, hip hop excludes as it includes and silences as it empowers. I deployed keywords, such as "moments" (Chapter 4) and "assembling" (Chapter 2), to capture after all these years of poststructuralism thought what is still fresh: culture as a generative process. Culture studies demands an attention to shifting emphases and sociogeographical terrains.

Since 2008, I have visited at least once all of the consultants whose life stories compose significant portions of *Brazilian Hip Hoppers Speak from the Margin: We's on Tape* and distributed book copies. While none of my interlocutors is a competent reader or speaker of the English language, they were all pleased to see a "product" of our time together. As we checked accuracy and reflected on new trends, we concluded that Brazilian hip hop, taken overall, still operates as an ideology of marginality made manifest in the "elements" of rap rhetoric, DJ sound engineering, graffiti images, and street dance moves. Certainly the connotations of marginality are multiple and such divergences lead to creative and even tense discrepancies among hip hoppers. Nevertheless, hip hop attracts and motivates thousands of young men and women who feel marginalized in some way to *believe* that hip hop holds a promise of change or *transformação*.

"I seek to always evolve as a person and maintain my posture as an 'artist', in the manner that I live on an everyday basis" (Rapper Nelsentimentum interview, 2010).

"I see gray portraits and colorful murals. All of that I absorb. I go on seeing, living, and realizing, as I exchange ideas with the city that I admire. All the hues and contrasts, that is art" (Lyrics from Nelsentimentum "There Is No Art vs. Art," 2006).

Nelsentimentum is a young rapper from Curitiba, the capital city of Paraná, the neighboring state to the south from São Paulo. His comments and lyrics are typical of a new minority voice in Brazilian hip hop's public pondering on the connections between "artist" and "identity." This section follows from interpretations expressed in Chapters 3 and 4 about "positive" hip hop and Chapters 1 and 6 about the significance of "artist" as a barometer of hip hop opinion on authenticity and "consciousness."

Identity starts with belief. Hip hoppers are *crentes*, akin to evangelical "believers," who use hip hop's "elements" to redesign the world around them. They begin with strong, dogmatic statements about the self and do the identity work necessary to achieve an attitude of confidence in espousing that what they know is valuable and deserves recognition. How should one represent the self? What is the connection between "self" and "reality"? Despite a general distaste felt by most hip hoppers around the term *artista* ("artist") due to its elite and thus exclusionary connotations, these questions speak to an artistic "problem," one that rappers, *grafiteiros*, street dancers, and DJs have explored with more intensity over the past years. That Brazilian "reality" discourses, such as *periferia* life, negritude, everyday street occurrences, public transportation stories, simulated "battles" (B-boy/B-girl), nondescript cement and metal surfaces (graffiti), or stylized signatures ("tags"), could be "art" is a transgression for many since hip hop's significance should be a measure of collective catharsis, a fun way to wake up and share one's recognition of self with others. In addition, many hip hoppers believe that hip hop is essentially "marginal" to corporate and state systems of culture. Any wholesale alliances between hip hop and art would ultimately form an exploitative relationship and distort the essence of hip hop. Nevertheless, the "art" industries of theater and galleries as well as the commerce of advertising and fashion have engaged the B-boy/B-girl and graffiti communities. For their part, DJs and rappers such as Parteum, Mzuri

Sana, Kamau, Black Alien, DJ Erry-G, Zinho Trindade, Nelsentimentum, and Shawlin have cast their nets ever wider and delved into European "classical" music such as Bach and canonic Brazilian singers and fiction authors such as Elis Regina and Machado de Assis, respectively.

In short, there is a productive yet precarious tension between the hardcore reality texts, sounds and images of marginalized, *periferia* life and experimental bricolage. Should hip hop be a culture about transparent or abstract representation? Can change or "solutions" (another stated goal of so many hip hoppers) come from nostalgia, spirituality, neologisms, samplings of "blackness," gun shots, and violence? The past few years have seen a proliferation of "positive" styles of hip hop in all of the "elements," yet the paradigm of Racionais MCs, DJ KLJay, Facção Central, Gog, and MV Bill remains steadfast and successful. The relationship between the orthodoxy of "marginal" rap and collective camaraderie of the B-girl/B-boy crews, on the one hand, and the multiplicity and crossover artistry of "positive" hip hop, on the other hand, is precarious because there is a sense the whole hip hop project could fall down, lose resonance in the communities where it was born, and thus ultimately "leave" the *periferia*. I argued in Chapters 3 and 4 that one can detect and feel a certain interdependency between the two sides. The empirical reality of (sub)urban life in Brazil makes it impossible for "positive" hip hoppers to simply leave the *perferia* behind for reasons of legitimacy and reputation. This is what happened, in effect, to Xis, a rapper who created popular poetics with fun, innocuous beats about mundane street corners and block parties. In 2002 he participated in the celebrity reality show, *Casa dos Artistas* (*Artists' House*), and quickly lost favor with the general hip hop community. He has not recorded a song since then and moved away from his East Side neighborhood. In recent years, entertainment industries of cinema and advertising have taken a greater interest in hip hop aesthetics as part of a larger canvas of pop culture. The center of meaning and production seems to be shifting and indeed leaving the *periferia*. How might such a shift affect hip hoppers' belief in hip hop's elements as the primary media of identity work and social change? What is at stake is the significance of hip hop as a form of "cultural design."

Let us remind ourselves of the elements of hip hop cultural design in the Brazilian case. In this book I described and interpreted the actions of São Paulo hip hoppers among three main axes: race, space, and gender with socioeconomic class as an entangled vector of stratification. In addition, I provided historical context to Brazilian hip hop not only as a frame to situate the reader but also to convey the general idea that popular culture is historically *rooted* in the past and dynamically *routed* through local actors' sense (a "historicity" of sorts) of change over time. In effect, hip hoppers take experiences of marginalization along the aforementioned axes and produce material and other types of commodified culture. "Culture" is discussed as "information," that property of knowledge that is only valuable to the extent that it is "exchanged." This is embodied in the ubiquitous saying of "*trocar ideia*" ("to exchange ideas") to evaluate a fellow hip hopper or judge an event. While hip hop continues to be of secondary importance in economic terms within the music and entertainment industries compared with popular genres such as samba, sertaneja (country music and culture), forró (regional folk dance music) and rock, its impact is not negligible.

For example, the impact of this design is visible in policies of culture and education at the municipal, state, and federal levels around *negritude*. That "blackness" can be modern, technological, and cosmopolitan is one of the foundational pillars of Brazilian hip hop. It is also the underlying logic of occasionally including rap lyrics as texts of comprehension on university entrance exams. It is one of the underlying reasons behind the development of a racial "quota" system to promote blackness and representation at the highest levels of formal education. Likewise, with space, hip hop has made an impact on the truth value of periphery urban neighborhoods. As an alternative to the poetic metaphors of samba, based in Rio de Janeiro, hip hoppers portray different contours of sprawling, improvised working-class communities as *quebradas*—"cracks" or fault lines of a system spatially grounded in a set of exclusive real estate practices. While the *sambistas* express the experience of pain and joy of the poor *morro* ("hill") dweller in abstract verse, the hip hoppers represent the systemic "cracks" of São Paulo spatiality as transparent—an unmistakable shattering of body and mind, the ultimate life challenge. During the first decade of the twenty-first century, hip hop has not only "spaced out" with its practitioners, "occupying" a wider and more expansive range of places in the São Paulo cultural landscape (including schools, downtown galleries, elite cinema), but it has also become more "national." Since the time that I conducted most of the fieldwork of *Brazilian Hip Hoppers Speak from the Margin*, vibrant hip hop communities have emerged in the Amazon region, smaller cities in the Northeast, and in towns near the Pantanal wetland region of the Centro Oeste ("Midwest") near the shared border with Paraguay and Bolivia. In part, the Ministry of Culture, under Gilberto Gil and his "cultural points" project starting in 2003 (discussed briefly in Chapter 6 and Pardue 2011), has been responsible for developing networks of popular culture, especially those forms practiced by marginalized communities. Such expansion marks a victory for hip hop aesthetics and the pleasure of popular culture. However, judging from my brief online conversations with hip hoppers from new spots of Brazil, this "spacing out" also reflects the general peripherization of Brazilian urbanization processes. One of my implicit conclusions from Chapter 3 remains current: if one follows the contours of hip hop, one can follow the dynamic links between urbanism (experience of architectural development) and urbanization (institutions and agencies of city organization).

The millions of residents in the urban peripheries of Brazil learn through popular discourses of legality and illegality, crime, disease, and relative intelligence that their place both physically and psychologically is precarious. This perceived truth adds another level of anxiety to periphery youth as they look for media and social networks through which they can discover, perform, and perfect themselves. Such identity work is no more present than with regard to gender. Hip hop is attractive to youth because it encourages dramatic performances of masculinities and femininities. I argued that hip hoppers have been least attentive to this field of representation by reinforcing long-standing notions of patriarchy, labor divisions, and physicality as definitive for hip hop masculinity. Concomitantly, particularly rappers and DJs have engendered hip hop in exclusive terms, in other words, what is a trait of masculinity cannot be feminine. In short, femininity exists as a "remainder" of hip hoppers' empowering work in masculinity. This is evident, for example, in the discussion around the rap group *Visão de Rua* ("Street Vision") in Chapter 5. However, as I signal toward the end of that chapter, São Paulo hip hoppers' perspective and accompanying actions around gender is dynamic.

The story of DJ Erry-G is exemplary. I have known Rogério for a decade and have accompanied his rollercoaster ride from moments of institutional status and personal pride to periods of individual shame and professional frustrations related to hip hop and life. Since 2007 we had discussed over e-mail and in person his project, *Dos Tambores aos Toca-Discos* ("From Percussion to Turntables"). As the title implies, the project is a historical performance tracing the roots of DJ hip hop turntable music from West African drumming through the Caribbean, the United States, and Brazil to the present sounds and styles of contemporary DJ skills. It is a multimedia affair with a host of participating emcees, graffiti artists, and street dancers—an all element hip hop spectacle. We worked together on its description as Erry-G applied for various international, domestic, and municipal grants. It was evident that this is his life project. In 2010, Erry-G and I scheduled a Sunday lunch. As we chatted and devoured a roasted chicken on the balcony of the improvised two-story house he financed on illegal watershed property on the banks of the Billings Reservoir, Erry-G recalled the moment of inspiration for the *Tambores* project.

> It was during Carnaval 2006. A cultural, percussion group of women from Bahia invited me and another guy to perform with them on top of one of those huge floats. You know one of those *trio elétricos* [slow moving truck or float with a massive sound system] they have in Salvador. It was amazing. There was an energy there. It reminded me of what I used to feel early on in hip hop in São Paulo, when I would look out to the crowd and feel that we're all here to sum up. Part of something greater. But, in Salvador it was more than that. I had interesting conversations with the women and they gave me inspiration to do something big, a new project. It wasn't just what they said; it was their presence and confidence up there that got me thinking about history and African pride. Whatever my pride is as a man, a black man, is linked to women, black women. I think we've forgotten this.

Erry-G's story is a feminist moment, as it provides insight into the structural force of gender inequality and reveals a recognition of the inextricable presence of femininity in hip hop, blackness, and masculinity. Erry-G continues to work out his debts to gender politics and his shortcomings in his own relationships to his ex-partner and their daughter. This pain and illumination comes through in certain moments of the *Tambores* project through samples of shouts and cries of anguish juxtaposed with images of female hands (on drums and turntables), fists, and hair.

Hip hop is ultimately about struggle for most of its practitioners: a struggle between the everyday structures of social exclusion and the belief in being able to parlay "attitude" into a profession. The classic binary of structure-agency becomes the experienced interdependency between *o sistema* ("the system") and public recognition. With this relationship in mind, I offer a final fieldwork anecdote from 2010 that represents this struggle. I began this book with the words of Brazilian hip hop legend Thaíde, "Do you know who I am? Then, tell me who you are." I end with the lived complexities of just telling.

Ângela, once billed as "Black Ângela" and now more known as Dyssa, is a dynamo. When we met in 2010 at the historic central train station in Campinas, a city of a million inhabitants 90 kilometers northwest of São Paulo, she was all smiles. The station was in transition, in between a pile of ruins and a resuscitated state project of patrimony. As urban historian Silvana Rubino (2006) explains, the train station, currently marketed as "The Cultural Station," has always been about maintaining social division between the ruling political and economic elite and the working classes. Dyssa confided, "This is exciting. I always get like this on 'battle' Saturdays." There was a general good vibe as young men and women arrived. Some knew each other well and others were meeting each other for the first time. Regardless, everyone seemed to be in good spirits, joking around, and making small talk about relationships and stylish dance moves. Over the next six months, I accompanied the group on "battle Saturdays" and found the same sense of camaraderie among the dancers. As Dyssa managed two cell phone conversations with a municipal bus driver and neighborhood organizer and simultaneously rounded up the troops, I was struck by the visual contrasts in the train station. My eyes focused on the slick, stainless steel backsplashes of a gourmet barbeque kiosk, in setup mode for a regional rock concert that evening, juxtaposed with the scraps of rusted iron and warped tracks impinging on the performance space. I took it as a metaphor for the intimate but stark relationship between hip hoppers and corporate entertainment mediated by the state and ideas of patrimony.

Roughly once a month, Dyssa leads a group of thirty to forty B-girls and B-boys to various periphery neighborhoods in the Campinas area to "battle" with other crews. She practices at least two times a week with any willing partners and finds a good place to spin, pop, and jump. Dyssa works a full-time job in a factory. Her mother serves food in public schools. They live in state-subsidized housing in a North Side periphery neighborhood. "It's always rush-rush here and there. It's always a mess of bureaucracy and organizing myself and these kids." Dyssa is now in her early thirties. She began as a rapper in the late 1990s and switched to street dance in 2003. On the bus ride out to the extreme East Side neighborhood of "New City," Dyssa let her smile down.

> Derek, you see the fun in their faces, right? They come from all over, we meet there at the station and we go to various impoverished neighborhoods and takeover space. It's an event and hip hop grows because of that. No doubt. That's good. Maybe it'll be different for them. Maybe they can break through all the *machismo* that is so much a part of hip hop. That's why I left rap. I had to depend on these ignorant boys and

their sense of authority. It was too much. There are some open guys like Kall and Preto Ghoéz[1], who I think are or were feminists. I think they worked for real inclusion. Maybe this new generation will feel that it is OK to really work together. Maybe they won't feel threatened. Like me, I am suspicious because I was betrayed by city politicians in their uses of hip hop and guys and girls in the movement who actually have no self-esteem and lash out at others in defense mode. It's either cooptation or silly jealousy. What I know how to do is try. I've got two new projects: D.I.V.A.S. (Integral Development of the Valorization of Social Self-Esteem) and M.U.D.A.R. (Evolved Women in Self-Made Revolution).[2]

Over the next months, Dyssa lost her day job and was an unfortunate runner-up for a social work job paying just above minimum wage. Her apartment was robbed and a foreign graduate student interested in hip hop education sabotaged her computer and threatened Dyssa's life. In April of 2010 Dyssa met a traveling dance troupe from Mali through her contacts with Campinas cultural bureaucrats and allies in the local black movement. She once again glowed as she showed me the images on a borrowed digital camera in a conversation we had in May. Despite her lack of language competency in French, Dyssa talked about multiple projects of idea exchange between Brazilian hip hop and Malian traditional dance. This vignette about Dyssa is not intended as a cautionary tale per se but rather a story of real frustrations and limitations within hip hop and its purview on gender, artistry, and its dependence on the state. Dyssa shows us that the representation of self and collectivity in hip hop involves a complex process of labor. Dyssa's telling of her story and current events demonstrates that hip hoppers in Brazil have accomplished much in exposing the values and truth of periphery life and blackness as modern elements of globally shared identities. However, these claims still remain fleeting and lack structural force. In sum, Dyssa and Erry-G and so many disenfranchised Brazilian youth continue to believe in hip hop, not so much because hip hop has the solutions, but sometimes it's because hip hop is all there is left.

Notes

Chapter 1

1. The term "hip hopper" is my attempt at a generic designation, not unlike legendary U.S. rapper and hip hop activist KRS-One's term "hip hoppa" (KRS-One 2003). The term "hip hop head" or "headz" strikes me as very American and is not part of the Brazilian hip hop vocabulary. From my experience, Brazilian hip hop participants do not have a catch-all term; they simply refer to each other in specific ways, such as DJ, rapper, *grafiteiro*, B-boy, and so on. In addition, they also use more politicized terms such as *aliado* and *consciente*, literally "ally" and "conscious (person)." My sense is that these terms would not translate very well into English as basic terms throughout an entire ethnography. Therefore, I have decided, despite the apparent awkwardness, to employ "hip hopper" as a general reference term.
2. I have argued elsewhere (2005) that Brazilian and other manifestations of hip hop strongly demonstrate the force of design in everyday life. As a comparison, one might refer to Mrazek 2002, a historical analysis of Dutch colonialism in Indonesia, and focus on his discussion of "engineers" as those "higher class of laborers" who invest their energies and discourse into the organized combination of material and ideology. My argument is similar to Mrazek's when he states that this is essentially the activity of *design*. While Mrazek focuses his analysis on the concept of "engineers," I frame such processes in hip hop as "cultural design."
3. I am referring to the work of many of the authors included in Tony Mitchell's edited volume *Global noise* 2001. Mitchell 2001 states that hip hop scholars' local and interpretive view of globalization and cultural practice has been influenced by the work of Roland Robertson 1992 and Featherstone, Lash, and Robertson 1995. Mitchell paraphrases Robertson in defining the "glocal" as "combining the global with the local, to emphasize that each is in many ways defined by the other and that they frequently intersect, rather than being polarized opposites" (Mitchell 2001, 11). "Reterritorialization" is a spatial articulation of the idea of cultural flows within globalization. It also implies a process and thus a dynamic sense of local agency as individuals and collectivities produce, in

this case, hip hop culture. In his ethnography *Phat beats, dope rhymes*, Ian Maxwell provides a useful discussion of how this current interpretation of the meaning and practice of global flows differs from both Arjun Appadurai's famous articulation of global flows and various "scapes" (1990, 1991) and much of the contemporary scholarship oriented around Marxist theories of culture (Maxwell 2003: 61–76).

4. See Paul Willis's discussion of "differentiation," in which he describes the "counter-school culture" of working class English "lads" as a set of activities, which potentially can "penetrate" hegemonic ideologies of the state, citizenship, and labor status (1981, 119–44).

5. The Brazilian historian Sérgio Buarque de Holanda, in his paradigmatic monograph *Raízes do Brasil* (*Roots of Brazil* 1936), characterized Brazilian society as effective at the level of intimacy rather than at the institutional level. He argued that Brazilians operated at the personal level, and it is here where the national archetype of the "cordial" man was born. Sixty years later, *Folha de São Paulo*, one of the leading daily newspapers in São Paulo, published a series of articles and an edited volume (1995) recuperating the theme of cordiality as the primary mark of Brazilian racism.

6. Sociologist Gilberto Freyre originally proposed the depiction of Brazilian society as a "racial democracy" during the dictatorship of Getúlio Vargas (1930–45). Freyre argued that Brazilians, especially urban elites, continued to be colonized, and this state of mind could be attributed to the long occupation of the Portuguese court in Rio de Janeiro (i.e., what Freyre termed the "Lusitanian invasion" [Freyre 1968]). This "invasion," Freyre contends, forced Brazilians to hide their mestizo nature and conceal their syncretic creativity. Therefore, under the idea of "racial democracy," the heightened presence of racial mixture was upheld as a distinguishing and empowering characteristic of Brazilian society. The fusing together of African spirit and creativity, indigenous local knowledge, and European intelligence would propel Brazil forward toward world prominence. Freyre explained this concept most systematically in *Casa grande e senzala* (1933).

7. "Tropicalism" is a long-standing historical reference to Brazil. It is the persistent residue of nineteenth-century theories espousing the deterministic relationship between geology and society. In short, proponents argued that the tropical climate of Brazil causes a "natural" tendency toward laziness, good nature, haphazard mixture, and syncretism.

8. "The system" is one of many powerful but often vaguely defined terms within Brazilian hip hop. Names of groups, posses, music titles, and CD titles often contain an oppositional position to "*o sistema*" usually literally indicting the concept. Examples include Anti-system Faction, Rational System, Black System, System Periferia, and Street System. For the MNU (United Black Movement), the "system" is a group of persons who are in control of society. "In control of communication, production, industry,

residential practices, the system is (re)constructed by the various levels of government and is institutionalized in places such as the (Catholic) Church, banks, and property ownerships. The system is naturally inclined towards a 'Catholic, white' perspective on morality and culture" (MNU 1997, pamphlet).
9. "Break dancing" is the recognized euphemism for hip hop dance. In the mid-1980s, break dancing became commercially successful through films such as *Breakin'* (1984). Many hip hoppers in Brazil cite this film as one of the first contact points they had with hip hop culture in general. I owe these clarifications to my conversations with friend and consultant Marcelinho Back Spin.
10. Of course, this term is a gesture toward the immense literature originating out of Indian and South Asian historians during the late 1970s and early 1980s. For my purposes here, I will cite Gayatri Spivak's central essay "Can the Subaltern Speak?" (1988) and Ania Loomba's *Colonialism/postcolonialism* (2005).
11. In 2006 the city administration under mayor José Serra finally began to address this eyesore and has finished part of the *Fura-Fila* project. According to critical journalists and a sample of thirty São Paulo residents I informally polled, the "fame" of *Fura-Fila* has now simply been transformed from one of something "ugly" and a sign of political corruption to one of "inefficiency" as the multi-million-dollar project serves a woefully miniscule percentage of the population as part of metropolitan transportation.
12. See Jessica's Helfland's essay "Sensory montage: Rethinking fusion and fragmentation" (2001, 53–58).
13. This situation is in flux. Since the end of 2002, hip hop consultants have sent me a number of newspaper and Internet articles about the rise of interest and investment among middle-class and elite, that is, non-*periferia* constituencies (see, for example, Athayde 2003). At this point it is difficult to tell what kind of ideological impact this sort of contact will have on hip hop in São Paulo. In their e-mails, consultants have prefaced the attachments and Web links with a range of sentiments. Some are worried that this is the end of "real" hip hop in Brazil, while others are more content with the cross-class exposure. Still others claim that they knew hip hop would become more commercial, because they saw Brazilian hip hop as tending toward that of the United States. Some consultants introduced these articles with phrases such as "*virou mercado*" ("[hip hop] has become a market"). In this gloss consultants analyze the current moment as a turning point, in which economic markets determine the lyrical content of rap and ideological practice of hip hop more generally.
14. See also Perry's depiction of U.S. hip hop as "celebrat[ing] Me and We, as opposed to You" (Perry 2005, 89ff).

Chapter 2

1. In particular, scholars analyzed "students" as a significant category in the evaluation of Brazil's relative level of modernization vis-à-vis their role as a political agent during the waning years of the military dictatorship (Abramo 1994, 21–26).
2. *Posse* is a term borrowed from U.S. hip hoppers, who borrowed it from Jamaican dance hall and dub traditions (mixture of reggae instrumentation and rap vocal style). According to Dick Hebdige 1987, Jamaicans had appropriated this term from the American Westerns. Similar to the United States, the Brazilian notion of posse is one of organization and camaraderie. The connotations of outlaws and criminality associated with "posse" are important in both the United States and Brazil. Hip hoppers use the discourse of violence and crime directed at them to create and produce life-affirming and poetic work (Forman 2002, 176–80).
3. Two exceptions to this rule are Rappin' Hood, who in 2001 (still late but relative to his colleagues, quick to the punch) recorded the song "De Repente," a title of double entendre meaning both "of repente," a poetic tradition from Northeastern Brazil, and "suddenly." Over the past decade, the rapper Thaíde has talked in his interviews and when he was the emcee for the television program *Yo! MTV Raps Brasil* about the link between repente and rap. More recently, the Brazilian Ministry of Culture and several hip hop and repente groups have come together to organize *RapRep*, the first meeting (*encontro*) of National Rappers and *Repentistas* to be held in the Northeaster State of Paraíba in October 2007 (http://raprep.com.br/).
4. Chico Science and *Nação Zumbi* were arguably the most successful groups of *mangue beat*, a local Recife mixture of folkloric rhythms and instrumentation with rap and trip hop. Trip hop involves fewer vocal tracks, higher BPM (beats per minute), and often more electronic sound production than rap. Their (*Nação Zumbi*) career changed dramatically when the front man Chico Science died in an automobile accident in 1997. Recently, *Nação Zumbi* has returned and released several CDs into the Brazilian music market.
5. In this text I do not discuss at any length the relationship between hip hoppers and local crime. Such ties, to borrow from network terminology, are distant and weak relative to hip hop ties to the state and NGOs. This is to say that ties to crime are not public and negotiations are frequently carried out via proxies. The fact is that to hold an event in the *periferia* often requires some sort of negotiation with local crime organizations. Scholar Enrique Arias 2006 has made the crucial point that the state and crime are not "parallel" but rather fundamentally intertwined networks of structure and practice. Although his research focuses on Rio de Janeiro, Arias's statements echo those made by representatives of social services (the state) and community groups in the São Paulo

metro area during my fieldwork. By necessity, at least for the time being, community activists, of whom many hip hoppers are one example, frequently engage local crime groups to operationalize their projects (hip hop events or otherwise). With that in mind, it is important to note that the term "posse," the category I mostly use with regard to Brazilian hip hop, is not the only one pertaining to hip hop groups or organizations. Others such as *banca* (crime ring) and *família* (family) have stronger connotations to *criminal* social groups. Within hip hop, "family" usually refers to a number of rap groups who use the same studio, who are friends, and who often have a foundational leader. An example is GOG, a legendary rapper from the satellite cities of Brasília, who in 2001 moved to Campinas and started to cultivate a "family" of younger rappers and DJs. There is a significant element of ideological, aesthetic, and financial paternalism. *Banca* within hip hop works similarly, although it is not usually associated with an individual per se. For example, *banca* has been mentioned related to a recording label: *Banca 7 Taças*, a leading evangelical rap label.

6. See Pardue 2004b for more on hip hoppers' negotiation with state agencies for employment as "professors" in programs of "alternative education" located in places such as youth prisons.
7. Studies concerning black dance parties in Brazil have focused on Rio de Janeiro and Salvador. The most important texts are by Vianna 1999 and Sansone 1997. See also Guasco 2001 for a more descriptive piece on how party participants get ready for weekend dance parties in São Paulo.
8. Erry-G is referring to his conflicted exit from the Casa de Hip Hop, a central focal point of hip hop workshops, community events, and visits from national and foreign educators, scholars, and filmmakers. For more on the Casa de Hip Hop and Erry-G's role there, see Pardue 2007.
9. The Sugar Hill Gang, so the story goes, were pretenders, Johnny-on-the-spot kids from New Jersey. The first recording of "Rapper's Delight" (1979) had nothing to do with the South Bronx or the pioneering figures of Afrika Bambaataa, Kool DJ Herc, and Grandmaster Flash. Most hip hop intellectuals and knowledgeable fans classify the Sugar Hill Gang as a flash in the pan and an unfortunate statistic in the history of hip hop culture.
10. For a cross-cultural comparison on the value of being informed, see Maxwell's discussion of the local importance given to doing "research" by hip hoppers in Sydney, Australia (Maxwell 2003, 52–56).
11. See also "nation conscious rap" as described by Eure and Spady 1991.
12. Samba-rock as a musical style is often attributed to Jorge Ben in his early 1970s recordings. Other groups include *Trio Mocotó* and *Bebeto*. One particular song comes to mind. The famous MPB (Brazilian Popular Music) performer and current Culture Minister Gilberto Gil recorded a cover of Jackson Pandeiro's song "Chiclete com Banana" (chewing gum with banana) in 1974, in the samba-rock style. In general, the music

contains an underlying samba rhythm, but performers play more "rock" instruments (electric guitar, bass, and conventional drums) rather than the *violão* and *cavaquinho* guitar instruments or the various Brazilian percussion instruments. For most Brazilians, samba-rock existed as a brief experiment and died by the mid-1970s; however, for hip hoppers, especially DJs and street dancers, it was an important period of musical production. In recent years groups such as *Trio Mocotó* and Gerson *King Combo* as well as younger groups have recuperated to some extent the spirit of samba-rock.
13. According to Prévos, tracking the circuits of hip hop "information" are also important in understanding the formation of hip hop in France. Unlike in the Brazilian scene, French music entrepreneurs Bernard Zekri and Jean Karakos facilitated the spread of hip hop ideas and tastes by living and participating and recording the local New York scene starting in 1980 (Prévos 2002, 2–3). Similarly, in Portugal, the access of local hip hoppers to focal points of hip hop, in this case Paris and London and to a lesser degree New York City, have provided important circuits of information (Contador and Ferreira 1997; Fradrique 2003; Calado 2007).
14. There are dozens of subcategories of samba. For the purposes of my argument, I include the following types of samba as "roots": *samba de morro, samba enredo, samba canção, samba de partido alto*. The point here is not that aficionados of Brazilian funk, soul, and samba-rock turned against samba, but rather they saw the soul sounds and later what would become the basis for hip hop in rap and DJ as more fresh and more "connected" to the world at large.
15. See Mitchell 2001 and Lull 2001 for a discussion of the importance of tracking "reterritorialization" within popular culture practices.
16. As an idea, Brasília, had existed for many decades prior to the 1950s and 1960s. See Holston 1989 for more detail on the various campaigns to relocate the capital inland and create a sentiment of "integration and interiorization."
17. This is a term used for northeasterners and other rural peasants who migrated to Brasília to construct the city.
18. Both Rio and São Paulo boasted important bands such as *Barão Vermelho* and *Titãs*, respectively. However, Brasília, perhaps due in part to its fresh status as a place of youth culture and not just an administrative outpost for the federal government, is generally acknowledged as the rock capital of Brazil.
19. SESC is an acronym that stands for Social Service for Commerce (*Serviço Social do Comércio*). These centers offer both physical education services and cultural programs.
20. The statistics were published on the following URL: http://www.universia.com.br/html/materia/materia_jcih.html. See also a 2003 study by IntegrAcão, a Brazilian publication of the "third sector" (http://integracao.fgvsp.br/ano6/06/pesquisas.htm). This report states that

12.5 percent of the Brazilian population "has access to a computer" and 8.3 percent "have access to the Internet."
21. The current local term for these places is "LAN House" (borrowed directly from the English acronym Local Area Connection). It is important to note that there are LAN Houses throughout the *periferia*, and they are relatively cheap. In July 2007 I visited one in a neighborhood that was less than two years old on the far south side of São Paulo and paid seventy-five *centavos* (forty cents) for thirty minutes.
22. There have been various campaigns to stomp out community radio stations. I remember a number of radio advertisements warning that the low frequency emissions of the so-called "pirate" radio stations interfered with air traffic controllers of both the local Congonhas Domestic Airport and the Governor André Franco Montoro International Airport, more popularly known as Cumbica airport. Both airports are located near large *periferia* areas, the former in the south side and the latter in the impoverished suburb city of Guarulhos. During the 1990s and early 2000s, these threats had little impact on the overall community radio scene. However, since 2004, the presence of community radio has changed significantly. The Federal Police with help from Anatel (National Agency of Telecommunications) has fortified its stance against community radio stations in the name of "national security." With such escalation, many hip hoppers have begun to transition out of community radio and into the virtual spheres of the Internet, as mentioned in the chapter text.
23. See also Pardue 2004a and 2008.

Chapter 3

1. "Autoconstruction" is a common practice in the Brazilian *periferia* that involves architectural improvisation based on available resources. I discuss this in more detail later in the chapter.
2. In my translation of *fundão*, I recall the work of Robin Kelley and his perspective on the "new social historiography" and "subaltern projects." Kelley's strength lies in his ability to take account of the complexity of black, working-class social positions and activities through the metaphor of the "way, way below" (Kelley 1994, 1–16). See also Kelley 1997.
3. For ethnographic descriptions of the *favela* in Rio as a product of various discourses of "danger" and "marginality," see Sheriff 2001 and Goldstein 2003.
4. For a classic argument of this spatiocultural tension, see Euclides da Cunha 1957. See also Andrade 1960 for a more general discussion.
5. This particular phrase comes from the song "Vida Loka" ("Crazy Life") by Brazil's most famous rap group *Racionais MCs* (2002).
6. See for examples the work of anthropologists William Kelleher 2003, Victoria Sanford 2003, and John Hartigan 2001, who work in Northern Ireland, Guatemala, and Detroit, respectively.

7. In recent years graduate students in the department of human geography in both Brazil (Rodrigues 2003) and Portugal (Calado 2007) have focused on the ideological dimensions of hip hop spatiality.
8. These acts are sometimes overtly political as in the case of MST (Landless Movement) who uses "invasion" tactics in order to raise issues concerning unequal land distribution. In other cases, "invasion" occurs frequently out of necessity.
9. The origin of the word *favela* is curious. Not surprisingly, the word was first used in Rio de Janeiro in reference to the place where builders scavenged for construction material. The story goes that it was a hill where a plant called *favela* grew. Ironically, upon consideration of the great northeast to southeast domestic migrations during the twentieth century, the plant's own origin is in the northeastern state of Bahia (Sachs 1999, 86n19).
10. BNH and SFH (National Bank for Residential Finance and Financial System of Residence) were created in 1964, operating at full force by 1967. As stated in their constitutions, the objective was to aid in home finance for low-income families. However, by the 1970s the BNH had become an important source for middle-class financial aid. Between 1965 and 1985, only 6.4 percent of funding went to families with an income lower than 3.5 times the minimum wage (calculated as a value per month) (Caldeira 2000, 226). The operation of BNH did not realize the socialist ideal of leveling the field of real estate and residential practices in São Paulo. Rather, BNH's biggest client was large real estate companies with development programs in the area of high-rise apartment buildings, by the 1960s the most common form of official building construction. 80.8 percent of residential apartment buildings placed on the real estate market between 1977 and 1982 received financial backing from BNH.
11. Rolnik, Kowarick, and Somekh 1991 describe the *periferia* and real estate as incorporated into mundane activities such as the weekly street fair. In their text they include stock photographs from newspaper agencies such as *Agência Estado*. One, in particular, is striking, as a sign reads, "houses, lots, and country homes . . . on-duty vendor" (1991: 89).
12. Sachs offers three categories of "autoconstruction." "Integral autoconstruction" refers to housing construction done completely outside the formal economy. Participants negotiate labor as amicable or neighborly reciprocity and procure materials outside the official market. "Self-help construction" relies on both informal labor relations and remunerated services by local artisans (see Tauschner and Mautner 1982). Finally, "assisted autoconstruction" consists of not only some remunerated, specialized labor but also some form of financial assistance from the public sector (Sachs 1999, 81–82).
13. Comparative charts from IBGE (Brazilian Institute of Geographical Studies) and PNAD (National Research on Domestic Statistics) from 1992 and 1999 show that overall the percentage of home ownership

in urban Brazil is quite high, in some cities such as Salvador with over 80 percent of the population. This is significant upon consideration of the history of "home ownership" discourses going back to the Vargas era as mentioned in this chapter. More specifically, the comparative data demonstrate that during the 1990s there was a considerable increase in home ownership. For example, in São Paulo, there was an increase of 6.5 percent. What these graphs do not show is the financial support of such ownership or location of ownership growth. As I argue in the text, bank loaning practices have historically benefited the middle and upper classes (mostly real estate entrepreneurs) and have thus forced those "dreaming" of their own home toward the *periferia* and potentially dangerous situations either regarding the land itself (precarious locations) or the legal status of the deeds and other paperwork.
14. Hip hop culture is a continuation of popular urban social movements in the negotiation of state recognition and structural change. The proliferation of *periferia* as a side effect of post-1964 economic policies was a concern not only of the emerging labor unions of the late 1970s but also of the CEBs (Ecclesiastic Community Bases) as part of the new progressive wing of the Brazilian Catholic Church. For a detailed account of the various social movements in São Paulo during the military dictatorship, see Singer and Brandt 1980 and Alvarez 1989, 1997.
15. The project was called "Vamos Ler um Livro: Centro de Documentação Jovem Agentes de Direitos Humanos."
16. See Hagopian's discussion of citizenship and democracy as it related to the early Greeks (2007, 21–22).
17. See, for example, Walzer 1995, 175–208.
18. The literature on these areas is quite extensive, but as an outline, for accounts in Guatemala, see Sanford 2003; for Bolivia, see Gill 2004 and Gustafson 2006; for Peru, see Garcia 2004; in Brazil, see Caldeira 1999. For more on the link between privatization of security and politics and the weakening of the State's hold on citizenship, see Oxhorn 2007.
19. See Dahl 1998. See also Jelin 2003.
20. Scholars often use the term "deindustrialization" to indicate a transition to the "postindustrial." This speaks to urban transformation as a function of capitalist reorganization practices. For more detailed analysis, see Castells 1991 and Harvey 1989.
21. It is important to note the difference between hotels and motels in Brazil. While the former holds the same basic significance as in the United States, patrons usually rent motel rooms by the hour for sexual encounters.
22. This phrase is very common in hip hop stories.
23. Some examples, as translated by the author, are: Of Little Crime, Targets of the Law, Criminal Command, and Point of Trafficking.
24. Some examples, as translated by the author, are: Verbal Violence, and Rhythm Trauma.

25. Some examples, as translated by the author, are: Rational System, Black System, Faction Anti-System.
26. Coolio's "Gangsta Paradise" (Tommy Boy, 1995) samples Stevie Wonder's "Pastime Paradise."
27. Apocalipse 16 refers to the biblical text with this name in which there is description of God's anger toward the pagan behaviors of earth's beings. According to the official Web site (http://www.7tacas.com.br), members chose the symbol of the seven chalices for its obvious relation to the Bible.
28. Readers can access this cover art on Web sites such as http://www.7tacas.com.br and http://www.tratore.com.br.

Chapter 4

1. In essence, I aim to extend important comments made by Stansfield with regard to race and racism: "Race-making is a mode of stratification . . . premised on the ascription of moral, social, symbolic, and intellectual characteristics to real or manufactured phenotypical features which justifies and gives normality to the institutional and societal dominance of one population over other populations materialized in resource monopolization, control over power, authority, and prestige, and ownership of the means of production and the State" (Stansfield 1985, 133). Hip hop in the United States and Brazil often reinforces certain modes of social stratification as it works to overturn or at least interrogate other modes.
2. Guimarães (2000, 31–48) shows that with regard to racial insults, registered in accordance with the new law of 1989, race overwhelmingly signifies skin color over other presumably race-based phenotypes, for example, hair type, lip or nose shape. In Brazil, recent "ethnicities" would include Japanese, South Korean, Chinese, and Lebanese. With regard to race and ethnicity in Latin America, see Wade 1997 among others. The study of whites (*brancos*) or better whiteness (*branquitude*), as Kabengele Munanga once whimsically pondered (1990, 109), has received little systematic scholarship. "Studying whites" did appear briefly after the 1940 census hailed as definitive evidence that indeed the Brazilian population was finally "whitening" and turning the corner toward "civilization." See Deffontaines 1945. In addition, Norvell 2001 investigates the inherent instability of "whiteness" as utilized by intellectuals from 1928–36. For the most part, whiteness has remained a silent and unproblematic partner of the "problem" of blackness. See Fernandes 1972, Piza 2000, Andrews 1988, Byrne 1993, among others.
3. Degler's theory of the "mulatto escape hatch" (1971) has since been criticized by a number of scholars and activists for the reason that it had little connection with reality in terms of employment, education, political power, and general discrimination. See, for example, Silva 1985; Marx 1999, 66–74; Nascimento 1989; Adorno 1996.

4. It is important to note that Batista referred to himself as *negro*. Anthropologist Robin Sheriff has argued that Brazilians utilize terms of "color" (*cor*) strategically as part of what she terms "pragmatic discourse" (2001, chap. 2). This is a complex process involving dozens of vocabulary terms and diminutive forms (suffixes such as *–inho*); however, certain terms, such as *negro*, she argues, retain an essentially negative connotation. While I agree with the spirit of Sheriff's ethnography, the meaning of *negro*, at least among hip hoppers in São Paulo, is significantly different from that of Sheriff's consultants in the ethnographically informed but fictitious neighborhood Morro de Sangue Bom in Rio de Janeiro. In São Paulo, *negro* is akin to "African American" in U.S. parlance, although many choose to identify with *preto* (black) (see, for example, Professor Pablo toward the end of this chapter). *Preto* is the term preferred by most hip hoppers of African descent. A few opt for *Afro-Brasileiro*, as this is a term that designates acute "consciousness." I make this point simply to contextualize my description of Batista, who identified himself as *negro*, and I have referred to him as such.
5. According to the IBGE census of 2000, of those Brazilians who finish the equivalent of high school, roughly 15 percent are of African descent, with 2 percent *pretos*, 13 percent *pardos* (racially mixed), and 82 percent *broncos* (whites). On the whole, *brancos* attend 2 more years of formal education than *pardos* and *pretos*, 6.6 years rather than 4.6 years. In a survey conducted by CPPN (Commission of Public Policies for the Black Population), published in the newspaper *Diário de São Paulo* (March 7, 2003), reports indicate that 1.3 percent of USP (University of São Paulo) students are *negros* and 8.2 percent *pardo*. Over 40 percent of the population of the São Paulo state is either *pardo* or *negro*. From my experience, the majority of *pretos* at USP are actually African students studying abroad in Brazil.
6. See Félix 2000.
7. This event took place around the time that Atlanta started to become an important place on the hip hop map and before the main impact of Master P and his New Orleans No Limit Records sound.
8. See Fanon 1967, 109.
9. With regard to the soul movement in the late 70s, Pedro de Toledo Pizza, then municipal secretary of tourism in Rio de Janeiro, was quoted in the newspaper *Jornal do Brasil* as stating that "Black Rio [the catch-all term for Rio's soul movement] is a commercial movement with a racist philosophy" (in Hanchard 1994, 114, his translation) with no trace of authenticity. Gilberto Freyre himself joined in attacking the soul movement as part of Yankee imperialism (1977). Journalists and cultural critics direct a similar attack, albeit with less frequency, against hip hop culture and particularly rap music. For an example that links blackness to violence to describe the problem rap causes with regard to police activity, see Edmundo Barreiros 1994, 1.

10. In 1976, PNAD (National Research per Residential Capita) published the results of a survey about focal vocabulary related to skin color. The compiled list includes 135 terms (reprinted in DataFolha 1995, 33–34; Schwarcz 1996, 172).
11. *Candomblé* is the syncretic religion that combines Catholicism and polytheistic West African religions. As an "invented tradition," *candomblé* represents the mediation of slavery and colonialism in the form of a cosmological system. *Terreiro* refers to the space of *candomblé* worship.
12. See Thaíde's account of the early days and the label of *tagarela* in Alves 2004, 34ff.
13. In addition to the political movements of *Frente Negra* in the 1930s and MNU since the late 1970s, the media phenomenon of *Raça* magazine is essentially a vehicle for the concerns of a small, black middle class. However, the significant difference between black middle-class political and media organization is that the latter succeeds in appealing to a wider audience by purposefully avoiding explicitly polemic issues of blackness. *Raça* overturns the stereotype that all Afro-Brazilians are dirt poor by highlighting the consumption practices and the success stories of those blacks, as chief editor Macedo described as, "already having self-esteem" (quoted in Kachami 1996, 112).
14. In his work on the soul movement in Rio, Hanchard mentions that participants were seen exchanging "copies of Stokely Carmichael's *Black Power* and Frantz Fanon's *Wretched of the Earth*" (Hanchard 1994, 116).
15. It is important to note the ways in which objectification of Africans results in linguistic forms in everyday Brazilian Portuguese usage. Portuguese colonials perceived physiological peculiarities in the cultural group *Quimbundo* and consequently created the word *bunda* referring to a person's hind parts. This word comes down in current usage as the popular term in favor of *nádegas*, a more technical term.
16. During a debate organized by the NGO *Ação Educativa* (Educative Action) on August 23, 2001, a local history professor cited that in a poll conducted in 1995, out of over six hundred adolescents interviewed in dance parties (*salões de baile*), 25 percent had heard of Zumbi. Of this 25 percent, approximately 20 percent learned this through some sort of contact with hip hop culture (as compared with 22 percent in schools). See also Silva for a description of the process by which São Paulo hip hoppers "come to know black history" through hip hop (1998, 98–101).
17. In 2003 under the mayor Marta Suplicy, the municipality of São Paulo recognized November 20 as a holiday. By November of 2006, there were 225 municipalities in Brazil (5,561 total) that recognized this day of Zumbi as a holiday.
18. See also Moura 1994 and Fontaine 1980.
19. *Posse Hausa* unofficially disbanded for a time in 2000–2002, but a year later returned to an active role within the hip hop and São Bernardo

community scene. In April of 2003, members Nino and Guriz sent me a flyer advertising an event in commemoration of the tenth anniversary of *Posse Hausa*. Since 2003 the posse has become more of a reference for young hip hoppers, especially in the São Bernardo area. Members such as Guriz, Skan, and Black have performed sporadically, but perhaps more importantly, they attend general hip hop events and conferences and attract young kids for a chat about experience.

20. It is important to note that unlike the United States, where hip hoppers had already established a solid relationship with the recording industry and produced hundreds of CD releases by the mid-90s, in Brazil the number of hip hop recordings was staggering low. According to official reports, between 1986 and 1996, just over a hundred rap CDs were released with the peak years of 1992–94, with sixty-eight recordings, respectively (Silva 1998, 110). Therefore, the fact that a *Posse Mente Zulu* CD exists as of 1994 is itself significant.
21. MPB (Popular Brazilian Music) became the overarching category to include popular music, which mixed bossa nova with rock and international popular musical trends (new wave, electronic music).
22. It is important to note that reggae in Brazil has a long tradition, especially in the northern state of Maranhão.
23. *Embolada* refers to a musical genre from the northeast of Brazil in which performers improvise rhymes, often in couplets, over *coco* or *baião* rhythms usually played on the *pandeiro* instrument.
24. The *cavaquinho* is a small, guitar-like instrument with four metal strings. In samba the *cavaquinho* provides rhythmic and harmonic support. *Repique de mão* is a percussive instrument invented by practitioners of the most contemporary form of samba—*samba pagode*. Normally, the player lays the instrument horizontally across his or her lap and articulates basic underpinning rhythms with one hand (*mão*) on the base of the instrument while the other hand strikes the instrument head in more complicated and periodically improvisatory rhythms. The *tan tan* is played in a similar fashion as the *repique de mão*. The difference is pitch, with the *tan tan* providing the low, bass pulse. In essence, the *tan tan* substitutes the more conventional *surdo* instrument.
25. See also Da Matta 1993, 180–97.
26. In the United States groups like Wu-Tang Clan are known for the lack of quantizing, yet in their case, they were able to become popular on a massive scale.
27. For example, the rhythm and timbre of "Fiquem Firmes," one of the trademark songs of leading positive and evangelical rap group *Apocalipse 16*, provide a jazzy feel as the instrumentation of acoustic guitar/ vibraphone and melismatic backup female vocals work with the multiple timbres of the hi-hat sound. The syncopated patterns of the vibraphone arpeggios and subsequent block chords complement the stepwise melismatic figures of the R-and-B-influenced female vocals. The male vocals

of *Apocalipse 16*, along with the hi-hat, ground the song into a seemingly straight-ahead format. Yet, it is the hi-hat figure at the end of various measures that contributes to a "human" feel and a momentary destabilization of the straight-ahead quantized pulse. There are, in fact, two hi-hat samples occurring in "Fiquem Firmes." The timbre is slightly and intentionally different, which elicits a "swing" or push and pull to the overall groove. *Apocalipse 16* producers did not exactly quantize the hi-hat pattern to the nearest sixteenth note. They complement the slipperiness in the hi-hat with a syncopated rhythm of the kick drum. The latter is a sound element frequently relegated to a more supportive role and thus stands in contrast to conventional "marginal" sound production techniques. Most probably, *Apocalipse 16* producers triggered this hi-hat pattern using two synthesizer keys.

28. Ketu and Honerê are names borrowed from one of the West African peoples located in Yorubaland in southwestern Nigeria and south-central Dahomey (Benin) who constituted a significant percentage of the slave population in Brazil. This group has been associated with the *candomblé* religion in terms of possible West African origins (Béhague 1984, 222). The choice of the group name is also revealing. "Banzo" refers to a sorrowful nostalgia felt by recent African slaves in Brazil of their homeland. "Bantu" is the name of a particular community located in what is today Angola, another significant point of Portuguese slave trade.

29. The phrase "*cair no mundo das drogas*" refers to the most popular consumer drugs in Brazil: cocaine, crack, and marijuana. Most hip hoppers do not discriminate among different types of drugs. Of course, marijuana and crack affect people in different ways both physically and psychologically. Unlike many U.S. hip hop *headz*, Brazilian hip hoppers, for the most part, do not recognize such differences. In recent years, there has been some change due to pro-marijuana rappers such as Marcelo D2, but I would argue that most of this influence is located in the emerging middle-class segment of hip hop consumption and not the majority of working-class hip hop performers.

30. The phrase "one race" is a popular gloss on race and nation both among policy makers and some pockets of hip hop culture. In 1972 the organization IBGE (Brazilian Institute of Geography and Statistics) actually eliminated the census category of color, the principal characteristic in Brazil's racial paradigm. This erasure was not unprecedented. In the Brazilian census of 1900 and 1910, racial specifications were omitted. And no census was conducted at all in 1920 and 1930. The president of IBGE stated in his defense that the item was spurious and thus omitted: "We [Brazilians] do not have a race problem, we are all one race" (quoted in Santos 1981, 44). Similarly, a number of hip hoppers responded to survey questions aimed at what I termed "social profile" with narratives expressing their objection to the very category of race. Such views are rooted in the national myth of racial democracy.

31. *Alternativa C* also used this image in the introduction to their Web site (http://www.alternativac.hpg.ig.com.br).
32. In his work, John Burdick (1998a, 1998b) details the disconnect between the *movimento negro* (black movement) in Rio de Janeiro and the black, working class due to a misrecognition of the importance of Christianity in people's lives.

CHAPTER 5

1. See Cooper, Kramer, and Rokafella 2005; Hopkinson and Moore 2006, chap. 5; Foster 2007; Sharpley-Whiting 2007, chap. 1; Rose 1994, chap. 5; Perry 2005; Toop 1984, 1991; Keyes 1991, 2004; Adler and Beckman 1991; Morgan 1999; Powell 1997; and Leadbetter and Way 1996.
2. Pough's discussion of the rhetoric of "wreck" is particularly convincing. She demonstrates that this general term from hip hop, "bringing wreck," understood as both disturbing the norm and displaying skills, is firmly located in the speech act tradition of "Black womanhood" including "talking back, going off, turning it out, having a niggerbitchfit, or being a diva" (2004, 78).
3. There are various reasons why hip hoppers and hip hop scholars have limited their criticism about gender. Of course, media pundits and journalists have consistently argued that this limitation is due to hip hop's exaggerated misogyny in rap lyrics and videos. Beyond this ahistorical response, writers and activists have explained that black popular culture has always been in dialogue with black popular politics, which has traditionally stressed "strategic essentialism" in its movement of "unity." More philosophical explanations include the gendering of public and private spaces. The argument goes that the decay of public spaces, particularly city streets and parks, has meant an attack on those who occupy these spaces, that is, young black men, and therefore hip hop, a street expression, is necessarily an expression of black males as victims.

   For heavy metal, Robert Walser's *Running with the Devil* (1993) still stands as a major contribution to the analysis of masculinity (see chapter 3 in Walser). For an equally compelling analysis of femininity in the "Riot Grrl Movement" of the early 1990s, see Gottlieb and Ward (1994). Imani Perry's *Prophets of the Hood* (2005) and Todd Boyd's *The New H.N.I.C.* (2002) represent the "new school" in gender analysis within U.S. hip hop scholarship. In particular, both authors imply that hip hop is an important discourse through which young men, specifically young black men, understand and "assert black male subjectivity and that it sometimes does so at the expense of black female subjectivity and by subjugating women's bodies, while at other times [hip hop] reveals the complexity of black male identity" (Perry 2005, 118). For an analysis of black masculinity at a more macro-level perspective of

contemporary U.S. society, that is, the "hip hop generation," see Hopkinson and Moore 2006.
4. See Ferguson 2001, Dimitriadis 2001, and Gilmore, 1985.
5. Literally, the Portuguese phrase means "truly of evil." I borrow the English phrase from Ferguson (2001, 77–96), especially in her concluding discussion about the struggle for many African American boys to avoid the label of "unsalvageable" (96). The phrase, "naughty by nature," is known within the global hip hop community due to the massive success of the rap group "Naughty by Nature" in the early 1990s.
6. See also Oliven 1996 and Archetti 1999 for insightful discussion into the articulation of masculinity to the nation through discourses of morality in Brazil and Argentina, respectively.
7. This statement is intended to contrast Brazilian hip hop gender dynamics from those in the United States, as articulated by scholars such as Imani Perry 2005, bell hooks 1995, and others following earlier *negritude* scholars such as Frantz Fanon 1967. Such scholars discuss hip hop performances of masculinity as first and foremost a reaction to white patriarchy and historical white fetish/disgust of the black body. As Perry states, "In order to understand this phenomenon [the assertion of black male subjectivity vis-à-vis the objectification of black women's bodies], we must first think about black masculinity in relation to white masculinity" (2005, 124).
8. See, for example, Warren 1988. See also McKeganey 1991.
9. Position has long been part of hip hop scholarship. Normally phrased in terms of race and class, scholarly representation of hip hop culture has only occasionally included gender as constitutive of analysis and analyst. Not surprisingly, black women scholars have been the ones to articulate such connections. See Keyes 1991 and Rose 1994.
10. It is important to note that authors such as Juan Flores (2000) and Raquel Rivera (2003) have struggled mightily to make space for the inclusion of Nuyoricans and *Latinidad* as part of the U.S. hip hop canon with respect to gender and performance. African American hip hop scholars have rarely acknowledged such histories. In particular, Rivera has provided great insight into the commodification of *Latinidad* in U.S. rap as "ghetto tropical"—a dynamic conflation of gender and race in which Latinas and Nuyorican Spanish-language phrases such as *mami, cholo, mira,* and *papi* intersect with African-American expressions (2003, 113–63).
11. The list of important literature on this subject is considerable. Some of the classic works include Freyre 1933; Candido 1951.
12. In this case, *posse* is the substantive form of the verb *possuir* ("to possess"). It is not to be confused with the borrowed term *posse* from English referring to an organized group in São Paulo hip hop culture.

13. In comparison, Perry describes black male hip hoppers as using black women "as a kind of commodity expression of wealth and sexual power in the face of racialized economic powerlessness" (2005, 126–27).
14. *Mina* is particular to São Paulo.
15. The Rio-based funk group *Tigrão* popularized this phrase in the beginning of the decade.
16. Brazilian men and women often employ the term *neguinha* to refer to subordinated women of any racial or ethnic classification. A pragmatic understanding of this ubiquitous term of address brings together Brazilian dynamics of race, class, and gender.
17. For a comparative example in the United States, see a similar story as told by Raquel Rivera in her interview with a Puerto Rican emcee/producer about the music of female rap artist Hurricane G. According to him, she was not "ladylike": "Women rappers have to be ladies to get treated like ladies" (in Rivera 2003, 142). See also Perry's discussion of MC Lyte and Boss in contrast to Salt-N-Pepa (2005, 155–57).
18. Imani Perry (2005, 164–65) and Gottlieb and Wald (1994, 254–55) analyze songs of rapper Lil' Kim and Grrl Rock band Bikini Kill, respectively, as an interrogation into the gendered notion that anger and rage are masculine domains.
19. *Axé* music is most widely associated with the northeast region of Brazil. In the 1990s groups such as *É o Tchan* recorded a series of popular songs that featured among other images women suggestively dancing over bottles.
20. "*Cerrado*" refers to the savannah plateau region that covers part of central Brazil and into Bolivia. This is where the capital city of Brasília was built during the 1950s. One can access the interview with Aninha from *Atitude Feminina* at http://www.realhiphop.com.br/colunas/djportela/index_17.html.
21. This was one of the primary points of interrogation by television journalist Paulo Amorim. In 1997 he invited Thaíde and X from *Câmbio Negro* to participate in a collective interview. When asked why hip hoppers always seem to be upset with a mean look on their faces, both X and Thaíde agreed that hip hoppers are that way because the culture is about *realidade*. They explained that for hip hoppers, reality is serious and that they are trying to differentiate themselves from conventional cultural depictions of the *periferia*, which focus on laziness, ignorance, and meaningless parties.
22. The feminist movement in Brazil is part of the more general MP ("Popular Movement") that emerged during the mid-1970s in reaction to the Brazilian military dictatorship. According to Alvarez (1990, 43) women, who had previously been a visible presence in the military *coup d'etat* (sometimes referred to as the "revolution" against a presumed communist threat) of 1964 and a constitutive part of the nationalist mantra of

"*A Família com Deus para Liberdade*" ("The Family, with God, for Liberty), in fact, made up 80 percent of the urban social movements of the late 70s and 80s. Feminism as a social movement is generally referred to as *movimento feminino* or *movimento de mulheres*. "Feminist" groups usually organize around issues specific to the female condition, for example, reproductive rights; while "feminine" groups normally mobilize around broader issues of gender such as the sexual division of labor. See Singer 1980 for a detailed description of "feminine" and "feminist" in the São Paulo context during the early period of the women's movement. See also Alvarez 1997, 95–101 and Alvarez 1990, 3–16.

23. See Alvarez 1998, 293–324 for a detailed analysis of how Latin American feminism "went global."
24. See, for example, the comments of leading Afro-Brazilian activist Joel Rufino dos Santos about black and white women. Santos *foi infeliz* ("lamentably decided") to choose the metaphor of cars to make his comparison; namely, that white women are like Monzas (mid-size luxury cars) and black women are like *fuscas* (Volkswagen bugs). These statements are reprinted in Silva 1995, 515.
25. See Collins 1991 and Weedon 1999 and Caldwell 1999 for detailed analyses of race and gender as structural and discursive forces in the formation of social stratification.
26. Much of *Visão de Rua*'s positioning is comparable to the trope of the "female badman" as described by Perry (2005, 156–57) in terms of women following "a masculinist form with masculinist aesthetics" (156).
27. See also Tricia Rose's interview with Beth Coleman (2001).
28. My perspective to contrast "inclusion" and "critique" come from Henry Giroux's discussion of these terms with regard to education, the classroom, and pedagogic curricula (Giroux 1985).

Chapter 6

1. The "cultural point" (*ponto de cultura*) campaign is one of Gilberto Gil's prize initiatives. Early in 2007 Diadema's *Casa de Hip Hop* was recognized as a "cultural point," and according to Nino Brown, this title has translated not only into extra funding for workshops, events, and infrastructure but has also meant greater access to a network of other cultural institutions, which may have an interest in the Hip Hop House. However, not everyone appreciates the "cultural point" program. On March 16, 2007, journalist Bárbara Gancia published an article in the newspaper *Folha de São Paulo* entitled "Cultura de Bacilos," in which she criticized hip hop for being sexist, violent, and musical trash. The target of Gancia's ire is the fact that the state subsidized hip hop and thus has categorically recognized hip hop as "Brazilian" and worth support. Many Brazilians denounced her article and her subsequent interview on Bandeirantes radio station. Hip hoppers were quick to utilize *their* Web

sites such as http://www.bocada-forte.com.br to register "manifestos" regarding hip hop's complex history and institutional work in various Brazilian communities. See, for example, Tina D's text, "Aplacando Ira de nossos Algozes" on the Web site.
2. Hip hop is a pop culture face of Brazilian social organizing, a force that continues to provoke representatives of Brazil's elite to take increasingly reactionary stances. One example that directly pertains to the *periferia* and hip hop is the recent return to "racial democracy." The political and scholarly documentation reinforcing "racial democracy" is perhaps best represented by the best-selling, anti-affirmative action book *Não Somos Racistas* (*We Are Not Racists*), written by Ali Kamel, director of journalism at Globo media corporation, with a preface by anthropologist Yvonnne Maggi.
3. Hip hop scholars Murray Forman (2002) and Bakari Kitwana (2005) have discussed these trends to show the expanding influence of hip hop outside of the music industry. See also Halifu Osumare's work, as she analyzed hip hop as the "collision and collusion between two powerfully global forces: transnational media and capital and African American popular culture that remains steeped in Africanist expressive modes" (2007, 2–3).
4. See Perry 2005, 186–89 for the hip hop application of a "spectacle" perspective within political-economic theory.
5. Such musico-racial positioning stands as an interesting comparison to Brazilian country artists. Alexander Dent in his work on *música sertaneja* (a genre term for commercial Brazilian country music) argues that part of the distinction that local "country" musicians try to create is vis-à-vis the national paradigm of "Brazilian" music, which is essentially the idea that "Brazilian" music is rooted in the Afro-Brazilian experience (samba dance, percussion, *axé*, trickster/hustler figure of the *malandro*, etc.). See Dent 2005.

Epilogue

1. Preto Ghoéz was a rapper and political activist who died tragically in a car accident in 2004 and in whose name the Brazilian Ministry of Culture as well as the commercial hip hop community has dedicated hip hop contests and awards. Kall founded one of the first hip hop posses in the 1980s, discussed in Chapter 2. He grew up in Capão Redondo in the extreme South Side of São Paulo. As an adult he entered college and graduated with a degree in social sciences. In 2005, he moved to Berlin, Germany, and is presently working on a Master's degree in anthropology. Kall maintains a vibrant listserv for global hip hop events and issues.
2. "Mudar" is the Portuguese verb meaning to "change" or to "move" in terms of residency.

References

Abramo, Helena Wendel. 1994. *Cenas juvenis: Punks e darks no espetáculo urbano.* São Paulo: Scritta.
Adler, Bill, and Jenette Beckman. 1991. *Rap: Portraits and lyrics of a generation of black rockers.* New York: St. Martin's.
Adorno, Sérgio. 1996. Violência e racismo: Discriminação no acesso à justiça penal. In *Raça e diversidade,* orgs. Lilia Moritz Schwarcz and Renato da Silva Queiroz, 255–75. São Paulo: EdUsp.
Alvarez, Sonia E. 1989. Politicizing gender and engendering democracy. In *Democraticizing Brazil: Problems of transition and consolidation,* ed. Alfred Stepan, 205–51. New York: Oxford University Press.
———. 1990. *Engendering democracy in Brazil: Women's movements and transition politics.* Princeton, NJ: Princeton University Press.
———. 1997. Reweaving the fabric of collective action: Social movements and challenges to "actually existing democracy" in Brazil. In *Between resistance and revolution,* ed. Richard C. Fox and Orin Starn, 83–117. New Brunswick, NJ: Rutgers University Press.
———. 1998. Latin American feminisms "go global": Trends of the 1990s and challenges for the new millennium. In *Culture of politics politics of cultures: Re-envisioning Latin American social movements,* ed. Sonia E. Alvarez, Evelina Dagnino, and Arturo Escobar, 293–324. Boulder, CO: Westview.
Alves, César. 2004. *Pergunte a quem conhece: Thaíde.* São Paulo: Labortexto Editorial.
Amaral, Tata. 2001. A cidade. In *Rede de tensão,* 85–89. São Paulo: Paço das Artes.
Andrade, Elaine Nunes de. 1996. Movimento negro juvenil: Um estudo de caso sobre jovens rappers de São Bernardo do Campo. Dissertation from Universidade de São Paulo, Faculdade de Educação.
———, ed. 1999. *Rap e educação, rap é educação.* São Paulo: Selo Negro.
Andrews, George Reid. 1988. Black and white workers: São Paulo, Brazil, 1888–1928. *Hispanic American Historical Review* 68 (August): 491–524.
———. 1992. Black political protest in São Paulo. *Journal of Latin American Studies* 24 (1): 147–71.
Andrade, Mario de. 1940. *Lira Paulistana.* Sao Paulo: Livraria Martins.
Appadurai, Arjun. 1990. Disjuncture and difference in the global economy. *Public Culture* 2 (2): 1–24.

———. 1991. Global ethnoscapes: Notes and queries for a transnational anthropology. In *Recpaturing anthropology: Working in the present*, ed. Richard G. Fox, 191–210. Sante Fe, NM: School of American Research Press.

Archetti, Eduardo. 1999. *Masculinities*. New York: Berg.

Arias, EnriqueDesmond. 2006. *Drugs and democracy in Rio de Janeiro: Trafficking, social networks, and public security*. Chapel Hill: University of North Carolina Press.

Ariefdien, Shaheen, and Nazli Abrahams. 2006. Cape Flat alchemy. In *Total chaos: The art and aesthetics of hip-hop*, ed. Jeff Chang, 262–70. Cambridge, MA: BasicCivitas Books.

Assef, Claudia. 2004. *Todo DJ já sambou*. Rio de Janeiro: Conrad.

Athayde, Phydia de. 2003. Hip-hop: Já se rendeu? *Carta Capital* 10(268), November 26.

Averill, Gage. 1997. *A day for the hunter, a day for the prey: Popular music and power in Haiti*. University of Chicago Press.

Azevêdo, Sandra. 1994. Teorizando sobre gênero e relações raciais. *Estudos Feministas*, October.

Barreiros, Edmundo. Rappers enfrentam a polícia. In *Jornal do Brasil*, Caderno B, Rio de Janeiro, December 11, 1994, p. 1.

Barreto, Lima. 1978. *The patriot (Triste fim de Policarpo Quaresma)*. Trans. Robert Scott-Buccleuch. London: Collings.

Barthes, Roland. 1957. *Mythologies*. Paris: Éditions du Seuil.

Basu, Dipannita, and Sidney J. Lemelle, eds. 2006. *The vinyl ain't final: Hip hop and the globalization of black popular culture*. Ann Arbor, MI: Pluto.

Béhague, Gerard, ed. 1984. *Performance practice: Ethnomusicological perspectives*. Westport, CT: Greenwood.

Blachman, Morris J. 1976. Problemas encontrados en la investigación de la actividad política organizada de la mujer en Brasil. In *Perspetivas femininas en América Latina*, orgs. Elu de Enero and Maria del Carmen, 125–49. Sepsetentas.

Boyd, Todd. 2002. *The new H.N.I.C.: The death of civil rights and the reign of hip hop*. New York: New York University Press.

Brancatelli, Rodrigo. 2005. Porque se mata menos em São Paulo. *Veja São Paulo*, July 6, 2006, http://veja.abril.com.br/vejasp/060705/criminalidade.html.

Brito, Maria Noemi Castilhos. 2001. Gênero e cidadania: Referenciais analíticos. *Estudos Feministas* 9 (1): 291–98.

Brusco, Elizabeth E. 1995. *The reformation of machismo: Evangelical conversion and gender in Colombia*. Austin: University of Texas Press.

Burdick, John. 1993. *Looking for God in Brazil: The progressive Catholic Church in urban Brazil's religious arena*. Berkeley: University of California Press.

———. 1998a. *Blessed Anastácia: Women, race, and popular Christianity in Brazil*. New York: Routledge.

———. 1998b. The lost constituency of Brazil's black movements. *Latin American Perspectives* 25 (January): 136–55.
Byrne, Bryan. 1993. Who are the whites? Imposed census categories and the racial demography of Brazil. *Social Forces* 72 (2): 451–62.
Calado, Pedro Miguel da Cruz. 2007. Não percebes o hip hop: Georgafia, (sub)culturas e territorialidade. Masters thesis in geography, Universidade de Lisboa.
Caldeira, Teresa P. R. 1985. *Mulheres, cotidiano e política*. São Paulo: CEBRAP.
———. 2000. *City of walls: Crime, segregation, and citizenship in São Paulo*. Berkeley: University of California Press.
Caldeira, Teresa P. R., and James Holston. 1999. Democracy and violence in Brazil. *Comparative Studies in Society and History* 41(4): 691–729.
Caldwell, Kia Lilly. 1999. *Ethnographers of identity: (Re)constructing race and gender in contemporary Brazil*. Ph.D. dissertation. University of Texas at Austin.
———. 2000. Fronteira da diferença: Raça e mulher no Brasil. *Estudos Feministas* 8 (2): 91–108.
Calvino, Italo. 1974. *Invisible cities*. New York: Harcourt.
Candeia. 1978. *90 anos de abolição*. Pamphlet. Rio de Janeiro: Gran Escola de Samba Quilombo.
Candido, Antonio. 1951 The Brazilian family. In *Brazil: Portrait of a half continent*, ed. T. Lynn Smith, 291–312. New York: Dryden Press.
Carneiro, Sueli, and Thereza Santos. 1985. *Mulher negra: Política governmental e a mulher*. São Paulo: Livraria Nobel, Conselho Estadual da Condição Feminina.
Castells, Manuel. 1991. *The informational city: Information technology, economic restructuring and the urban-regional process*. New York: Blackwell.
Castro, Roberto C. G. 1996. Ainda temos muito a realizar. *Jornal da USP* (November): 18–24, p.3.
CEAPN (Coordinating group concerning topics of the black population). 2003. A população negra e o orçamento participativo da cidade de São Paulo. Meeting minutes, Mário de Andrade Public Library, March 15.
Chang, Jeff, ed. 2006. *Total chaos: The art and aesthetics of hip-hop*. Cambridge, MA: BasicCivitas Books.
Cheney, Charise L. 2005. *Brothers gonna work it out: Sexual politics in the Golden Age of rap nationalism*. New York: New York University Press.
CNMB (National Conferences of Brazilian Women). 2002. Plataforma política feminista—Primeira versão. Document published on April 20, http://www.articulacaodemulheres.org.
Collins, Patricia. 1991. *Black feminist thought: Knowledge, consciousness, and the politics of empowerment*. New York: Routledge.
Condry, Ian. 2006. *Hip-hop Japan: Rap and the paths of cultural globalization*. Durham, NC: Duke University Press.
Contador, Antonio, and E. Ferreira. 1997. *Ritmo e poesia: Os caminhos de rap*. Lisbon: Assírio & Alvim.

Cooper, Martha, Nika Kramer, and Rokafella. 2005. *We B*Girlz*. New York: Powerhouse Books.

Costa, Tina Gonçalves. 1993. Mulheres no rap. *Pode crê* 1 (August/September): 33–35. São Paulo: Geledés.

Cunha, Euclides da. 1957. *Os sertões*. Rio de Janeiro: Livraria F. Alves.

Dagnino, Evelina. 1998. The cultural practices of citizenship, democracy, and the state. In *Culture of politics, politics of culture: Re-visioning Latin American social movements*, ed. Sonia Álvarez, Evelina Dagnino, and Arturo Escobar, 33–63. Boulder, CO: Westview.

Dahl, Robert. 1998. *On democracy*. New Haven: Yale University Press.

Damasceno, Caetana Maria. 2000. "Em casa de enforcado não se fala em corda": Notas sobre a construção social da "boa" aparência no Brasil. In *Tirando a máscara: Ensaios sobre o racismo no Brasil*, orgs. Antonio Sérgio Alfredo Guimarães and Lynn Huntley, 165–99. São Paulo: Paz e Terra.

DataFolha. 1995. *Racismo cordial*. São Paulo: Editora Ática.

Deffontaines, Pierre. 1945. A População branca no Brasil. *Boletim Geográfico* III, no. 32.

Degler, Carl N. 1971. *Neither black nor white: Slavery and race relations in Brazil and the United States*. Madison: University of Wisconsin Press.

Dent, Alexander Sebastian. 2005. Cross-cultural "countries": Covers, conjuncture, and the whiff of Nashville. *Musica Sertaneja* (Brazilian Commmercial Country Music). *Popular Music and Ssociety* 28 (2): 207–27.

Dimitriadis, Greg. 2001. *Performing identity/performing culture: Hip hop as text, pedagogy, and lived practice*. New York: Peter Lang.

Durand, Alain-Philippe, ed. *Francophone world*. Oxford: Scarecrow.

Dyson, Michael Eric.1993. *Reflecting black: African-American cultural criticism*. Minneapolis: University of Minnesota Press.

Eagleton, Terry. 1991. *Ideology: An introduction*. New York: Verso.

Ebron, Paulla. 1991. Rapping between men: Performing gender. *Radical America* 23 (October–December 1989): 23–27.

Eure, Joseph D., and James Spady. 1991. *Nation conscious rap*. New York: PC International.

Fanon, Frantz. 1967. *Black skin white masks*. New York: Grove Weidenfeld.

Featherstone, Mike, Scott Lash, and Roland Robertson, eds. 1995. *Global modernities*. Thousand Oaks, CA: Sage.

Felinto, Marilene. 1997. Participação de negros ainda é vetada. *Folha de São Paulo*, November 16.

Félix, João Batista de Jesus. 1996. Pequeno histórico do movimento negro contemporâneo. In *Negras imagens*, org. L. Schwarcz and L. Reis, 211–16. São Paulo: Editora USP.

———. 2000. Chic show e Zimbabue: a construção de identidade nos bailes black de SP. Master's thesis. Department of Anthropology. University of São Paulo.

———. 2005. *Hip hop e política no contexto Paulistano*. Masters thesis, USP, São Paulo.

Ferguson, Ann Arnett. 2001. *Bad boys public schools in the making of black masculinity*. Ann Arbor: University of Michigan Press.
Fernandes, Florestan. 1972. *O negro no mundo dos brancos*. São Paulo: Difusão Européia do Livro.
Fernandes, Sujatha. 2003. Fear of a black nation: Local rappers, transnational crossings, and state power in contemporary Cuba. *Anthropological Quarterly* 76 (4): 575–608.
———. 2006. *Cuba represent! Cuban arts, state power, and the making of new revolutionary cultures*. Durham, NC: Duke University Press.
Ferreira, Tânia Maria Ximenes. 2005. *Hip hop e educação: Mesma linguagem múltiplas falas*. Masters thesis, Department of Education, State University in Campinas, São Paulo.
Flores, Juan. 2000. *From bomba to hip-hop: Puerto Rican culture and Latino identity*. Columbia University Press.
Fontaine, Pierre M. 1980. Research in the political economy of Afro-Latin America. *Latin American Research Review* 15 (2): 111–42.
Forman, Murray. 2002. *The "hood" comes first: Race, space, and place in rap and hip-hop*. Middletown, CT: Wesleyan Press.
———. 2010. Hip-hop culture, youth creativity and the generational crossroads. In *Art and human development*, ed. Constance Milbrath and Cynthia Lightfoot, 59–82. New York: Psychology Press.
Forman, Murray, and Marc Neal, eds. 2004. *That's the joint: The Hip-Hop Studies reader*. New York: Routledge.
Foster, Makiba J. 2007. Gettin' busy, goin' global: A hip-hop feminist experiences Ghana. In *Home girls make some noise*, eds. Gwendolyn D. Pough, Elaine Richardson, Aisha Durham, and Rachel Raimist, 449–62. Mira Loma, CA: Parker.
Fradrique, Teresa. 2003. *Fixar o movimento: Representações da música rap em Portugal*. Lisbon: Publicações D. Quixote.
Fraser, Nancy. 1990. Rethinking the public sphere: A contribution to the critique of actually existing democracy. *Social Text* 25/26 (56–80).
Freyre, Gilberto. 1968. *Sobrados e mucambos*. Rio de Janeiro: José Olympio.
———. 1969. *Casa-grande e senzala*. Lisbon: Editora Livros do Brasil.
———. 1976a. Aspectos da influência africana no Brasil. *Cultura* 6 (23). Brasília: Ministry of Education and Culture (October–December).
———. 1976b. Atenção Brasileiros. *Diário de Pernambuco*. A (13).
Garcia, Maria Elena. 2004. The challenges of representation: NGOs, education, and the state in highland Peru. In *Civil society or shadow state?: State/NGO relations in education*, eds. Margaret Sutton and Robert Arnove. Information Age Publishing, 45–70.
Gil. 2001. Entrevista com La Bela Mafia. http://www.manuscrito.com.br.
Gill, Lesley. 2004. *School of the Americas: Military training and political violence in the Americas*. Durham: Duke University Press.
Gilmore, David D. 1990. *Manhood in the making: Cultural concepts of masculinity*. New Haven, CT: Yale University Press.

Gilmore, Perry. 1985. "'Gimme room': School resistance, attitude, and access to literacy." *Journal of Education* 167 (1).
Gilroy, Paul. 1992. It's a family affair. In *Black Popular Culture*, ed. Gina Dent, 303–16. Seattle: Bay.
———. 1993. *The black Atlantic: Modernity and double consciousness*. Cambridge, MA: Harvard University Press.
Giroux, Henry A. 1985. Introduction. In *The politics of education*, by Paulo Freire. Boston: Bergin and Garvey.
Glen, John M., Stephen G. Mcshane, Brenda Nelson-Strauss, Paul C. Heyde, and Wilma L. Gibbs. 2004. Indiana archives: African American history. *Indiana Magazine of History* 100 (4): 46 pars. http://www.historycooperative.org/journals/imh/100.4/glen.html (accessed January 10, 2006).
Goldstein, Donna. 1999. "Interracial" sex and racial democracy in Brazil: Twin concepts? *American Anthropologist* 101 (3): 563–78.
———. 2003. *Laughter out of place: Race, class, violence and sexuality in a Rio shantytown*. Berkeley: University of California Press.
Gonzalez, Lélia, and Carlos Hasenbalg. 1982. *Lugar de negro*. Rio de Janeiro: Editora Marco Zero Limitada.
Gottlieb, Joanne, and Gayle Ward. 1994. Smells like teen spirit: Riot grrrls, revolution and women in independent rock. In *Microphone fiends: Youth music and culture*, 250–74. New York: Routledge.
Guasco, Pedro Paulo M. 2001. Num país chamado periferia: Identidade e representação da realidade entre os rappers de São Paulo. Masters thesis, Department of Social Anthroplogy, University of São Paulo.
Guimarães, Antonio Sérgio Alfredo. 1999. *Racismo e anti-racismo no Brasil*. 34th ed. São Paulo: Fundação de Apoio à Universidade de São Paulo.
———. 2000. O insulto racial: As ofensas verbais registradas em queixas de discriminação. *Estudos Afro-Asiáticos* 38 (December): 31–48.
Guimarães, María Eduarda. 1998. *Do samba ao rap: Música negra no Brasil*. Dissertation, University of Campinas.
Gustafson, Bret. 2006. Spectacles of autonomy and crisis: Or, what bulls and beauty queens have to do with regionalism in eastern Bolivia. *Journal of Latin American Anthropology* 11(2): 351–79.
Hagopian, Frances. 2007. Latin American citizenship and democratic theory. In *Citizenship in Latin America*, ed. Joseph S.Tulchin and Meg Ruthenberg, 11–56. Boulder, CO: Lynne Rienner.
Hanchard, Michael. 1994. *Orpheus and power: The movimento negro of Rio de Janeiro and São Paulo, 1945–1988*. Princeton, NJ: Princeton University Press.
Hansen, Thomas Blom, and Finn Stepputat, eds. 2001. *States of imagination: Ethnographic explorations of the postcolonial state*. Durham, NC: Duke University Press.
Hartigan, John, Jr. 1999. *Racial situations: Class predicaments of whiteness in Detroit*. Princeton, NJ: Princeton University Press.

Hartmann, Heidi I., and Donald J. Treiman, eds. 1981. *Women, work, and wages: equal pay for jobs of equal value.* Committee on Occupational Classification and Analysis. Assembly of Behavioral and Social Sciences. National Research Council. Washington, D.C.: National Academy Press.

Harvey, David. 1989. *The conditions of postmodernity.* Oxford: Blackwell.

Hebdige, Dick. 1987. *Cut 'n' mix: Culture, identity, and Caribbean music.* New York: Methuen.

Hecht, Tobias. 1998. *At home in the street.* Cambridge University Press.

Helfland, Jessica. 2001. Sensory montage: Rethinking fusion and fragmentation. In *Screen: Essays on graphic design, mew media, and visual culture,* 53–58. New York: Princeton Architectural Press.

Holanda, Sérgio Buarque de. 1936. *Raízes do Brasil.* Rio de Janeiro: José Olympio.

Holloway, Lynette. 2002. Hip-hop sales pop: Pass the courvoisier. *New York Times,* September 2.

Holston, James. 1989. *The modernist city: An anthropological critique of Brasília.* Chicago: University of Chicago Press.

———. 1991a. Autoconstruction in working-class Brazil. *Cultural Aanthropology* 6 (4): 447–65.

———. 1991b. The misuses of law: Land and usurpation in Brazil. *Comparative Studies in Society and History* 33 (4): 695–725.

Hooks, Bell. 1984. *Feminist theory from margin to center.* Chicago: South End.

———. 1991. Choosing the margin as a space of radical openness. In *Yearning: Race, gender and cultural politics.* London: Turnaround.

———. 2003. *We real cool; Black men and masculinity.* New York: Routledge.

Hopkinson, Natalie, and Natalie Moore. 2006. *Deconstructing Tyrone: A new look at black masculinity in the hip-hop generation.* San Francisco: Cleis.

IBGE (Brazilian Institute of Geography and Statistics). Data taken from http://www.ibge.gov.br.

Jameson, Frederic. 1981. *The political unconscious.* Ithaca, NY: Cornell University Press.

Jelin, Elizabeth. 2003. Citizenship and alterity: Tensions and dilemmas. In *Latin American Perspectives* 30 (2): 309–25.

Kachami, Morris. 1996. Sucesso Negro. *Veja,* September 18, p. 112.

Keil, Charles. 1984. Music mediated and live in Japan. *Ethnomusicology* 28 (1): 91–96.

Kelleher, William F. 2003. *The troubles in Ballybogoin: Memory and identity in Northern Ireland.* Ann Arbor: University of Michigan Press.

Kelley, Robin D. G. 1994. *Race rebels: Culture, politics, and the black working class.* New York: Free Press.

———. 1997. *Yo mama's disfunktional: Fighting the cultural wars in urban America.* Boston: Beacon.

Keyes, Cheryl. 1991. Rappin' to the beat: Rap music as street culture among African Americans. PhD dissertation, Indiana University.

———. 2004. *Rap music and street consciousness*. Urbana: University of Illinois Press.
Kirschner, Tony. 1998. Studying rock: Towards a materialist ethnography. In *Mapping the beat: Popular music and contemporary theory*, ed. Thomas Swiss, John Sloop, and Andrew Herman, 247–68.
Kitwana, Bakari. 1994. *The rap on gangsta rap*. Chicago: Third World.
———. 2005. *Why white kids love hip hop*. New York: Basic Books.
KRS-One. 2003. *Ruminations*. New York: Welcome Rain.
Kulick, Don. 1998. *Travestí*. Chicago: University of Chicago Press.
Lancaster, Roger. 1992. *Life is hard: Machismo, danger, and the intimacy of power in Nicaragua*. Los Angeles: University of California Press.
Leadbetter, Ross, Bonnie J., and Niobe Way. 1996. *Urban girls: Resisting stereotypes, creating identities*. New York: New York University Press.
LeFebvre, Henri. 1991. *The production of space*. New York: Blackwell.
Limón, José E. 1994. *Dancing with the Devil: Society and cultural poetics in Mexican-American south Texas*. Madison: University of Wisconsin Press.
Lipsitz, George. 1994. *Dangerous crossroads: Popular music, postmodernism, and the poetics of place*. London: Verso.
Lloyd, David, and Paul Thomas. *Culture and the state*. New York: Routledge.
Lodi, Célia Amália. 2005. *Manifestações culturais juvenis: O hip hop está com a palavra*. Thesis, PUC, Rio de Janeiro.
Lomnitz, L. A. 1977. *Networks and marginality: Life in a Mexican shanty town*. New York: Academic.
Loomba, Ania. 2005. *Colonialism/postcolonialism*. New York: Routledge.
Lull, James. 2001. Superculture for the Communication Age. In *Culture in the Communication Age*, ed. James Lull, 132–63. New York: Routledge.
Maggie, Yvonne, and Claudia Rezende. 2002. Raça como retórica: A construção da diferença. In *Raça como retórica: a construção da diferença*, orgs. Maggie and Rezende, 13–25. Rio de Janeiro: Civilização Brasileira.
Magnini, Jose Guilherme Cantor. 1985. Espaco e Debates. *Revista de estudos regionais e urbanos* 6 (17): 127–30.
———. 1992. Quando o campo e a cidade: Fazendo antropologia na metropole. In *Na metropole. Sao Paulo*. ED. USP, pp. 15–53.
Manuel, Peter. 1993. *Cassette culture: Popular music and technology in North India*. Chicago: University of Chicago Press.
Maricato, Ermínia. 1979. Autoconstrução, a arquitetura possível. In *A produção capitalista da casa (e da cidade) no Brasil industrial*, ed. Ermínia Maricato, 71–93. São Paulo: Alfa Omega.
Marshall, T. H. 1950. *Citizenship and social class and other essays*. Cambridge: Cambridge University Press.
Marx, Anthony. 1999. *Making race and nation: A comparison of South Africa, the United States, and Brazil*. New York: Cambridge University Press.
Massey, Doreen, and N. A. Denton. 1992. A place called home. *New Formations* 17 (Summer): 3–15.
Matta, Roberto da. 1993. *Conto de mentiroso: Sete ensaois de antropologia brasileira*. Rio de Janeiro: Rocco.

———. 2000. *A casa e a rua: Espaço, cidadania, mulher, e morte no Brasil*. Rio de Janeiro: Rocco.
Maxwell, Ian. 2003. *Phat beats, dope rhymes: Hip hop down under coming upper*. Middletown, CT: Wesleyan University Press.
McLaren, Peter. 2000. Gangsta pedagogy and ghettocentricity: The hip-hop nation as counterpublic sphere. In *Challenges of urban education sociological perspectives for the next century*, ed. Karen A. McLafferty and Carlos Alberto.
McKeganey, Neil, and Michale Bloor. 1991. Spotting the invisible man: The influence of male gender on fieldwork relations. In *British Journal of Sociology* 42(2): 195–210.
Meintjes, Louise. 2003. *Sound of Africa! Making music Zulu in a South African studio*. Durham, NC: Duke University Press.
Mitchell, Tony, ed. 2001. *Global noise: Rap and hip-hop outside the USA*. Middletown, CT: Wesleyan University Press.
Morgan, Joan. 1999. *When chickenheads come home to roost: My life as a hip-hop feminist*. New York: Simon & Schuster.
Morgan, Marcyliena. 2002. *Language, discourse and power in African American culture*. Cambridge: Cambridge University Press.
———. 2005. Comments as respondent during the AAA (American Anthropological Association) panel entitled "Hip hop and globalization."
Moura, Clovis. 1988. *Sociologia do negro brasileiro*. São Paulo: Editora Ática.
———. 1994. *Dialética radical do Brasil negro*. São Paulo: Ática.
MNU. 1996. As eleições, o negro, e a sociedade que queremos. *Movimento Negro Unificado Boletim Informativo* 5 (July–September): 2–3.
———. 1997. Pamphlet circulated by *Posse Hausa* member Honerê.
Mrazek, Rudolf. 2002. *Engineers of happy land*. Princeton: Princeton University Press.
Munanga, Kabengele. 1990. Negritude Afro-Brasileira: Perspetivas e dificuldades. *Revista de Antropologia* 33:109–17.
Nascimento, Abdias do. 1980. *Quilombismo: Documentos de uma militância pan-africanista*. Petrópolis, RJ: Vozes.
Nascimento, Maria Ercília do. 1989. A estratégia da desigualdade: O movimento negro dos anos 70. Masters thesis, Pontifica Universidade Católica.
Nascimento, Nívio Caixeta do. 1995. Movimento hip-hop: A busca da cidadania. Senior thesis, Universidade de Brasília.
Neal, Mark Anthony. 2007. Foreword: A few words on hip-hop feminism. In *Home girls make some noise*, ed. Gwendolyn D. Pough, Elaine Richardson, Aisha Durham, and Rachel Raimist, i–iv. Mira Loma, CA: Parker.
Norvell, John M. 2001. A Brancura desconfortável das camadas medias brasileiras. In *Raça como retórica*, 245–67. São Paulo: Civilização Brasileira.
Novaes, Regina. 1999. Ouvir para crer: Os racionais e a fé na palavra. *Religiãoe Sociedade* 20 (1): 65–92.
O'Donnell. Illusions about consolidation. *Jounral of Democracy* 7 (2): 34–51.
Oliveira. 1996. Vale do Paraíba, Movimento hip-hop. *Notícias*, November 22, p. 4.

Oliven, R.1996. *Tradition matters: Modern gaucho identity in Brazil.* New York: Columbia University Press.
Osumare, Halifu. 2007. *The Africanist aesthetic in global hip-hop power moves.* New York: Palgrave Macmillan.
Oxhorn, Philip. 2007. Neopluralism and Citizenship in Latin America. In *Citizenship in Latin America*, eds. Tulchin Joseph S. and Meg Ruthenberg, 123–48. Boulder, CO: Lynne Rienner Publishers.
Pardue, Derek. 2004a. Putting *Mano* to music: The mediation of race in Brazilian rap. *Ethnomusicology Forum* 13 (November): 253–86.
———. 2004b. "Writing in the margins": Brazilian hip-hop as an educational project. *Anthropology and Education Quarterly* 35 (4): 411–32.
———. 2005. Brazilian hip-hop material and ideology: A case of cultural design. *Image and Narrative* 10 (February), http://www.imageandnarrative.be/worldmusica/worldmusica.htm.
———. 2007. Hip hop as pedagogy: A look into "Heaven" and "Soul" in São Paulo, Brazil. *Anthropological Quarterly* 80 (3): 673–708.
———. 2008. Sou marginal mesmo (I am the real hoodlum): Using violence as an aesthetic resource in Brazilian hip-hop. In *Ruminations on violence*, ed. Derek Pardue, 159–72. Waveland.
———. Forthcoming. *Conquistando espaço*: Hip-hop occupations of São Paulo. In *Brazilian music and citizenship*, ed. Christopher Dunn and Idelber Avelar. Duke University Press.
Pardue, Derek, Charlene Christman, and Molly Sheehan. 2002. It's on the cover. Interactive CD-Rom developed for AAA conference, November.
Parker, Richard. 1991. *Bodies, pleasures, and passions: Sexual culture in contemporary Brazil.* Boston: Beacon.
Perry, Imani. 2005. *Prophets of the hood: Politics and poetics in hiphop.* 2nd ed. Durham, NC: Duke University Press.
Perry, Marc D. 2008. Global black self-fashionings: Hip-hop as diasporic space. *Identities* 15 (6): 635–64.
Pieterse, Edgar. 2010. Hip-hop cultures and political agency in Brazil and South Africa. *Social Dynamics: A Journal of African Studies* 36 (2): 428–47.
Pimentel, Spensy Kmitta. 1997. *O livro vermelho do hip-hop.* Journalism thesis, Universidade de São Paulo, Escola de Comunicações e Arte.
———. 1998. Microfone aberto à população. *Caros Amigos* 3(9).
Piza, Edith. 2000. Branco no Brasil? Ninguém sabe, ninguém viu. In *Tirando a máscara: Ensaois sobre o racismo no Brasil*, orgs. Antonio Sérgio Alfredo Guimarães and Lynn Huntley, 97–125. Rio de Janeiro: Paz e Terra.
Pólis (Institute of Research, Formation and Assistance in Social Politics). 2000. http://www.polis.org.br.
Ponciano, Levino. 2001. *Bairros Paulistanos de A a Z.* São Paulo: SENAC.
Pough, Gwendolyn D. 2004. *Check it while I wreck it: Black womanhood, hip-hop culture, and the public sphere.* Boston: Northeastern University Press.
Powell, Kevin. 1997. *Keepin' it real—Post-MTV reflections on race, sex, and politics.* New York: Random House.

Prévos, André J. M. 2002. Two decades of rap in France: Emergence, developments, prospects. In *Black, blanc, beur: Rap music and hip-hop culture in the Francophone World*.
Probyn, Elspeth. 1990. Travels in the postmodern: Making sense of the local. In *Feminism/postmodernism*, ed. Linda J. Nicholson, 176–89. New York: Routledge.
Ramos, Guerreiro. 1959. *Introdução crítica à sociologia brasileira*. Rio de Janeiro: Editora Andes.
Rebelo, Marques. 2001. Interview with Visão de Rua. *Planeta hip-hop* 1(4).
Rivera, Raquel Z. 2003. *New York Ricans from the hip hop zone*. New York: Palgrave Macmillan.
Robertson, Roland. 1992. *Globalization: Social theory and global culture*. London: Sage.
Rocha, Janaina, Mirella Domenich, and Patrícia Casseano. 2001. *Hip-hop: A periferia grita*. São Paulo: Editora Fundação Perseu Abramo.
Rodrigues, Glauco Bruce. 2003. *Uma geografia do hip hop*. Senior thesis, Department of Geography, the Universidade Federal Fluminense, Niterói, Rio de Janeiro.
Roland, Edna. 2000. O movimento de mulheres negras brasileiras: Desafios e perspectivas. In *Tirando a máscara: Ensaios sobre o racismo no Brasil*, orgs. Antonio Sérgio, Alfredo Guimarães, and Lynn Huntley, 237–56. São Paulo: Paz e terra.
Rolnik, Raquel, Lúcio Kowarick, and Nádia Somekh. 1991. *São Paulo: Crise e mudança*. São Paulo: Brasiliense.
Rose, Tricia. 1994. *Black noise*. Hanover: University Press of New England.
———. 2001. Sound effects. In *Technicolor: Race, technology, and everyday life*, ed. Alondra Nelson, Thuy Linh N. Tu, and Alicia Headlam Hines, 142–53. New York: New York University Press.
Rubino, Silvana. 2006. Os dois lados da linha do trem: História urbana e intervenções contemporâneas em Campinas, SP. In *As cidades e seus agentes: Práticas e representações*, ed. Heitor Frúgoli Jr., Luciana Teixira de Andrade, and Fernanda Arêas Peixoto, 68–97. São Paulo e Belo Horizonte: EDUSP e Editora Puc Minas.
Sachs, Céline. 1999. *São Paulo: Políticas públicas e habitação popular*. Translated into Portuguese by Cristina Murachco. São Paulo: Editora USP.
Sanford, Victoria. 2003. *Buried secrets: Truth and human rights in Guatemala*. New York: MacMillan.
Sansone, Lívio. 1982. *O que é racismo*. São Paulo: Editora Brasiliense.
———. 1997. Funk Baiano: Uma versão local de um fenômeno global? In *Abalando os anos 90 funk e hip hop, globalização e estilo cultural*, ed. Michael Herschmann. Rio de Janeiro: Rocco.
———. 2002. Não-trabalho, consumo e identidade negra: Uma comparação entre Rio e Salvador. In *Raça como retórica: A construção da diferença*, orgs. Maggie and Rezende, 155–83. Rio de Janeiro: Civilização Brasileira.
———. 2003. *Blackness without ethnicity*. New York: Palgrave Macmillan.

Santos, Joel Rufino dos. 1981. *História política do futebol brasileiro*. São Paulo: Editora Brasiliense.
Santos, Milton. 1979. *The shared space: The two circuits of the urban economy in underdeveloped countries*. New York: Methuen.
Scandiucci, Guilherme. 2005. *Juventude negro-descendente e a cultura hip hop na periferia de São Paulo: Possibilidades de desenvolvimento sob a ótica da psicologia analítica*. Masters thesis, USP, São Paulo.
Schloss, Joseph Glenn. 2004. *Making beats: The art of sample-based hip-hop*. Middletown, CT: Wesleyan University Press.
Schwarcz, Lilia Moritz. 1993. *O espetáculo das raças: Cientistas, instituiçoes e questão racial no Brasil, 1870–1930*. São Paulo: Companhia das Letras.
———. 1996. A questão racial no Brasil. In *Negras imagens*, orgs. Lilia Moritz Schwarca and Letícia Vidor de Sousa Reis, 153–77. São Paulo: EdUsp.
Schwarz, Roberto. *Misplaced ideas: Essays on Brazilian culture*. Ed. John Gledson. New York: Verso.
Sedgwick, Eve Kosofsky. 1985. *Between men: English literature and male homosocial desire*. New York: Columbia University Press.
Sevcenko, Nicolau. 1993. São Paulo: The quintessential uninhibited megalopolis as seen by Blaise Cendrars in the 1920s. In *Megalopolis: The giant city in history*, ed. Theo Barker and Anthony Sutcliffe. New York: St. Martin's.
Sharpley-Whiting, T. Denean. 2007. *Pimps up, ho's down: Hip hop's hold on young black women*. New York: New York University Press.
Sheriff, Robin E. 2001. *Dreaming equality: Color, race, and racism in urban Brazil*. New Brunswick, NJ: Rutgers University Press.
Silva, José Carlos Gomes da. 1998. Rap na cidade de São Paulo: Musica, etnicidade e experiência urbana. Dissertation, Universidade de Campinas, Departamento de Ciências Sociais.
Silva, Maria Aparecida Bento da. 1995. O rap das meninas. *Estudos Feministas* 3 (2): 515–24.
———. 1999. Projeto Rappers: Uma iniciativa pioneira e vitoriosa de interlocução entre uma organização de mulheres negras e a juventude no Brasil. In *Rap e educação Rap é educação*, org. Elaine Nunes de Andrade, 93–101. São Paulo: Selo Negro.
Silva, Nelson do Valle. 1985. Updating the cost of not being white in Brazil. In *Race, class and power in Brazil*, ed. Pierre-Michel Fontaine, 42–55. Los Angeles: Center for Afro-American Studies, UCLA.
Singer, Paul, and V. C. Brandt, eds. 1980. *São Paulo: O Povo em movimento*. Petrópolis: Vozes/CEBRAP.
Soares, Luiz Eduardo. 2000. *Casaco de general; 500 dias no front da segurança pública do Rio de Janeiro*. São Paulo: Editora Companhia das Letras.
———. 2002. *Bus 174*. Oral comments as part of the documentary film. Directors, José Padilha and Felipe Lacerda.
Soihet, Rachel. 1999. Symbolic violence: Male lore and female representations. In *Estudos Feministas*, 125–39. Rio de Janeiro: IFCS/UFRJ.

Spivak, Gayatri Chakravorty. 1988. Can the subaltern speak? In *Marxism and the interpretation of culture*, ed. Cary Nelson and Lawrence Grossberg. Urbana: University of Illinois Press.

Stansfield, John. 1985. Theoretical and ideological barriers to the study of race-making. In *Research in race and ethnic relations: A research annual*, ed. C. Marrett and C. Leggon, 161–81. Greenwich, CT: JAI.

Stocking, George. 1968. *Race, culture, and evolution*. Chicago: University of Chicago Press.

Tauschner, Suzana, and Y. Mautner. 1982. Habitação da pobreza: Alternativas de moradia popular em São Paulo. *Cadernosde Estudo e Pesquisa* 5: 238. São Paulo: FAU-USP.

Toop, David. 1984. *Rap attack*. London: Pluto.

———. 1991. *Rap attack 2: African rap to global hip-hop*. New York: Serpent's Tail.

Trindade, Solano. 1961. *Cantares ao meu povo*. São Paulo: Editora Fulgor.

Vianna, Hermano. 1999. *The mystery of samba: Popular music and national identity in Brazil*. Chapel Hill: University of North Carolina Press.

Wade, Peter. 1997. *Race and ethnicity in Latin America*. Chicago: Pluto.

Wallace, Michelle. 1979. *Black macho and the myth of the superwoman*. New York: Dial.

Walser, Robert. 1993. *Running with the Devil: Power, gender, and madness in heavy metal music*. Hannover: Wesleyan University Press.

Walzer. 1995. Rhythm, Rhyme, and Rhetoric in the Music of Public Enemy. *Ethnomusicology* 39, no. 2 (Spring, 1995): 193–217.

Warren, C. 1988. Gender issues in field research. *Qualitative Research Methods Series No. 9*. London: Sage.

Waxer, Lise. 1999. Consuming memories: The record-centered salsa scene in Cali. In *Sound identities: Popular music and the cultural politics of dducation*, ed. Cameron McCarthy, Glenn Hudak, Shawn Miklaucic, and Paula Saukko, 235–51.

Weedon, Chris. 1999. *Feminism, theory and the politics of difference*. New York: Blackwell.

Willis, Paul. 1981. *Learning to labour: How working class kids get working class jobs*. New York: Columbia Press.

Zaluar, Alba. 1999. Women of gangsters: Chronicle of a less-than-musical city. In *Estudo feministas*, trans. Christopher Peterson, 109–15. Rio de Janeiro: IFCS/UFRJ.

Discography

Apocalipse 16. *Antigas idéias novos adeptos*. 7 Taças.

Atitude Feminina. 2005. "Rosas." On *Rosas*, Marola Discos e Porte Ilegal records.

The Best Beat of Rap. 1989. Kaskatas Records.

Black Juniors. 1984. *Black juniors*. CBS Records.

Código 13. 1988. "Código 13." On *Hip-hop: Cultura de rua*, Eldorado.
Consciência Black. 1989. Volume 1. Kaskatas Records.
———. 1991. Volume 2. Kaskatas Records.
Coolio. 1995. "Gangsta paradise." On Rhino Records.
Cultura de rua. 1988. El Dorado Records.
The Culture of Rap. 1989. Kaskatas Records.
Dead Prez. 2000. *Let's get free*. Relativity Records.
Equipe Gallote. 1990. FAT Records.
Facção Central. 2000. "Vidas brancas." On *Versos sangrentos*.
Filosofia de rua (Ugli C and Man). 1996. *Valeu a experiência*.
509-E. 2001. "Saudades mil." On *Movimento de rua*, CD compilation, Atração.
Genival Oliveira Gonçalves Album. 1994. *Dia-a-dia da Periferia*. Gravadora: So Balanco.
Gilberto Gil. 1972. "Expresso 2222." Philips Records.
Hills, Ieda. 2001. "Som de preto." On *Movimento de rua*, CD compilation, Atração.
Hip Rap Hop. 1988. Região Abissal.
Ice-T. 1991. *OG: Original gangster*. Sire Records.
Jamal. 2002. *Sem medo de errar*. Independent.
Jorge Bem. 1971. "O Negro é Lindo." Philips Records.
Lino Crizz e Gueto Jam. 2001. *Um, dos, três*. FMN records.
Mira Direta. 1996. "A suposta democracia racial." Live recording from *Posse Hausa* anniversary event, April.
Mos Def. 1999. *Black on both sides*. Priority Records.
Nelsão and Funk CIA. 1990. *Se liga meu*. TNT Records.
Neps. 1991. Ritmo negro. In *ABC rap. Coletânea de poesia rap*. São Bernardo do Campo: SECE.
New Edition. 1983. "Candy Girl." Streetwise Records.
O Som das Ruas. 1988. Chic Show.
Ousadia do Rap. 1987, Kaskatas Records.
Pete Rock and CL Smooth with the YG'z. 1993. "Death Becomes You." On *Menace to society*, Original Motion Picture Soundtrack, Jive Records.
Planeta Hip Hop Coletânea #8. 2002. Gravadora: Editora Escala.
Posse Mente Zulu. 1994. "Sou negão." On *Revolusom parte 1*, Raizes.
Professor Pablo. 2002. "Quem é preto." On *Estratégia, 7 Taças*.
Racionais MCs. 1993. "Pânico na Zona Sul." On *Raio X do Brasil*, Zimbabwe Records.
———. 1997. "Rapaz comum." On *Sobrevivendo no inferno*, Cosa Nostra Records.
———. 2002. *Chora agora ri depois*. Cosa Nostra Records.
Rappin' Hood. 2001. "Sou negão." On *Sujeito homem*, Trama.
———. 2005. *Sujeito homem 2*. Trama.
RZO. 1997. *Todos são manos*. Cosa Nostra.
Sampa Crew. 1995. "Aroma." On *Aroma*, Big Posse Records.

Sistema Negro. 1997. *A jogada final*. Zimbabwe Records.
Sistema Racional. 2002. "É assim que tem que ser." Independent.
Situation Rap 1988. FAT Records.
Somos Nós A Justiça. 1999. "No mundo da lua." On *SNJ*, Big Posse Records.
———. 2000. *Somos nós a justiça*. Atração.
Spice-1. 1993. "A nigga gots no heart." On *Soundtrack for Menace 2 society*, Jive Records.
Stevie Wonder. 1976. "Pastime Paradise." *Songs in the Key of Life*. Motwon Records.
Sugar Hill Gang. 1979. "Rapper's Delight." Sugar Hill Records.
Thaíde e DJ Hum. 1988. "Corpo fechado." On *Hip-hop: Cultura de rua*, Eldorado.
———. 1996. "Afro-Brasileiro." On *Preste atenção*, Eldorado.
———. 2001. *Assim caminha a humanidade*. Trama.
Tim Maia. "Racional." 1975. Seroma Records.
Visão de Rua. 2001. "Sangue B." On *Movimento de rua*, CD compilation, Atração.
Xis. 1999. *Seja como for*. 4P.

Interviews and Public Speeches

Akan, O.A.D.Q. July 22, 1999. Community leader and hip hop organizer in Diadema, São Paulo. Conversation during hip hop event.
Alam Beat. June 29, 1999. Informal conversation with member of Sampa Crew in their downtown studio.
Aldimir. December 10, 2001. Speech given during inauguration event for Cidade Tiradentes Community Library.
André. February 22, 2002. A founder of Bocada Forte. Informal conversation in the downtown *galerias* of May 24th Street.
———. May 11, 2002. Phone conversation about Web sites and the future of hip hop in São Paulo.
Batista. November 1995. Conversations at the State University of São Paulo, MNU headquarters in São Bernardo do Campo, near nightclub *SambaLove*.
Black. July 24, 1999. Member of *Posse Hausa*. Recorded interview as part of FEBEM document for *Posse Hausa*.
Borges, Neuza. November 3, 2001. Former secretary of culture in São Bernardo do Campo. Downtown public park conversation.
Brown, King Nino. April, 1997. Zulu King, first Brazilian member of the Universal Zulu Nation since March 1994. Informal interview in Nino's home in São Bernardo do Campo.
———. July 15, 1999. Soul and funk activists, hip hop historiographer. Recorded interview in Nino's home in São Bernardo do Campo.
———. August 22, 2001. Informal visit and conversation in author's apartment.

———. April 11, 2002. Conversation at Casa de Cultura Hip Hop in Diadema.
———. November 20, 2002. President of Zulu Nation Brasil. E-mail conversation.
Cafu. January 10, 2002. Rapper. Conversation in Santo André home.
Casa de Cultura Hip Hop. February 27, 2002. Participation in steering committee meeting for the upcoming *Hip-hop em ação* (Hip hop in action).
Cleberson. January 22, 2002. Conversation with state employee at the Regional Administration office in Campo Limpo district of São Paulo.
Comando Negro. February 1997. Conversation with members of rap group and their girlfriends in São Bernardo do Campo home of rapper Nepalm.
C.O.T. A Fusão. April 11, 2002. Rap Group. Casa de Cultura Hip Hop, Diadema.
Cris. July 1999. Rapper. Conversation in "black" beauty salon in downtown mall (*galeria*).
DJ Éboni. March 1, 2002. Graphic designer and hip hop activist. Conversation in Éboni's home in Parque Santo Antônio on the south side of São Paulo.
DJ Erry-G. April 16, 2002. Founder of Guerreiros Produções, member of Zulu Nation Brasil, and director of Projeto Dos Tambores aos Toca Discos. Conversation with DJ and pedagogue Érry-G in his south side residence.
———. December 29, 2005. Conversation at Casa de Cultura Hip Hop in Diadema.
———. May 25, 2007. Phone conversation.
———. July 15, 2007. Conversation in his south side residence.
DJ Hum. March 9, 2002. DJ and producer Hum from the duo Tháide e DJ Hum. Phone conversation.
DJ Ícaro. May 12, 2002. DJ in São Paulo community radio station. Informal conversation at the radio station.
DJ Jair. May 10, 2002. DJ in São Paulo community radio station. Informal conversation at the radio station.
DJ Lâmina. October 21, 2001. Conversation at east side posse meeting.
DJ Marcão. June 22, 1999. DJ and hip hop activist. Informal conversation in his home on the east side of São Paulo.
DJ Marquinhos. September 20, 2001. Visit to east side home.
DJ Q-Suco. July 2007. Conversation in south side home.
DJ Simplício. July 1999. Conversation in downtown studio of rap group Sampa Crew.
DJ Tanque and Wesley. March 7, 2002. Informal conversation at Casa de Cultural Hip Hop, Diadema.
Drica. March 3, 2002. Conversation during the Hip hop in action event dedicated to gender issues and the role of women in Brazilian hip hop.
Edilane. December 10, 2001. Informal conversation at inauguration of Cidade Tiradentes Community Library.

Edivelton. December 12, 2001. Member of Aliança Negra Posse and rapper for Shalom Adanai. Cidade Tiradentes residence.
Fábio Féter. April 9, 2002. Leader, composer, and main rapper of Sistema Racional. Personal conversation in downtown Santo André.
Fantasma. March 22, 2002. Member of Zulu Nation Brasil and DJ professor at Casa de Cultura Hip Hop in Diadema. Conversation in his home in the district of Pedreira on the south side of São Paulo.
Fran. July 15, 2005. Organizer of Rap em Festa of CEDECA.
Giro. February–March 2002. Rapper. Conversations in car and his south side home.
Gordo. March 29, 2002. Conversation with rapper Gordo at the Casa de Cultura Hip Hop in Diadema.
Gregório. April 1997. DJ and Producer. Conversation at this east side home.
Ice Bronx. November 20, 2001. President of Posse União da Periferia. Conversation before weekly meeting.
Ice-Ice. June 21, 1999. Member of CEDECA and Força Ativa. Conversation at CEDECA meeting in São Paulo.
Jabu. February 7, 2002. Conversation with Jabu in his south side São Paulo home/studio.
Jamal. March 10, 2002. Rapper and producer. Conversation in his south side home.
Jay, Bob. November 14, 2001. DJ of the group RDM. *Galerias* in downtown São Paulo.
Kall. December 20, 2003. Member of posse Conceitos de Rua. Conversation at Hip Hop em Ação event at the Casa de Hip Hop in Diadema.
Manga. May 12, 2002. Zine producer/rapper for RU10. Studio of producer Fegato, Santo André.
Marquinhos Funky Soul and Nino Brown. April 6, 1997. Two transitional figures who link funk, soul, and hip hop in São Paulo. Conversation after posse meeting.
Maulana. November 27, 2001. Conversation outside of nightclub regarding the hip hop contest.
———. July 7, 2002. Phone conversation about the future of Brazilian hip hop.
Moisés. December 9, 2001. Member of *Força Ativa*. Phone conversation.
Natto, Antonio. July 7, 1999. Building superintendent and local historian of the downtown *galerias de 24 de Maio*. Informal conversation.
Nepalm. December 2004. Rapper. Conversation in his home in São Bernardo do Campo.
Pedro and Gil. December 17–18, 2001. Social workers for the city of São Bernardo do Campo. Interviews conducted in their city office spaces.
Periferia em Chamas. September 2001. Rap group. Conversation with DJ Canhoto and rapper Jefferson in downtown May 24th *galeria*.

Pimentel, Spensy. October 12, 2001. Informal conversation with political and community activist and graduate student about his partnership with CEDECA in Jardim Sapopemba.
Pregador Luo. February 15, 2002. Rapper of the group Apocalipse 16. Phone interview.
Rappin' Hood and Nino Brown. August 12, 2001. Informal conversation during public hip hop event on south side of São Paulo.
Santos. July 1999. Rapper. Conversation at Diadema event.
Sharylaine. December 2004. Rapper. Conversation in a workshop sponsored by CEU (Unified Educational Centers) on the east side of São Paulo.
Simara. December 20, 2005. Conversation at the Casa de Cultura Hip Hop in Diadema.
Soul Sisters. January 19, 2002. Interview with the members of Soul Sisters in Nino Brown's office inside the Canhema Cultural Center in Diadema.
Talis. October 22, 2005. B-boy and graffiti artist. Conversation at a show at east side public park.
Thaíde. May 4, 2002. Rapper of pioneering group Thaíde e DJ Hum. Phone interview.
Triunfo, Nelsão. July 17, 1999. Video recorded interview as part of FEBEM document for *Posse Hausa*.
———. October 12, 2001. B-Boy and hip hop historian/activist. Casa de Cultura Hip Hop, Diadema.
———. November 22, 2004. Conversation during the event organized by Kall at Pontificate Catholic University in São Paulo.
X. September 22, 2001. Member of the Brasília group Câmbio Negro. X among others participated in a public debate about the role of hip hop in the media and Brazilian popular culture at the SESC (Social Service for Commerce).

Videos and Films

Beat street. 1984. Directed by Stan Lathan.
Brazil: An inconvenient history. 2000. BBC.
Breakin'. 1984. Directed by Joel Silberg.
SAMPOP. 2001. Documentary film produced by TV Cultura.
Style wars. 1983. Directed by Henry Chalfant and Tony Silver.
Wild style. 1982. Warner Bros.

Web Sites, Newspapers, and Magazines

Caros amigos (magazine)
Carta capital (magazine)
Estação hip hop (hip hop newspaper)
Estado de São Paulo (newspaper)
Folha de São Paulo (newspaper)

Folhas de atitude (hip hop zine)
Mente poderosa (hip hop zine)
Piauí (magazine)
Rap Brasil (hip hop magazine)
Veja (magazine)
http://www.alternativac.hpg.ig.com.br
http://www.articulacaodemulheres.org
http://www.bocada-forte.com.br
http://integracao.fgvsp.br/ano6/06/pesquisas.htm
http://www.manuscrito.com.br
http://raprep.com.br
http://www.realhiphop.com.br (accessed March 27, 2003). Article about the public debate "A mulher no hip-hop" (Women in hip-hop).
http://www.realhiphop.com.br/colunas/djportela/index_17.html. Interview with nominees, including Atitude Feminina, for the annual Prêmios Hutus hip hop awards, 2005.
http://www.7tacas.com.br
http://www.tratore.com.br
http://www.universia.com.br/html/materia/materia_jcih.html

Index

The letter n *following a page number denotes an endnote. The letter* f *following a page number denotes a figure.*

Ação Educativa, 55, 88, 134, 138, 178n16
Afrika Bambaataa, 76, 88, 107f, 108, 171n9
Afro-centricity, 92, 102, 111, 115, 117
alienation, 14, 15, 75, 151
artist, 5, 23, 86, 100, 101, 155, 162, 183n17
attitude, 6, 11, 15, 18, 29, 40, 43, 45, 86, 87, 91, 94, 98–99, 102, 108, 114, 117, 135, 141, 143, 144, 147, 151, 153–54, 156, 158, 160, 163–65
autoconstruction, 20, 61, 69–70, 173n1, 174n12

baile, 32, 46, 50, 60, 178n16
blackness, 11, 17, 24, 27, 29–30, 33, 45–47, 53, 70, 91–92, 94–96, 101, 106, 108, 111, 115, 119–20, 130, 146, 176n2, 177n9, 178n13

candomblé, 46, 97, 100, 118, 162, 178n11, 180n28
Casa de Cultura Hip Hop (Hip Hop House), xi, 88, 155, 164, 184
CEDECA, 3–5, 14, 16, 55, 75, 106, 138

citizenship, 5, 21, 36, 39, 46, 55, 64, 74, 76–78, 92, 160–61, 165, 168n4, 175n16, 175n18
consciousness (*consciência*), 14–15, 17, 37, 39–44, 55, 69, 72, 76, 102, 104–6, 110, 134, 148, 177n4
crente, 4, 111

design, 3, 6, 18, 30, 48, 50, 71, 88–89, 116, 123, 126, 128, 130, 159–60, 163, 165, 167n2
DJ Erry-G, xi, 37
DJ Hum, 1, 17, 37, 38, 46, 85, 98–101, 110, 138, 145

Evangelical (*Evangélica*), 3, 7, 26, 56, 85–87, 102, 111, 117–18, 120, 170n5, 179n27

Fanon, Frantz, 24, 104, 178n14, 182n7
favela, 20, 28, 64f, 66–70, 82, 88, 136, 173n3, 174n9
Força Ativa, 52, 55–56, 71–72, 74–76, 78, 88, 106

galeria, 34, 38, 49, 52–53, 53f, 54, 56, 93, 116, 128, 161
Geledés, 43, 122, 126–27, 148–49, 152

gender, 3, 9, 11, 21, 72, 122, 125, 127, 142, 158, 160; as discourse, 2, 6, 30, 43, 91–92, 95, 121, 123, 126–27, 130, 133, 137–38, 142, 144, 146, 150, 153, 156, 158, 181n3, 182n9, 182n10, 183n17, 184n25; femininity, 91, 121, 127, 130, 138, 141, 146–47, 149, 150–52, 156, 158, 184n22; homosociality, 126, 136, 158; *machismo*, 122, 126, 130–31; masculinity, 91, 121, 127, 129, 134, 141, 146, 158, 182n7
global hip hop, 146, 182
globalization, 8, 9, 11, 26, 78, 167n3
gringo, 3, 15, 95, 123, 129, 133, 160

hegemony, 12, 27, 30, 54, 56, 76–78, 126, 129, 146, 168n4
hip hop, elements, 11, 37; as Brazilian, 16, 156–57; as a "movement," 88, 156–57; as "solution," 76, 155, 157
humility (*humildade*), 40–42

ideology, 3, 6–7, 12, 17, 24–27, 29, 31, 33, 36, 38, 47, 52, 56, 61, 63, 70, 79, 82, 91, 98, 117, 120–21, 126, 130, 135, 142, 151, 160–161, 167n2
information (*informação*), 5, 7, 11, 23–24, 26, 28, 30, 34, 38–40, 42, 44–47, 50–52, 56–57, 61, 66–67, 87, 92, 95, 98, 101, 120, 122, 125–26, 143, 148–49, 155, 160, 163, 165, 172n13

mana, 22, 92, 121–22, 137, 141

mano, 11, 19, 22, 27, 91–92, 97, 111, 117, 119, 121–23, 125, 137, 140–41, 153
Mano Brown, 17, 65, 111
marginal, 6–7, 11, 16, 24–25, 34, 47–48, 57, 61, 66, 69, 79–80, 83–84, 88–89, 102, 111–13, 115–17, 136, 142–43, 152, 160, 163, 180n27
marginal hip hop, 7, 16, 113, 116, marginality, 2–3, 5–6, 26–27, 30, 56, 63–64, 82, 84, 86–89, 97, 110–11, 124–25, 158, 165, 173n3
Marquinhos Funky Soul, 41–42, 46, 51, 63f, 94, 106–7
MNU (United Black Movement), 43, 45, 93–95, 102, 105–6, 108, 134, 140–41, 153, 168n8, 169n8, 178n13
música black, 45–47, 153

negritude, 24, 27, 29, 43, 45–46, 91–92, 94, 97–100, 102, 104, 108, 110–11, 113, 115–16, 118–20, 127, 147–48, 154, 156, 165, 182n7
negro, 34, 38, 39, 47, 49, 52, 83, 92–93, 98–102, 105–6, 111, 120, 133–34, 177n4, 177n5, 181n32, 183n21
NGOs, role of, 3–4, 14, 23, 34, 52, 54–56, 111, 126, 134, 178
Nino Brown, xi, 7, 17, 19, 44, 46, 59, 83, 97, 106, 107f, 108, 113, 120, 184n1
nordestino, 40–41

Os Alquimistas, 22, 80–81

periferia, v, xi, 2–3, 6, 11, 15, 20–21, 25–27, 30–31, 34–37, 39–42, 44–48, 50, 52–57, 59–63, 63f, 64–66, 68–76, 78–79, 81–89, 91–92, 94–95,

97–100, 105, 111–13, 115–17, 119, 121–25, 127–28, 131–32, 135, 137–39, 141–42, 145, 151–53, 155–56, 158–59, 162–63, 165, 168n8, 169n13, 170n5, 173n21, 173n22, 173n1, 174n11, 175n13, 175n14, 183n21, 185n2
personality (*personalidade*), 59, 70, 93
"positive" hip hop, 5, 67, 85, 112, 115,
"positivists," 7, 11, 26, 119, 163
posse, 1, 29, 52, 55–56, 72, 87, 93, 108, 111, 123, 136, 170n2, 171n5, 179n19, 182n12
Posse Hausa, 39, 42, 45, 55, 76, 94–95, 104, 106, 108, 113–14, 139f, 140f, 141, 153, 178n19, 179n19
preto, 39, 92, 111, 119, 120, 142, 177n4
professionalization, 71, 154, 156

quantizing, 112, 179n26, 180n27
quebrada, 51, 67–68, 78, 83, 116, 151
quilombo, 103–4, 108

race, 3, 5, 6, 9–11, 21, 24, 30, 43, 45, 47, 70, 78, 83, 91–95, 99–100, 104–6, 111, 116–17, 119–20, 159–60, 162, 176n1, 176n2, 180n30, 182n9, 182n10, 183n16, 184n25
racial democracy, 12, 30, 47, 98–100, 102, 116, 120, 126, 168n6, 180n30, 185n2
racial formation, 92
racialization, 8, 24, 65, 91, 98, 117
Racionais MCs, 37, 46, 50, 65, 95, 110–12, 115, 119, 138, 145, 173n5
radio, 34, 41, 50–52, 56, 105, 108, 116, 125, 165, 173n22, 184n1
Rappin' Hood, 17, 47, 50, 67, 108, 109, 170n3
reality, 1, 3, 5–7, 11, 15, 21, 25–27, 29, 35, 39, 46, 56–57, 69, 79, 82–83, 86, 91, 102, 111, 115, 118–19, 123, 125, 136–38, 145–46, 151, 162, 164–65, 176n3, 183n21

saudade, 144–45
skill, 1, 10, 15–16, 23, 25, 28–29, 33, 40, 43, 71, 93, 111, 121, 124, 152, 155, 160, 162, 164–65, 181n2
social change (*transformação*), 15, 26, 30, 36, 45, 75, 83, 89, 121, 131, 153, 162, 165,
space, xi, 3, 6, 8, 17, 18, 23, 24, 49, 56, 60, 72, 78, 81, 84, 133, 135, 147–48, 162, 182n10; "conquest" of, 52, 60–61, 70, 76–79, 81, 87; occupation of, 34, 52, 61, 65–66, 71, 76, 87, 151, 158; territorial claims of, 27, 56, 69, 74, 113, 157, 164, 178n11
state, the, xi, 7, 9, 15, 16, 20–21, 23, 26, 28, 34–36, 43, 47, 52, 55, 56, 61, 63, 70–71, 76–78, 80–81, 88, 96, 99, 104–5, 108, 119, 159–60, 168n4, 170n5, 171n6, 175n14, 176n1, 184n1
style, 5, 11, 15–16, 23–24, 28, 33, 35, 44, 52, 67, 83, 91, 99, 100, 108–9, 111–13, 123, 135, 138–40, 143, 151–52, 154–57, 170n2, 171n12
system (*o sistema*), 12, 15, 25–27, 34, 39, 61, 63, 66, 76–77, 80, 82–84, 111–14, 120, 125–26, 131, 133, 135, 143, 150–51, 155, 158, 168n8, 169n8

Thaíde, 1, 7, 17, 38, 44, 46, 83, 85, 98–102, 110, 119–20, 138, 142, 145, 170n3, 183n21
Trindade, Solano, 97–98, 104, 120

unity (*união*), 7, 14–15, 22, 26, 57, 82, 91, 99, 101, 108, 116, 119, 123–25, 156, 163, 181n3
urbanization, 20, 25, 36, 42, 47, 56, 66, 68–69, 89

Vargas, Getúlio, 47, 69, 70, 168n6, 175n13

violence, 4, 6, 13, 27, 41, 42, 55, 59–61, 64–66, 77, 79, 82–84, 87–89, 102, 105, 110–12, 114, 116, 122, 131, 135–36, 142–43, 151, 155, 157, 170n2, 175n24, 177n9

Zulu Nation, 7, 8, 23, 24, 26, 78, 108
Zulu Nation Brasil, 64f, 76, 88, 107f, 153, 162
Zumbi, 35, 104, 114, 170n4, 178n16, 178n17

GPSR Compliance

The European Union's (EU) General Product Safety Regulation (GPSR) is a set of rules that requires consumer products to be safe and our obligations to ensure this.

If you have any concerns about our products, you can contact us on

ProductSafety@springernature.com

In case Publisher is established outside the EU, the EU authorized representative is:

Springer Nature Customer Service Center GmbH
Europaplatz 3
69115 Heidelberg, Germany

www.ingramcontent.com/pod-product-compliance
Lightning Source LLC
LaVergne TN
LVHW040615250326
834688LV00035B/577